Political Theory After Deleuze

Political Theory After Deleuze

NATHAN WIDDER

Deleuze Encounters

continuum

Continuum International Publishing Group
The Tower Building　　　　　80 Maiden Lane
11 York Road　　　　　　　　Suite 704
London　　　　　　　　　　　New York
SE1 7NX　　　　　　　　　　NY 10038

www.continuumbooks.com

© Nathan Widder 2012

All rights reserved. No part of this publication may be reproduced or transmitted in any form or by any means, electronic or mechanical, including photocopying, recording, or any information storage or retrieval system, without prior permission in writing from the publishers.

Nathan Widder has asserted his right under the Copyright, Designs and Patents Act, 1988, to be identified as Author of this work.

British Library Cataloguing-in-Publication Data
A catalogue record for this book is available from the British Library.

ISBN: HB: 978-1-4411-9795-5
PB: 978-1-4411-5088-2
e-ISBN: 978-1-4411-1687-1

Library of Congress Cataloging-in-Publication Data
Widder, Nathan, 1970–
Political theory after Deleuze/Nathan Widder.
p. cm. – (Deleuze encounters)
Includes bibliographical references (p.) and index.
ISBN 978-1-4411-9795-5 (hardcover) –
ISBN 978-1-4411-5088-2 (pbk.) –
ISBN 978-1-4411-1687-1 (ebook (pdf)) –
ISBN 978-1-4411-9260-8 (ebook (epub))
1. Political science–Philosophy.
2. Deleuze, Gilles, 1925–1995–Political and social views.
3. Deleuze, Gilles, 1925–1995–Influence. I. Title. II. Series.
JA83.W52 2012
320.01–dc23
2011036461

Typeset by Deanta Global Publishing Services, Chennai, India

To my mother, Rachel Widder

Contents

Preface ix
List of abbreviations xii

1 The ontological turn in political theory 1
  'Strong' versus 'Weak' ontology 8
  Abundance and lack 11
  Immanence and transcendence 17

2 Deleuze's ontology 21
  An ontology of 'sense' 21
  Difference in itself 27
  Virtual and actual; differentiation and differenciation 35
  Repetition and the event 41
  The simulacrum and the simulation of identity 53

3 Deleuze's Nietzsche 61
  A new ontology of sense and force and a new method
  of critique 63
  Nietzschean and Hegelian masters and slaves 71
  The will to truth and nihilism; the Overman and eternal return 79

4 Desire and desiring-machines 89
  Desire as lack and the subject of lack 94
  Desiring-machines; social machines 105
  Territorial, despotic and capitalist social machines 114

5 Micropolitics 123

    Thought's dogmatic image 125
    The many levels of politics 129
    The place of the subject? 135
    The ethics of making yourself a body without organs 141

6 Conclusion: Pluralism and 'a life' 149

Notes 155
Bibliography 181
Index 189

Preface

This book examines Gilles Deleuze's philosophy in relation to political theory. In this respect, it aims to show how Deleuze's thought is cashed out through a number of political and ethical themes. But it is also meant to contribute to current debates and trends in political theory by offering a reading of the field of political theory from a perspective Deleuze's philosophy provides. In this respect, it aims to show why those who are interested and involved in these debates and trends ought to be interested in reading Deleuze. With this in mind, the opening chapter positions Deleuze in relation to what has become known as the 'ontological turn' in political theory, outlining a set of debates concerning 'strong' versus 'weak' ontology, the possible ontological foundations of 'radical democratic theory', and the nature of immanence and transcendence in political and philosophical thought. Four subsequent chapters then explore the major components of Deleuze's ontology, his reading of Nietzsche, the politics of desire he develops primarily in collaboration with Félix Guattari, and finally the idea of micropolitics. The conclusion addresses ethical issues linked to Deleuze's last publication, 'Immanence: a Life'.

Inasmuch as a number of political theorists are already influenced by Deleuze, there is no need to introduce a Deleuzian perspective into political theory, as many versions of it already exist. But I hope that readers will find the Deleuzianism offered here to be distinctive, and that, by showing how Deleuze's thought challenges aspects of the existing framework of political theory, this work can both shift that framework and free Deleuze's thought from some of the usual interpretations and appropriations. Throughout the book, I have sought to introduce Deleuze's thought by relating it to key figures who are not only important interlocutors for him but also major influences in contemporary political thought. These include Hegel, Foucault, Lacan, and, as indicated above, Nietzsche. But many other classical and modern thinkers make appearances, including Aristotle, Plato, Spinoza, Leibniz, Bergson, Sartre, Freud, and Melanie Klein. While references to these other thinkers may challenge some readers – and if so, I can only hope it will be taken as a welcome challenge – the intention is to provide multiple avenues into Deleuze's very complex thought. Deleuze develops his philosophy through creative engagements with a wide range of philosophers, writers, artists, filmmakers, scientists and mathematicians. It would be impossible to trace all of these in a single book. But an accurate portrayal of both his ideas and his philosophical approach dictates that any work on Deleuzes take into account as many of them as possible, provided it can do so without losing sight of the main themes of its exposition.

If I were to sum up in a few words what this book takes to be the centre of Deleuze's contribution to contemporary political theory debates, it would be this: we are micropolitical before we are political. The micropolitical is a domain of constitutive relations, and Deleuze's philosophy is an unwavering attempt to expose this domain, investigate its mechanisms and dynamics (which, for Deleuze, are fundamentally different than those found in the macropolitical domain), show how it unfolds to form the concepts and categories that define so much of personal, social, and political life, and explore how it can be engaged and adjusted. In this last respect, the micropolitical is also a realm of self-problematization and of critical and creative self-formation, where this 'self' is as much collective and social as it is individual. We have the political and social lives and values that we ought to have given the micropolitics that constitute us, and if we wish to move our politics beyond what it is at its most spiteful, vindictive, and reactionary, we must begin here. Only in this way, for Deleuze, can a political and ethical pluralism be truly affirmed and realized. And Deleuze is, despite the view of some very strange yet influential interpretations of his work, above all a pluralist thinker, in his ontology, epistemology, politics, and ethics.

I would like to thank Ian Buchanan for giving me the opportunity to contribute to his new series, and for also being one of many scholars who have added to my understanding of Deleuze's thought. I began reading Deleuze some twenty years ago, but I could not have come to understand him, or the political theory debates engaged in this book, without the help of many others. In addition to Ian, I would like to thank Jeff Bell, Jane Bennett, William Connolly, Johnny Golding, Matthew Hammond, Ed Kazarian, Will Large, Iain MacKenzie, John

Protevi, Daniel W. Smith, and James Williams, who have been particularly important influences. I would also like to thank my colleagues, and in particular political theorists Michael Bacon and Jonathan Seglow, for making Royal Holloway's Department of Politics and International Relations a wonderful home for my scholarly work. And I would like to thank the research students and young scholars, from Royal Holloway and elsewhere in London, who have been active participants in the work of my Department's Contemporary Political Theory Research Group, in particular Shaul Bar-Haim, Clayton Chin, Nathan Coombs, Robin Dunford, Bobby Farnam, Craig Lundy, Julia Osborn, Victoria Ridler and Rory Rowan. Finally, I would like to thank Li-E Chen for all her love and support throughout this project.

List of abbreviations

Abbreviations of works by Deleuze (including those written with Guattari and Parnet)

AO	*Anti-Oedipus: Capitalism and Schizophrenia*
ATP	*A Thousand Plateaus: Capitalism and Schizophrenia*
B	*Bergsonism*
C1	*Cinema 1: The Movement-Image*
C2	*Cinema 2: The Time-Image*
D	*Dialogues*
DI	*Desert Islands and Other Texts, 1953–1974*
DR	*Difference and Repetition*
ECC	*Essays Critical and Clinical*
EPS	*Expressionism and Philosophy: Spinoza*
F	*Foucault*
FLB	*The Fold: Leibniz and the Baroque*
KCP	*Kant's Critical Philosophy*
LS	*The Logic of Sense*
N	*Negotiations*
NP	*Nietzsche and Philosophy*
TRM	*Two Regimes of Madness: Texts and Interviews, 1975–1995*
WIP	*What is Philosophy?*

1

The ontological turn in political theory

Ontology, the 'science of being', is the philosophical study of the basic categories of existence or reality – such as identity and difference, subject and object, essence and appearance, necessity and accident, substance, quantity, quality, space and time – and their relations to one another. The Latin *ontologia* originates in seventeenth-century scholastic writings, but the ideas and questions associated with ontology are found in key statements in ancient philosophy, including Aristotle's definition of metaphysics as the science of being *qua* being; the declaration in Plato's *Sophist*, which opens Heidegger's *Being and Time*, that the meaning of being remains perplexing; and the pre-Socratic Parmenides's claims that only the one being 'is' and that nothingness does not exist.[1] A recent 'ontological turn' in political theory has focused not on the science of being per se but rather on our human being, or, to borrow a phrase from the early Heidegger, on our 'being-in-the-world'. It has therefore explored fundamental aspects of human existence such as the role of language, death, the unconscious and relations to others in the constitution of the self, linking these to questions of both ethics and politics, although these explorations have often involved both nonhuman being and more general and abstract areas of ontological speculation. The category of identity has become particularly important in this ontological turn, as a thing's identity, which can be understood as the essential traits or characteristics the thing retains over time, is usually said to define what it *is*. Ontology is often associated, and sometimes even identified, with metaphysics, understood as the study of the domain transcending the physical world, and thus with concerns about the relationship between spirit and matter, the nature of eternal truths and highest goods, the existence of free will versus determinism and other issues prevalent in premodern philosophical and theological doctrines. For this reason, the most prominent forms of contemporary political theory have generally dismissed ontology and declined engagement with ontological matters. But this avoidance has been problematic.

Dominant forms of postwar liberal political thought have frequently conceived the human self in minimalist terms, often justifying this move on grounds that it avoids controversial, baseless and ultimately metaphysical speculations about human nature or the good life. An example is found in Isaiah Berlin's famous critique of 'positive' concepts of freedom, which define freedom as autonomy or self-governance and link it to internal capacities such as reasoned judgement, strength of will and self-reflection, which cannot be grasped directly: I cannot know, for example, that someone's actions are based on reasoned judgement, only at best that they accord with my own sense of what actions reasoned judgement compels. Theories of positive freedom, Berlin argues, hold individuals to be unfree if their actions and goals do not meet certain requirements of rationality and human fulfilment, engendering the paradox, famously articulated by Rousseau, that an individual may be 'forced to be free' – that is, denied freedom of action in order to be compelled to conform to the standards deemed necessary for autonomy.[2] A singular notion of the good life is thereby enforced on all in the name of ensuring their liberty. This utopian thinking, which seems to celebrate human freedom as a high moral achievement, is easily perverted, Berlin maintains, into the kind of fascist and totalitarian politics that destroyed freedom in the first half of the twentieth century. Its error lies in idealizing a 'notion of total human fulfillment [that] is a formal contradiction, a metaphysical chimera' (Berlin 1969: 168). Positive concepts of freedom in this way betray a kind of religious longing for a 'harmonious state of affairs

[that] was sometimes imagined as a Garden of Eden before the Fall of Man' (146). Against this, Berlin holds that the only coherent conception of freedom is a 'negative' one that defines it as the absence of external interference or restraint, which is observable and in principle measurable, making the existence and the degree of negative freedom purely empirical matters. The negative definition of freedom, Berlin admits, is as compatible with an authoritarian view that the space of individual freedom should be highly restricted as it is with a liberal view that it should be as wide as possible, but it is not complicit with authoritarianism. Its coherence and consistency come from its refusing to assess either the nature of the human agent acting within the space where restraint is absent or the value of the ends this agent pursues (153n). For Berlin, this makes the negative concept appropriate to 'the empirical, as against the metaphysical, view of politics' (1969: 171n. 1). But it also means that, in the name of avoiding metaphysical speculations about human fulfilment, it refuses to explore the domain of human ontology generally.[3]

The minimalist approach also predominates in political theories that deploy the kind of abstract rational chooser found in economic theory and much empirical political science. These theories usually leave it an open question as to whether they are really making the strong claim that human subjects are nothing more than rational interest-maximizers or simply holding the construct to be useful in modelling human behaviour or grounding normative claims. However, this ambiguity is often useful for avoiding engagement with issues of human ontology, whether or not they are conceived in metaphysical terms. The development of John Rawls's thought illustrates this point well. The early Rawls's *A Theory of Justice* (1971) seeks to articulate and ground principles of justice that ensure the fair distribution of social goods within the basic institutions of society. It does so by introducing a device Rawls calls the 'original position', in which the principles of justice are to be chosen from within a presocial condition analogous to the state of nature scenarios of early modern social contract theories. In this hypothetical situation, rational agents placed behind a 'veil of ignorance' are stripped of knowledge of their values and religious beliefs, their skills and talents, their place in society and anything else comprising their comprehensive social identities. Under such conditions of ignorance, Rawls argues, these actors would choose his principles of justice over a small group of competitors, his principles being, first, that each person has equal right to the maximum of (negative) individual liberty compatible with similar liberty for all others; and, second, that unequal distributions of other primary social and economic goods must accord with a 'difference principle' wherein this inequality works to the benefit of the least well off in society and is attached to offices and occupations open to all.[4] With the veil of ignorance ensuring that the agents in the original position cannot know the place they will have in actual society, Rawls holds that they cannot be motivated to choose principles benefitting particular social groups or values. He therefore concludes that these agents must follow the 'maximin' rule – they will 'maximize the minimum' – and agree to social arrangements that make society's least well off as well off as possible. Among the principles of justice considered, only Rawls's are designed to offer this guarantee.

Critics have frequently attacked the conception of the self at the heart of Rawls's theory, doing so in ways that force issues of human ontology onto the table.[5] Michael Sandel (1998), for example, holds Rawls's self to be one that is prior not only to society, but to its attributes, experiences and ends, such that everything from its talents, skills and knowledge to its beliefs, aspirations and values must be treated as what this self *has* rather than what it *is*. That human subjects can somehow stand apart from these aspects of their existence is certainly not an empirical fact; rather than connoting an absence of metaphysics, then, the minimalist conception of the self embodies substantial metaphysical commitments to a subject that, while disconnected and disengaged from its substantial identity, can still act as a subject by, for example, freely choosing principles of justice. But this is incoherent, Sandel argues, because choice requires a density of character that is linked to one's concrete sense of self. 'Pure' rational choice is a chimera, as genuine choice is based on values, experiences and self-knowledge, which are usually not chosen but are instead linked to a context of social relations, traditions, linguistic practices and institutions that together constitute the chooser. Society must therefore be prior to the individual, not the reverse. Unsurprisingly, Sandel maintains, Rawls himself cannot remain consistently true to the methodological individualism framing his approach. On the one hand, his difference principle depends on holding society to be prior to the individual, since only then can it be justified in controlling the unequal distribution of social goods that arise through differences in individual talents, skills and fortune; on the other hand, Rawls's argument for his principles of justice works only by structuring the original position so that no choice is really being made, the superiority of the principles following as obviously as the answer found when working out a mathematical algorithm.[6] For Sandel, these deficiencies in Rawls's liberal approach compel a reorientation of political theory towards a communitarian focus on the shared histories and traditions that constitute both individuals and the groups to which they belong.

The later Rawls (1985) responds to these criticisms by holding his original theory to be 'political not metaphysical': it neither rests on truth claims about justice or human nature nor purports to resolve fundamental disputes between religious or metaphysical positions (230–1). Instead, he claims, it invokes a set of 'basic intuitive ideas' and an 'overlapping consensus' purportedly found in contemporary democratic states (225). These agreed ideas must of necessity steer clear of comprehensive claims about human beings and their good, which are areas of irreconcilable dispute; they therefore amount to a political consensus on fair and just ways to manage a pluralistic society divided on fundamental moral and religious questions (230). In this way, Rawlsian justice 'deliberately stays on the surface, philosophically speaking' (230). Regarding human subjects, it assumes only that there exists consensus 'implicit or latent in the public culture of a democratic society' (231n. 14) that having rationality and the 'moral powers' to feel a sense of justice and to hold a conception of the good are sufficient conditions for being part of a political system of mutual cooperation (233); regarding the original position, it holds it merely to be 'a device of representation' that 'serves as a means of public reflection and self-clarification' (238) and that reflects agreed assumptions about the conditions required to judge principles of justice fairly. No metaphysical claims are made, Rawls insists, about real human agents being prior to their comprehensive social identities (239n. 21); instead, the theory simply acknowledges the fact that real humans can and do suspend their commitments to their deeply held but controversial values in order to consider what would be fair to perspectives other than their own. The original position's structure is thus derived on the basis of an existing but implicit social understanding that motivations and values linked to particular social identities should not govern the elaboration of principles of justice.[7] And this, for Rawls, reflects an underlying view in contemporary democracies that while comprehensive social identities are deeply important, in their public personae as citizens individuals should decide political questions through rational argument and with equal respect for others as free rational and moral beings.

So the first strategy to avoid ontological issues about human being, shared by Berlin and the early Rawls, involves adopting a minimalist conception of the self on grounds that it is free of substantive metaphysical commitments; when this move comes under pressure, a second strategy, which the later Rawls's 'political liberalism' adopts, displaces the matter onto assertions about generally accepted starting points for answering purely political problems. Both strategies tend to conflate ontology and metaphysics. But even if that conflation were to be accepted, is all this enough to vindicate the neglect of the ontological? Many would refuse to accept that irreconcilable diversity and overlapping consensus can be treated as straightforward 'facts' that require no further elaboration as to the reasons for and conditions of their emergence and persistence. Based on such an analysis, some would challenge Rawls's assertions that consensus on the nature of public citizenship really exists and that controversial values and motivations do not regularly infiltrate and shape public political debate in democratic societies; others would hold that any existing consensus rests on relations of power that hide the dominance of particular values and ideologies in purportedly free societies; and still others would argue that Rawls's entire position reflects a liberal bias in favour of individualism to the detriment of alternative social understandings, and that the current consensus in actual liberal states simply expresses an underlying anomie and alienation in these individualistic societies, an inability to see beyond the status quo. The level of theorization these challenges invoke is inseparable from comprehensive engagement with ontological questions about the constitution of the human self, which in turn necessitates engagement with a broader array of political questions.

Unsurprisingly, the refusal of Rawls, Berlin and others to address issues that they dismiss as metaphysical sets the horizon of the space they accord to the political. If Rawls's thought deliberately 'stays on the surface' philosophically, it is no less superficial politically, its image of politics being one of already established constituencies with divergent interests competing over the distribution of goods in a public institutional setting, where the primary concern is to ensure neutrality and fairness in procedures. As significant as this domain of politics is, it hardly exhausts the field in which politics, broadly understood as a contest involving differences and power relations, applies, as evidenced by the way one speaks of a politics of the family, church, school, workplace or boardroom, and as evidenced by the explorations of feminist, Marxist, communitarian, New Left and other strands of political theory that are critical of Rawlsian-style reductions. As Deleuze himself says, there are many layers to political and social life, and while the level of institutional politics is certainly important, it presupposes other levels that require different terms of analysis and engagement.

The ontological turn in political theory has sought to explore these levels, and has stretched and revised the terms of political thought in the process. Its origins can be traced to the early 1980s with the publication of several prominent communitarian critiques of Rawlsian liberal thought and the introduction of the work of Nietzsche and various Nietzsche-inspired philosophers into a variety of political theory debates. It has continued to gain momentum, particularly in the last fifteen to twenty years, and has been further influenced by a broad range of nineteenth- and twentieth-century philosophers who refuse to shy away from ontological speculation and who have sought to break ontology free from a metaphysical tradition linked to Plato, Aristotle, Augustine and Hegel, to which ontology is often reduced. The key inspirational figures have come from a variety of traditions, such as phenomenology, existentialism, pragmatism, psychoanalysis and what is often labelled postmodernism or poststructuralism, and they include – but are certainly not limited to – Nietzsche, William James, Heidegger, Adorno, Derrida, Foucault and Lacan. Deleuze too has certainly established his presence in this group, but at least within Anglo-American political theory this has happened comparatively late, and largely after the parameters of this ontological turn have been consolidated. In many respects Deleuze's thought does not fit neatly into these parameters. For this reason, however, it helps reshape them, pushing the ontological turn in new directions.

'Strong' versus 'Weak' ontology

Stephen White's *Sustaining Affirmation: The Strengths of Weak Ontology in Political Theory* (2000) aims to grasp the character of political theory's ontological turn. Holding the turn to be motivated by dissatisfaction with both mainstream theory's 'disengaged subject' (the subject of Rawls's original position) and the relativism that seems to follow from this subject's deconstruction, White argues that new theories develop ontological themes by offering portrayals of a 'stickier subject', which they delineate through 'figurations of human being in terms of certain existential realities, most notably language, mortality or finitude, natality [or 'the capacity for radical novelty'], and the articulation of "sources of the self"' (9).[8] White names the current trend 'weak ontology', maintaining that it navigates a middle road between 'strong ontologies' and 'antimetaphysical or postmodern views' (8). The former's certainty about ontological principles and the moral and political imperatives it derives from them works by reference to an 'external ground' (6) and involves 'too much "metaphysics"' (7); the latter's scepticism about ontological, moral and political truth claims leaves it so preoccupied 'with what is opposed and deconstructed' (8) that any affirmative positions it might take can only be 'bald assertions of *my* perspective' (16). Against these alternatives, weak ontologies seek to affirm political and ethical positions without returning to premodern foundationalism or a problematic modern or postmodern minimalism.

Weak ontologies, for White, hold ontological foundations to be indispensable but problematic. Thus they proceed cautiously by acknowledging the contestability of their claims, 'folding' this contestability into their self-reflections so that it is 'enacted rather than just announced' (White 2000: 8) and holding moral and political principles to be 'prefigured, not simply determined' (44) by ontological speculations. White identifies William E. Connolly as 'perhaps the most conscious contemporary articulator of weak ontology' (13). Connolly himself declares that all political interpretation is 'ontopolitical' in that it 'invokes a set of fundaments about necessities and possibilities of human being' (Connolly 1995a: 1), and he holds that all such political ontologies, including his own, are 'contestable responses to persistent mysteries of existence' (28). He further maintains that his own ontological and political thinking must be offered to others as 'a solicitation rather than a command' (Connolly 1993: 144), as he doubts 'that any transcendental argument in the late-modern context can foreclose the terms of ontopolitical contestation' (Connolly 1995a: 15). For White, Connolly's approach embodies 'what weak ontology means, an interpretation of being that is not provisional or thin, but rather deeply affirmed and rich, yet ultimately contestable' (White 2000: 114). White thereby distinguishes 'weakness' from 'thinness'. The latter shows 'a reticence to affirm very much ontologically' (76) and thus maintains a bias towards ontological minimalism that parallels mainstream theory's. A 'felicitous' weak ontology like Connolly's, according to White, has a richness that makes it 'satisfying' (76), though it reflexively folds self-contestation into its challenges to other theories.

White's thesis certainly captures a great deal of how Connolly and other political theorists seek to deploy ontology in a way that affirms the political and ethical implications of basic foundational claims without falling into dogmatism. But his strong/weak division is often ambiguous and forced. On the one hand, if acknowledgement of contestability is taken to mean openness to fallibility and revision, then few if any thinkers really qualify as strong ontologists in the first place, making that side of the binary little more than a straw figure;[9] on the other hand, it is far from certain that any weak ontology could ever fully problematize its own foundations, making it something of an idealization.[10] This has not stopped many contemporary theorists from adopting White's terminology and often explicitly identifying their own style and approach with 'weak ontology'. But like most binary oppositions, this one is unhelpfully reductive. It seems not to distinguish clearly between an ontology's content and its presentation, treating strong ontologies as necessarily both stringently metaphysical in their doctrine and dogmatic in their stance, and weak ontologies as both softer in their metaphysics and self-problematizing in their approach. For White himself, strong ontologies make metaphysical appeals to an external ground, draw direct connections between ontological claims and moral/political imperatives and are unable to signal their limits, while weak ontologies are pretty much the opposite on all these fronts. Yet the history of Western thought is full of metaphysical ontologies that refuse to derive political and ethical certainties in this way,[11] just as anti-metaphysical and anti-foundationalist political philosophies can be extremely dogmatic. Moreover, it seems perfectly possible for a political ontology to make strong claims that reject metaphysical or transcendent foundations, or to articulate 'foundations' that make it impossible to derive clear-cut moral and political principles. Such an ontology would differ from those 'weak' ones that affirm but also constantly problematize their claims and signal their limits. Instead, it would be a strong ontology *of* uncertainty and indeterminacy, one that, in exploring rich ontological depths, demonstrates how political and ethical principles can only be contoured but never determined by considerations of human (and extra-human) being. This kind of ontology does not fit onto White's strong/weak binary. It is the kind Deleuze offers.[12]

Deleuze, in other words, presents a 'strong' ontology that underpins political and ethical formulations of the type White and others associate with 'weak' ontology. It is not a science of being that is offered and then problematized, but rather a science of 'the being of the problematic, the being of problem and question' (*DR* 64). And it goes well beyond the figurations of language, death and novelty that for White are essential components of an ontology of human being, towards an ontology of the 'nonhuman' or 'extra-human' and towards concepts of difference, space and time that are clearly metaphysical in scope, even if they differ from traditional metaphysical versions of these concepts. With Guattari, Deleuze declares that 'the death of metaphysics or the overcoming of philosophy has never been a problem for us: it is just tiresome, idle chatter' (*WIP* 9); and with respect to questions of ethics and politics, he writes with Claire Parnet: 'There is no general prescription. We have done [*sic*] with all globalizing concepts' (*D* 144). Deleuze's ontology is certainly presented in the form of a classical 'strong' ontology, even if its content differs fundamentally. In this respect, it offers an alternative to the way recent trends in political theory have sought to navigate a return to ontology that does not also return to an old metaphysics.

Abundance and lack

Within the broader ontological turn in contemporary political theory – which, for White, includes representatives of mainstream liberal and communitarian thought[13] – is a group of theories known as 'theories of radical democracy'. Aspiring to move democratic thought and practice beyond existing models of democracy, which reduce democratic practice to interest groups competing within an institutional framework and ground this practice in appeals to universal standards of human rights or principles of rationality, these theories have sought to develop pluralist conceptions of being that can inform new conceptualizations of political and ethical pluralism. Often these theories have been framed in relation to a critique of Hegel's dialectical thought, and from this ontological backdrop a series of debates has emerged concerning issues of difference and its role in the constitution of language, the self and complex social and political structures. Deleuze has become a key figure in these debates, which represent an important presence his work currently has in political theory.[14]

Similar to Sandel's critique of Rawls's original theory, the ontologies involved in these radical democratic theory debates argue that the disengaged subject is incoherent because a subject is constituted by its traits or properties, which must be more than what it *has* because they comprise what it *is*. Moreover, they hold these properties to be necessarily relational and differential: saying that a subject is 'green', for example, signifies a relation to another subject (it is green for another who perceives this quality) and to other things that have the same or a different colour or no colour at all, and the same can be said about politically salient traits such as religious beliefs, values and so forth – namely, that they are defined in relation to the traits that define others and hence relate the subject to difference at a constitutive level. However, these ontologies go beyond Sandel's communitarian position by distinguishing two types or orders of constitutive difference. The first, which can be associated with Hegel, might be called an oppositional or dialectical difference. It is a relation of negativity or contradiction, but it functions ultimately to secure identity. A subject's identity is defined in relation to others that it is not and that negate it, in the same way that the meaning of 'white' is determined by its difference from 'black', which opposes or negates it: white cannot be where black is – blackness negates it – but white is white by virtue of not being black, and so forth. This negation and determination, however, is reciprocal: black's identity, its meaning or place on the colour spectrum, is likewise defined by its relation to a whiteness that negates or contradicts its being. As a result, each term in this opposition, being at once separate from and part of the identity of the other, is, through a process of synthesis, raised up into a higher unity: the initial negation between the opposites is thereby negated and sublated in what Hegel calls the 'Identity of Identity and Difference'. Underpinning this Hegelian logic is the idea that contradictions or polar opposites, taking the form of X and not-X, have the greatest distance and difference from each other, and that other differences, like shades of grey, fall into intermediate positions and are identified according to their proximity and distance from one or the other extreme. In all cases, however, while identity is displaced in so far as it depends on difference for its definition, the end result is a return to identity, established across these negative and negating differences.

The second type of constitutive difference relates the subject not to others who are also identified through the relation, but to a second-order difference or Otherness that is enigmatic and indefinite, and that is thereby unable to serve as an anchoring point that would define the subject's identity through contradistinction. This Other is not an opposite, a not-X, but is more appropriately understood as *neither X nor not-X*, as something that does not fall within the 'space' of opposing terms and their intermediaries. While this difference is part and parcel of the being of language, it is never fully expressible in it: in so far as language is structured through relations of opposition, wherein each word gains its definition in relation to what it is not, it can beckon towards this second-order difference but never grasp it completely. In this way, Otherness escapes the order of representation and so calls into question the adequacy of organizing differences by degrees ranging from similarity to polar opposition. It thereby displaces the subject in a fundamental way: as Otherness cannot be identified or fixed itself, it calls into question the possibility of a subject's identity ever being finally settled.

The debate, then, concerns how this Otherness is understood, with diverging positions sometimes categorized as radical democratic theories of lack and of abundance.[15] The former often draw directly from Jacques Lacan's thought and particularly his thesis that the psychoanalytic subject is constituted 'on the terrain of the Other'. For Lacan, the subject, lacking a complete identity, is driven by a desire for fullness towards the impossible task of completing itself by filling a void that negates it beyond any dialectical opposition. The subject is in this way led to pursue an inexplicable object of desire (the *objet a*) that seems to promise it the sought-after fulfilment but also appears to be prohibited to it by an equally mysterious authority (the paternal Law, signified for Lacan by the phallus). For political theories indebted to Lacan, unrepresentable Otherness appears in the form of a lack or interruption within a structure in which meaning and identity are established through opposition: the subject's relation to Otherness ensures that these meaningful structures upon which its identity depends inevitably fail. These theories treat lack as ontological (in many respects, as will be seen later, Lacan does not), holding that the subject suffers from a *lack of being* and thereby equating being with a fullness that is never really achieved. Individual and collective subjects secure their identities and thus attain being through opposition, but only to the extent that Otherness can be excluded or repressed, often by always inadequate attempts to substitute for it fixed and identifiable others, so that the subject defines itself as a being that desires *this* object, forbidden to it by *that* authority, rather than by trying to fix itself in relation to something indefinite.

A collective political subject, for example, might consolidate itself around a desire for freedom or democracy that seems to be denied to it by an oppressive dictatorial authority. At the same time, however, this idea of emancipation must remain vague, as it would surely mean different things to different individuals and groups. It will always be unclear the degree to which this opposing authority is really what blocks the group's fulfilment – in some ways it is not the dictator but the people themselves who have created their lack of freedom; indeed, as Deleuze and Guattari argue, often people come to *desire* the very kind of authority that represses them. Nor will it be certain that eliminating this authority will resolve the complex problems of how collective freedom and sovereignty might really be attained. In these kinds of ways, the object of desire that seems to complete the subject's identity and the authority that seems to negate it must remain ambiguous – their Otherness will not be eliminated. And precisely because the subject is necessarily related to enigmatic difference, the exclusion of Others in favour of identifiable others cannot be final, leaving the desire for fullness and identity forever unsatisfied. For political theorists of lack who treat identity in this way, the stability of identity is indispensable, as meaning depends upon the establishment of 'an ontological centre that could guarantee the completeness of any social identity' (Tønder and Thomassen 2005: 3). But identity is also problematic, as it is always compromised by the way its being is always already lacking. The main political thrust of these theories of lack is that this paradox must be negotiated so as to achieve temporary constructions of efficacious collective subjectivity. This requires consolidating the constitutive exclusions needed to constitute meaningful identity through a stable set of oppositions, making politics a struggle over how these exclusions and oppositions are defined and over which ones become dominant.[16] As suggested by the dictator example above, often it is held that on the political register these exclusions must take the ultimate form of an antagonistic friend/enemy distinction. The Other's ambiguous and alien character is thus considered to be such that it necessarily negates a collective identity within which different individuals and groups might negate but nonetheless also recognize and affirm one another. In this way, Otherness must be defined as an absolute threat to this collective. Antagonism thereby goes beyond opposition – one can see oneself in one's opponent, and thereby recognize the opponent and affirm oneself – but it is also necessary for it, and in this way antagonism constitutes the possibility of politics as such.[17]

If Otherness entails the incompleteness of structures of identity, it also implies its excessiveness in relation to these structures. If the language of representation and meaning is lacking in relation to it, it suggests that Otherness is actually 'too great' for language to capture its meaning. In this respect, its indefiniteness implies its infinitude, and also, perhaps, its transcendence. For this reason, theorists of lack often hold Otherness to designate both lack and abundance.[18] In relation to this, political theories of abundance might at first glance seem simply to represent a perspective on Otherness that emphasizes its character of excessiveness over that of lack, and thus might seem not to offer any significant ontological or political differences from theories of lack. But their political orientation and the connections they make between ontology and politics make these theories of abundance quite different to their counterparts. Theories of abundance are concerned primarily with how excessive Otherness, by disrupting settled patterns of identity, works productively to generate 'networks of materiality, flows of energy, processes of becoming and experimenting modes of affirmation' (Tønder and Thomassen 2005: 6) in such a way that it 'keeps propelling new things into being' (7). The thrust of these theories, therefore, does not concern how temporary collective unities are established through friend/enemy antagonisms. Instead, they are focused, on the one hand, on how the continual and often unpredictable pluralization of differences outstrips, compromises and resists large-scale contemporary forms of power, and, on the other hand, on how this pluralization requires a political sensitivity to the relations of agonism – rather than antagonism[19] – among existing identities and to the ways that new constituencies and identities are brought into being. Michael Hardt and Antonio Negri (2000) develop the first of these with the idea of a 'multitude' that exceeds the formations of an Empire of global capital whose dynamics both create the multitude and struggle to incorporate it; William Connolly (1995a, 2005) develops the second through his calls for 'agonistic respect' among existing identities and 'critical responsiveness' towards emerging differences. For Connolly, agonistic respect and critical responsiveness are political virtues that go beyond the liberal virtue of tolerance, and they follow from the contestability of all political ontologies, including his own. He holds their development to be crucial for building a democratic pluralism that avoids antagonistic postures that can develop from the agonism inherent in relations that constitute social identities. In other words, Connolly does not treat antagonism as ontologically foundational, but instead considers it a potential product of the agonistic pluralization of differences – it results from this pluralization being pressed into two opposing camps. Unsurprisingly, Connolly finds political theories of lack generally unable to recognize or affirm the pluralist political virtues that can be figured by this ontology of abundance, since they treat antagonism as the unavoidable basis for politics as such.[20]

Holding that difference cannot be understood as negation, rejecting the idea that desire is fundamentally focused on lack and offering an ontology and an ethics of creative and unpredictable becoming, Deleuze certainly belongs on the 'abundance' side of the abundance versus lack debate. Nevertheless, he also breaks with a tendency among theorists on both sides of the division to continue to centre their politics on the formation of identity and subjectivity. On the abundance side, this tendency is clear in Hardt and Negri's call for the dispersed multitude to become a collective political subject, by which they reinstate a simple opposition between the multitude and Empire.[21] It also seems to be implied in many of Connolly's formulations of critical responsiveness as a care for new identities coming into being.[22] In the introduction to *Difference and Repetition*, Deleuze declares that 'all identities are only simulated, produced as an optical "effect" by the more profound game of difference and repetition' (*DR* xix), and in his later writings on micropolitics and the many levels of politics, he continues to treat the stability of identity as a notion applicable only to the most superficial levels of political life. Precisely what Deleuze refuses here is the definition of being as fullness (identity) and non-being as lack or absence. Such an ontology, he argues, invokes a 'summary law of all or nothing' (*LS* 306) and a false alternative between 'a supremely individuated Being' and 'only chaos' (106). Deleuze also refuses the relationship between difference and Otherness in which difference, as opposition, defines and consolidates identity and meaning while the Otherness that dissolves relationships of identity is held either to be a meaningless lack or to be 'too meaningful' to be defined or expressed in language. Instead, he maintains that Otherness has a meaning or sense, that a thing's relations to Others as much as its relations to what opposes or negates it constitute its being and its sense, but that this sense cannot be understood under the terms that link meaning to identity and opposition. Indeed, for Deleuze, the reason sense cannot be represented is because identity and representation have almost nothing to do with the expression of sense, because they can capture only its most superficial aspects. In this respect, Deleuze's thought is not on one side of an ontological division between the consolidation and hegemonization of identity and the pluralization of identities, because it is not oriented towards the constitution of identity, or of subjectivity as it is traditionally understood, in the first place. Against these alternatives, Deleuze presents an ontology and a politics that proposes in many respects to leave problematics of identity behind.

Immanence and transcendence

Another debate that is prevalent more generally in contemporary philosophy and to an extent overlaps with and impinges on the political theory debate between abundance and lack concerns the distinction between immanence and transcendence. Here too Deleuze is an influential figure in the debate, and quite clearly a philosopher of immanence.[23] In the most basic terms, immanence refers to a state of being internal or remaining within, free from external conditioning, while transcendence concerns that which conditions from above, beyond or outside. In theology, for example, an immanent conception of the divine might hold God to be an energy or spirit infusing the world, rather than a Creator beyond and independent of the universe. Spinoza and the ancient Stoics, who figure prominently in Deleuze's thought, both assert versions of an immanent divinity. Immanence and transcendence also appear in three main fields of philosophy - the subject, ontology, and epistemology (see Smith 2003a) - and in these fields too Deleuze's engagements fall on the side of immanence. Deleuze defines the philosophical task of immanence as the overturning of Platonism and its 'poisoned gift' of introducing transcendence into philosophy. He associates this task with a philosophical heritage that includes the Stoics, Spinoza and Nietzsche (*ECC* 136–7).

Unlike their earlier counterparts, contemporary philosophies of transcendence deny that transcendence can be understood in positive terms, along the lines of Plato's ideal Form of the Good or Judeo-Christianity's perfect and heavenly divinity. Instead they hold it to be a radical lack or an absolute negativity. This lack, they maintain, can certainly be indicated through an immanent philosophical critique – that is, a critique that evaluates and criticizes a domain from within that domain's internal logic.[24] But whether it is envisaged in terms of an Other that exceeds the conscious self (subjectivity), one that lies beyond being (ontology), or one that cannot be given as an object of possible experience (epistemology), transcendence refers to a fundamental break that ruptures what would otherwise be a closed and insular domain of immanence. In this respect, even while these theories abandon the traditional content of transcendence, they retain its formal structure (Smith 2003a: 54), insisting that a sense of transcendence is both irreducible and indispensable, so that a subject cannot *be* without a relation to something transcendent and inexplicable to it, and so forth. The error of philosophies of immanence, according to these theories, is that they deny the necessity of this moment of transcendence and the corresponding antagonisms and exclusions that make subjectivity possible, consequently asserting a pipedream of complete inclusivity. As a result, immanence is held to be unable properly to grasp the conditions of knowledge, change and subjectivity – particularly political subjectivity – as these require something both paradoxical and external to them.[25] Indeed, philosophies of immanence are often held either to be incapable of mounting a politics or to be manifestly apolitical.[26]

However, although the terminology he uses, such as 'pure immanence' and 'smooth space', might suggest otherwise, Deleuze's immanence does not posit such an ideal of simple inclusion, and it certainly does not deny the violence and rupture that is associated with politics. Indeed, Deleuze criticizes the 'beautiful soul...who sees differences everywhere and appeals to them only as respectable, reconcilable or federative differences, while history continues to be made through bloody contradictions' (*DR* 52).[27] And he maintains that a certain kind of thought, which he associates with immanent critique, emerges 'from a violence suffered by thought' and is 'defined as a function of an Outside' (*D* 24).[28] What is crucial in this regard is that this Deleuzian 'Outside' is not exterior in the sense that a garden is outside a house or God is outside the cosmos – that is, it is not transcendent. Here Deleuze opposes a transcendent conception of the Other, which treats it as either an absolute fullness or an absolute lack beyond being, to an immanent one in which Otherness is a conduit – or, better, a *fold* – that structures relations of difference in ways that exceed the terms of identity and opposition, interiority and exteriority. If one takes a piece of paper and marks two opposite corners, the difference between the marks – the negative difference, that is, that establishes their respective locations or identities – might be conceived in terms of the distance between them – about 36 centimeters in the case of a standard A4 sheet. However, if one then folds the paper so that the corners approach each other, the marks remain on opposite corners when following the paper's surface, but they are also now closer along another dimension. Assuming more than three spatial dimensions, one can imagine even more complex folds, including folds immanent or internal to the marked corners themselves. Otherness, for Deleuze, is precisely this kind of folding. It complicates relations of difference in such a way that the opposition between two things is never enough to delineate their respective meanings or senses: although two things may be distant and opposed in one respect, they may be much more intimately related in another, or even related in ways that are neither intimate nor opposed, and the full sense of something must refer to all these axes of difference taken together. Deleuze's most fundamental criticism of dialectical understandings of identity and opposition is that they are abstract or one-sided. In other words, they treat a single side of reality as the whole of reality, and thereby lose sight of more complex aspects that do not appear from this limited perspective. In the case of dialectics and opposition, they abstract away the folds that contour meaning and sense, leaving only a 'flat' terrain of opposing and identifiable differences that may be portrayed in terms of their proximity to or distance from one another: 'Dialectic thrives on oppositions because it is unaware of far more subtle and subterranean differential mechanisms: topological displacements, typological variations' (NP 157). Philosophies of transcendence may go beyond this dialectical understanding of difference by gesturing towards an unrepresentable Otherness that surpasses opposition, but these philosophies, for Deleuze, continue to abstract away crucial aspects of the character of this Otherness by conceiving it in terms of lack.

Deleuzian immanence is thus a domain of complex and subtle folds, which are both spatial and temporal in nature, and whose 'exteriority' is unlike that posited by philosophies of transcendence. Indeed, for Deleuze, transcendence is nothing more than an erroneous interpretation of these folds, one that misconstrues them as ruptures or breaks that point to a beyond. This error, however, emerges from immanent conditions: 'Transcendence is always a product of immanence' (TRM 388). This is not to say that philosophies of transcendence are baseless. Indeed, breaks or ruptures certainly appear in relation to structures of identity. But that is precisely the point: only from an abstract perspective still oriented towards identity does transcendence present itself as a necessity, and, conversely, transcendence, however it is conceived, treats the consolidation of identity, even if it is ephemeral, as a precondition for meaning and sense. The stakes involved in treating folds as breaks that imply transcendence are therefore more than ontological: for Deleuze, they hold profound consequences for how political and ethical possibilities and necessities are construed. Philosophies of transcendence can certainly mount a politics, but it is one that treats identity as a political *sine qua non*. Unlike a liberal politics that, avoiding questions of human ontology, treats identities in terms of pre-existing groups with competing interests, political theories that invoke both lack and transcendence focus on how individual and collective identities are constructed. In this way, they go beyond the level of institutional politics that dominant traditions in political theory have usually taken to be their main focus, towards levels that require more complex forms of analysis. But for Deleuze, these theories still abstract away relations in a way that limits their analysis of these other levels. As will be seen, they fail to explore properly a 'micropolitical' domain that for Deleuze has little to do with the constitution of identity, successful or otherwise, but instead concerns other kinds of fundamental transformation. Political theories of lack and transcendence have tended to treat the transformations Deleuze calls micropolitical as being merely personal or aesthetic and having little to do with politics. But for Deleuze, as we will see, they are a crucial political upshot of the ontology of pure immanence, and one that takes the recent ontological turn in political theory in an important alternative direction.

2

Deleuze's ontology

An ontology of 'sense'

Deleuze's ontology is often called an 'ontology of difference'. This is certainly accurate, as Deleuze holds difference to be foundational and identity, along with the categories of being traditionally associated with it, to be engendered by difference. But the label is also generic and can be applied to a variety of Deleuze's contemporaries, including Heidegger, Lacan, Derrida, Lyotard and Foucault. A more specific term frequently attributed to Deleuze is 'vitalist', which is often used to describe the ontologies of many thinkers who inspire his thought, particularly Nietzsche's and Bergson's, and which Deleuze himself does adopt.[1] A vitalist ontology infuses being with a living force or energy – what Bergson calls *élan vital* – so that being's fundamental nature is found in *becoming*. Within current political theory debates some theorists have adopted the vitalist idea to put forward a 'new materialism', which they set against dominant scientific and technological approaches that treat the material world as an inert and pliable clay, as well as traditional Marxist views that treat human mastery over the natural and material worlds as the key to human emancipation.[2] Deleuze, Bergson and Nietzsche are certainly important figures in the formulation of this new materialism, which often also stresses the importance of time as an active and creative force in change and becoming. But the vitalist term has also been used as a disparaging one, as it suggests a kind of mysticism that is certainly attributable to Bergson, particularly in his late writings, but that is anathema to Deleuze (and to Nietzsche).[3] Yet another reading of Deleuze's ontology holds it to be an ontology not of difference or multiplicity but of the One. While Deleuze does at times refer to the Oneness of being, this description of his ontology is frequently based on misunderstandings concerning his relationship to Spinoza and his thesis of the 'univocity of being'. Often these readings of Deleuze as a philosopher of the One also take him to be a philosopher of transcendence and an apolitical thinker.

One of Deleuze's first publications is a review of *Logic and Existence*, written by his Hegelian teacher, Jean Hyppolite. In the opening paragraph Deleuze declares that Hyppolite founds his investigation of Hegel's thought on 'a precise point: *Philosophy must be ontology, it cannot be anything else; but there is no ontology of essence, there is only an ontology of sense*' (*DI* 15). It is easy to see in Deleuze's later writings that his thought carries forward this same thesis, and that like Hyppolite's Hegel, philosophy for him must be an ontology of sense. The theme of sense is as prominent as any other in Deleuze's work, and is closely related to the concepts of univocity, difference and vitalism that have been the focus of many interpretations of his thought. Yet in many respects it is less appreciated than the other ideas, despite its presence from Deleuze's earliest writings.

The term 'sense' appeared several times in the previous chapter, but it did not receive a proper elaboration. While it is most directly and obviously associated with meaning, for Deleuze it has much broader significance. An ontology of essence is one of identity, traditional philosophy holding essence to be delineated by a substance's fundamental attributes, which it retains over time and through its various forms or appearances and which thereby constitutes what it is. Being, as static essence, thus remains distinct from becoming, events and changing appearances. But while essence is opposed to appearance and, as Deleuze states in his review of Hyppolite's book, an ontology of essence is opposed to one of sense, sense and appearance must not be equated: an ontology of sense does not affirm the being of appearances against that of essences. As one side of an opposition, appearance presupposes essence hidden behind or beneath it, as when it is said that underneath a thing's appearance is the thing-in-itself or the thing as it really or essentially is. An ontology of sense, on the contrary, denies this division any foundational status, and holds instead that appearances, such as they exist, present only the illusion of essences lying underneath them, when in fact there is nothing underneath: '"Behind the curtain there is nothing to see," or as Hyppolite says: "the secret is that there is no secret"' (*DI* 17). But to say that there is no essence beneath appearance does not mean that only appearance remains or has being, because the traditional concept of appearance is defined in contradistinction to essence and cannot persist without this opposition. Nor does it mean that the notion of essence is wholly invalidated; instead, it now refers to the predominant sense among many a thing expresses, a predominance that is a function of power (*NP* 4–5). If appearance and essence have being, it is only in so far as they are also different from the appearance and essence of traditional philosophy. Against such a philosophy and its essentialist ontology, Deleuze holds that being is neither essence nor appearance, but rather sense, which is expressed through the world's appearance and which includes the way this appearance seems to conceal another, essential world.

Deleuzian sense is a synthetic concept. It constitutes and brings together domains that essentialist philosophies hold in opposition, such as the material and the conceptual, the particular and the universal, the external and the internal and so on. For this reason, however, sense is also something more than these opposites. On the one hand, as Hyppolite notes, sense denotes both the apprehension of particular physical phenomena (such as the sense of smell) and the universal significance of a thought or idea (the meaning or sense of a word). In Hegel's language, sense indicates both the thing's immediate external existence and its meaningful inner essence.[4] The French *sens* and the German *Sinn* also indicate direction, a meaning not entirely absent in the English word in so far as 'the sense of history', for example, can be considered the direction history is moving. On the other hand, in *The Logic of Sense*, Deleuze describes sense in terms of a *surface* that separates seemingly opposite domains, constitutes and defines those domains through this separation, but also exceeds their terms. Similar to the way the surface of the ocean separates air from water, yet its surface tension makes it different from the water beneath it without it becoming anything like the air above, sense is 'the frontier, the cutting edge, or the articulation of the difference between the two terms, since it has at its disposal an impenetrability which is its own and within which it is reflected' (*LS* 28). An ontology of sense therefore concerns an excessive and constitutive difference or Otherness that engenders and weaves together differences. However, contra Hegel, Deleuzian sense does not establish identity through these differences. Sense, Deleuze maintains, is not a synthesis of connection or conjunction but rather one of *disjunction*: it folds differences together such that they never simply correspond to or oppose one another. The material and conceptual, for example, fold into each other in such a way that 'there is a disjunction between speaking and saying, between visible and articulable: "what we see never lies in what we say", and vice versa' (*F* 64). Deleuze refers to this Otherness serving as a conduit for these disjoined differences as a 'differenciator'. It effects a 'differentiation' and a 'differenciation' of differences, both of which will be discussed below. Sense is engendered by these two processes, and differences, in turn, are sensible – they 'make sense' – because of them. The processes of differentiation and differenciation constitute being as a vibrant multiplicity and establish the direction of its dispersed and multiple becomings.

Sense is not absent from essentialist ontologies, but they assign to it a derivative status. Physical sense is taken to be nothing but a thing's changing phenomenal appearance. Universal sense, expressed in language, is separated from and in some cases subordinated to the thing that is its referent. An ontology of essence, for Deleuze, is always part and parcel of a humanist philosophy in which essence, appearance, identity and related ontological concepts are given forms appropriate to a view of the human as observer, knower and actor in the world, even when these concepts take human being as their object. Humanist philosophy aspires to be a form of anthropology, 'a discourse *on* humanity', but in doing so 'it presupposes the empirical discourse *of* humanity, in which the speaker and the object of his speech are separate. Reflection is on one side, while being is on the other' (*DI* 15). Humanism, in other words, limits expression to human language and thought, treating the human as subject in relation to an objective and inexpressive world of being. But an ontology of sense refuses this foundational division too: being is neither distinct from nor prior to its expression, nor is it expressed by something or someone else; rather, being is immediately expressive and, indeed, *it is nothing but its expression.* The anthropological focus of humanist philosophy is thereby displaced.

Deleuze links this conception of expressive being to Spinoza,[5] holding that Spinozist expression includes not only the manifestation or signification of meaning, but also involvement and explication.[6] Spinoza's one, infinite substance, Deleuze argues, expresses itself through an infinity of attributes, and is further explicated in its modes, in accordance with the proposition that from substance's necessity follow infinite things in infinite ways.[7] Substance remains immanent to its attributes and modes, and they amount to its 'own evolution, its very life' (*EPS* 18). Substance is thereby an immanent cause, meaning a cause that remains within itself – it does not become different in causing something else – but also one whose effects are not external to it even though they do not change the cause within which they remain. 'What defines an immanent cause', Deleuze declares, 'is that its effect is in it – in it, of course, as in something else, but still being and remaining in it. The effect remains in its cause no less than the cause remains in itself. From this viewpoint the distinction of essence between cause and effect can in no way be understood as a degradation' (172). Where an effect is held to be external to its cause and the cause is taken to be superior in being to its effect, the result is transcendence (172–4). This is illustrated by the traditional Judeo-Christian view of an unchanging and perfect God who stands above and beyond a creation made in His image. Conversely, an ontology of immanence maintains the internal relation of effect and cause, whereby the cause has its own impenetrability – it remains within itself – but it nonetheless differentiates and differenciates itself in effects that are immanent to it and that are equal to it in being. God understood as an immanent, living energy remains the *same* energy (what Spinoza calls *natura naturans*) even while the world it infuses (*natura naturata*) continually changes, without the world ever being separate or separable from its energetic source.

In this way, substance is immanent but also *univocal*: its sense expresses a 'single voice' through the changes and becomings it engenders. Deleuze attributes a univocal conception of being to Spinoza, holding his thought to mark a middle point in a legacy that can be traced from the medieval theologian John Duns Scotus to Nietzsche (*DR* 35–42). Those who treat Deleuze as a thinker of transcendence usually hold his thesis of being's univocal expression to amount to the assertion of a transcendent voice akin to Plato's Form of the Good or the 'One beyond Being' of neo-Platonist philosophy – that is, to amount to an identity-in-itself that establishes unity and hierarchy among subordinate differences. The irony of this interpretation is that univocity originates in Aristotelian philosophy and concerns not some unity among differences but rather a connection across differences that maintains their discontinuity – that is to say, univocity has always designated a disjunctive synthesis.[8] Duns Scotus, for example, adopts the thesis of univocity in order to show that God and His creations can *be* in the same sense – that is, that the statements 'God is' and 'Socrates is' can express the same sense of being – even though God, being infinite and transcendent, is completely distinct from finite creatures. Deleuze maintains that despite Duns Scotus's attempt to use the univocity of being to sustain divine transcendence, the concept really lends itself to an ontology of immanence, and that this is the direction it takes with Spinoza. Again, Spinoza's substance implicates and explicates itself in all differences without standing above or beyond them. Nevertheless, Spinoza's adaptation of univocity remains inconsistent, Deleuze contends, as it retains a moment of equivocation – an ambiguous duality of voices or senses – between substance and modes, leaving them distinct expressions of being. Substance continues to express identity, Spinoza defining it as that which exists and is conceived only through itself, so that it is also said only of itself: only substance *is* substance. Modes, on the other hand, express difference and are subordinated to substance precisely by being *substance's* modes:[9] 'Spinoza's substance appears independent of the modes, while the modes are dependent on substance, but as though on something other than themselves. Substance must itself be said *of* the modes and only *of* the modes' (*DR* 40). Genuine univocity, Deleuze argues, therefore requires 'a more general categorical reversal according to which being is said of becoming, identity of that which is different, the one of the multiple, etc. That identity not be first, that it exist as a principle but as a second principle, as a principle *become*; that it revolve around the Different' (40). It is only difference, Deleuze contends, that can be said in a univocal manner of both itself and what differs from it (difference said of what differs from difference). A univocal ontology of sense must therefore be an ontology of difference in which what is expressed in a 'single voice' is nothing but difference itself. Deleuze associates this univocal difference with Nietzsche's doctrine of eternal return, which will be addressed in greater detail later. The eternal return, Deleuze argues, concerns the production of difference by difference rather than, as dominant interpretations claim, the eternal repetition of identical events. The univocity of this eternal return requires a concept of difference that does not allow itself to be subsumed by any order of identity, a constitutive and excessive Otherness implicating and explicating itself in all beings and their becomings. Alain Badiou, who offers one of the most prominent readings that attributes to Deleuze an ontology of a transcendent One, quotes a declaration from the closing page of Deleuze's *Difference and Repetition*: 'A single and same voice for the whole thousand-voiced multiple, a single and same Ocean for all the drops, a single clamour of Being for all beings' (*DR* 304, quoted in Badiou 2000: 10). But Badiou fails to complete the passage, ignoring how Deleuze continues by holding this univocity to obtain only 'on condition that each being, each drop and each voice has reached the state of excess – in other words, the difference which displaces and disguises them and, in turning upon its mobile cusp, causes them to return' (*DR* 304). The single voice of univocal being is not a transcendent One but an excess immanent to all beings that propels them towards their self-overcoming. For Deleuze, eternal return is the structure of this overcoming, and it is the expressive sense of being as such.

Difference in itself

Difference has obviously been thematized in philosophy for as long as identity has been. Nevertheless, Deleuze contends, traditional philosophy from Aristotle to Hegel never reaches a concept of 'difference in itself' because it confuses it with 'a merely conceptual difference' (*DR* 27). In other words, it understands difference only in relation to the identity of a concept that it divides or that it constitutes, restricting its sense in ways that retain its compatibility with identity or return it to identity. Philosophy thus remains 'content to inscribe difference in the concept in general', which is to say that it finds only 'a difference already mediated by representation' (27). Ultimately, traditional philosophy conceives difference as the determination of identity. Deleuze outlines two paradigms of representation that subordinate difference in this way: organic and orgiastic. Aristotelian organic representation uses difference to specify identities within larger indeterminate classifications. Thus, for example, the general category, or genus, 'animal' is differentiated by traits such as 'winged' and 'rational' into the specific identities, or species, 'bird' and 'man'. Birds are winged animals and humans are rational animals, making birds and men the same in respect of being animals but different in regard to what makes them one animal species rather than another. Their difference is thus conceived in terms of a higher sameness. This higher sameness, the genus, has no concrete existence absent its specification, so that these 'specific differences', literally 'cutting up' the genus, 'make the difference' between species by constituting their respective essences: as Deleuze writes, 'genera are not divided into differences but divided by differences which give rise to corresponding species' (*DR* 31). Difference is thus constitutive, but what it constitutes is identity. Furthermore, specific differences are all positive – negative predicates such as 'not-winged' cannot specify, as being not-winged leaves completely undetermined what a thing actually is. Aristotle thus holds that these differences must take the form of contraries, which are the positive predicates demarcating the various forms that real species can take while remaining within a common generic identity: an animal can be winged, bipedal, quadrupedal and so forth. Contraries stand at only finite and limited distances from one another, allowing them to 'become a harmonious organism and relate determination to other determinations within a form' (29). Nevertheless, because they express 'the capacity of a subject to bear opposites while remaining substantially the same' (30), Aristotle holds contrariety to be the greatest and most perfect difference.[10]

As Deleuze notes, Aristotle's thesis on contraries is conditional, as they are the greatest differences only in respect to the requirements set out for the self-identity of substance. Strictly speaking, contradiction – the relation between, say, existence and non-existence, where the terms cannot both be designated positively because one is the absolute negation of the other – is a greater difference than contrariety.

But since contradictories cannot be predicated of species within the same genus, they are imperfect and extraneous to definition and essence (*DR* 31–2).[11] Aristotle can thereby dismiss contradiction as playing no role in giving a thing its being or its sense. Nevertheless, within Aristotle's own scheme there are still other differences that are neither contraries nor contradictories, that cannot be dismissed as extraneous and that interfere with organic representation's treatment of differences as different only in relation to some overarching identity. These differences too are constitutive and 'make the difference' between beings. But they do not serve identity.

On the one hand, there are the individuating differences that distinguish members of a species. These are indispensable to the individuals themselves – an individual would not be *this* individual without them – but they do not affect their common essence. Socrates and Plato, for example, are distinct individuals due to real and material differences in height, hair colour, age and so forth, and finally due to a difference that is unique to each one – Socrates is made of *this* material or is standing *right there*, and so forth. But while a generic essence is modified by the differences that constitute species – an animal becomes *this* type of animal rather than another – Socrates and Plato's shared essence as human beings is in no way altered by their respective individual traits. Individuating differences thus have an ambiguous relationship to the species they divide: while they make the members of a species fully concrete, their indifference to the common essence they individuate means that they also make individuals ultimately distinct. While two individuals may in one sense belong to the same species, in another sense that speaks genuinely to their differences, they are irreducibly diverse.

On the other hand, above the level of species and genera are the categories, which include substance, quantity, quality, space, time and relation. However, there is no ultimate identity that unifies them, for even though they are all categories of being, Aristotle acknowledges that being is not a 'highest genus'. Deleuze highlights Aristotle's reason: 'because differences *are*' (*DR* 32). In other words, while the genus is predicated of species but not of specific differences, being is said of all genera and differences: we say 'man is an animal' but not 'winged is an animal', but we do say 'winged is'. Being, in this way, designates both sameness and difference, and for this reason it cannot act as a common identity. This status of being indicates that its categories too are irreducibly diverse. Nevertheless, as both Aristotle and Deleuze argue, being still has a common sense. For Aristotle, this is glimpsed in the universality of the law of non-contradiction: whether it is a substance or quality, a category or an individual, no being can both be and not be at the same time and under the same relation. For Deleuze, the thesis of univocity, which develops as a response to this predicament concerning the categories, leads to a conception in which differences remain irreducibly diverse but still related in such a way that they express a single sense.

Where organic representation aims to restrict difference for the sake of identity, Deleuze finds in modern philosophy an attempt to make difference and its representation infinite. This orgiastic representation takes two forms, exemplified by Hegel and Leibniz. Both forms seek to close the gap between concept and individual – the way individuals stand apart from the identities meant to define them – that characterizes organic representation. Hegel's dialectical conception of difference, introduced in the previous chapter, promises to synthesize differences across the seemingly infinite distance between contradictories, thereby guaranteeing the determination of identity. For Hegel, even polar opposites or contradictories, taking the form of X and not-X, reciprocally determine each other's identity and thereby supersede their difference. Hegel refers to the higher-order form this engenders as the Absolute, the Notion, the Concept or the Identity of Identity and Difference. It is simply a matter of showing how an assertion of a thing's identity always negates itself and invokes the thing's opposite, but that the opposite's identity too is self-negating and refers back to the first identity. Opposition in this way becomes no opposition at all, making synthesis 'the infinite movement of evanescence as such – that is, . . . the moment at which difference both vanishes and is produced' (*DR* 42). Following Hyppolite's reading of Hegel, Deleuze sees this dialectical project as one that aims to 'push. . .alterity up to contradiction' (Hyppolite 1997: 113). However, just as he saw with contrariety in Aristotle, Deleuze maintains that the thesis that negative contradiction extends difference to its absolute limit 'is true only to the extent that difference is already placed on a path or along a thread laid out by identity' (*DR* 49–50). Against this, he asks 'whether an ontology of difference couldn't be created that would not go all the way to contradiction, since contradiction would be less and not more than difference' and whether it is 'the same thing to say that Being expresses itself and that Being contradicts itself?' (DI 18). Deleuze responds to these questions with the idea of an immanent Otherness that folds differences in such a way that while opposition may be able to delineate their identity, it cannot fully express their sense.

In contrast to Hegel, Leibniz's orgiastic representation thematizes the infinitely small rather than the infinitely large. This direction is set by Leibniz's development of differential calculus, although, Deleuze notes, 'for Leibniz no less than for Hegel, infinite representation cannot be reduced to a mathematical structure' (DR 310n. 9). Finite analysis can estimate the vector of a curved line at some point A by determining the change from A along its y-axis for a given change along its x-axis ($\Delta y/\Delta x$) (see Figure 1). But this remains a coarse approximation because the curve changes continuously at each point. The determination of the curve's direction at the exact point in question

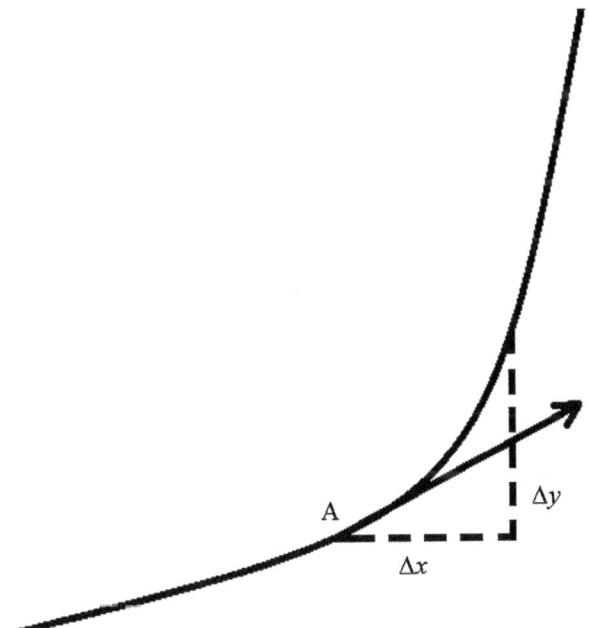

Figure 1

becomes more refined as Δx becomes smaller, with infinite analysis obtaining as the difference approaches zero. Complete determination thus involves, on the one hand, a reciprocal determination of two differences (Δy and Δx) that need not correspond to the particular x and y numerical values for any of the curve's points even though their ratio is a derivative of the curve's function, and, on the other hand, a convergence of each of these differences towards an infinitely small differential that, like Hegel's infinitely large contradiction, is a vanishing difference (46). Deleuze contends, however, that the infinitely small is not simply the inverse of Hegel's infinitely large. Rather, it differs from it fundamentally in so far as it determines by reference to the inessential rather than the essential, the latter invoking the internal contradiction by which an essence gives rise to its opposite and is then mediated with it.[12] The determinate differential ratio that emerges from infinitesimal analysis points to a difference that is *intensive* rather than extensive; it is not the difference between distinct points but a difference within the singular point itself. In this respect, the infinitely small is more than just another conceptual difference that invokes an extensive space between the essences it mediates. To capture this intensive difference, Deleuze holds that infinitely small difference 'vice-dicts' rather than contradicts that from which it differs (46). He maintains that Leibniz's move in this direction remains important for an ontology of difference irrespective of the quandaries around infinitesimals that plagued his and other early formulations of the calculus (170–1, 176–7).[13]

This infinitely small and vanishing difference ensures both the continuity of the curve and the discreteness of each of its points. But it also establishes the criteria for judging this world as the best among all possible worlds that God could create. Here Deleuze sees Leibniz continuing to subordinate difference to the principles of representation and identity. Contra Spinoza's single infinite substance, Leibniz's metaphysics presents an infinity of discrete and absolutely individual substances or monads. Though indivisible and therefore simple, each monad includes within it a multiplicity of affections and relations, which, though entirely internal to it – 'Monads have no windows, by which anything could come in or go out' (Leibniz 1973: §7) – constitute its perception of the world it inhabits. However, in accordance with Leibniz's principle of sufficient reason, whereby 'no fact can be real or existing and no proposition can be true unless there is a sufficient reason, why it should be thus and not otherwise, even though in most cases these reasons cannot be known to us' (§32), the unique existence of each monad requires that in its own singular way it 'has relations which express all the others, and that consequently it is a perpetual living mirror of the universe' (§56). Each monad, in other words, must be distinguished from all others so that it cannot be confused with any of them, and this can only be accomplished by establishing its unique place in and perspective on its universe, through an elaboration of its perspectival relations to all other monads, a task of which only a divine intellect is capable. In this way, each monad must reflect the universe as a whole through its affectations and perceptions. This does not mean that each monad perceives the entire world clearly; rather, its clear perception covers only that part within its 'neighbourhood' or 'vicinity', though it emerges from within a larger domain of hazy and confused perceptions. Together, the totality of the monads' perceptions express the entirety of the universe, and, like the sum total of images of a single town viewed from every possible angle and distance, while many of these perceptions look nothing alike, they still remain 'different perspectives of a single universe in accordance with the different points of view of each monad' (§57). What makes the existing world the best one, for Leibniz, is that it combines 'as much variety as possible, but with the greatest order possible' (§58), this being the sufficient reason for God to have chosen it over all other possibilities. Creating a world where suffering is least present, therefore, is not a criterion for the choice. Order is determined by a continuity that links all relations and events together in harmony; that this order is the greatest possible is demonstrated by the way an infinite analysis of Adam and the event of his sin shows a continuity with Eve and her temptation and all else that came before, and with Christ and his redemption and all that comes in between and afterwards. In this way, each individual and event expresses the whole of creation within it.

The fact of Adam's sin is a matter not of his essence but rather of his existence, which means that the predicate 'does not sin' can be attributed to Adam without any logical contradiction. The Adam who does not sin, however, implies a completely different world, and in this way, Adam the non-sinner is 'incompossible' with this world:

his possible existence is incompatible with the existing individuals and events of the actual world, these individuals and events being compossible only with the sinning Adam. Deleuze maintains that incompossibility in no way implies contradiction, but rather divergence from a continuous series of compossible individuals and events (*DR* 48). Nevertheless, he argues, Leibniz treats incompossibility as if it were contradiction, holding incompossibilities such as Adam avoiding sin simply to be false, in opposition to the truth of the best possible world. Leibniz thus uses incompossibility to exclude divergence from the world, treating it as a 'negative of limitation, because he maintained the dominance of the old principle' (51) that prioritized convergence and identity. As a result, Leibniz could not envision a scenario in which 'incompossibles belonged to the same world' (51). Once the theological requirements governing Leibniz's thesis are removed, however, Deleuze maintains that 'divergence and disjunction are . . . affirmed as such' (*LS* 172). A world of incompossibles is one where 'Adam sins' and 'Adam does not sin' both have truth, not because the sinning Adam's identity must relate to its contradictory, but because its sense requires a relation to differences that are incompossible with it, differences that for Deleuze are fully real but *virtual*. The divergence of incompossibles expresses a relation of irreducible diversity comparable to that which exceeds organic representation, and a folding of heterogeneities comparable to that which exceeds dialectics. But it is also an infinitely small that is wholly different from the infinitely small that Leibniz uses to sustain continuity. The Adam who sins 'vice-dicts' the Adam who does not sin, but against the vice-diction of the continuous line or the continuous world, this smallest difference is at the same time the greatest chasm. Like a science fiction story about parallel universes, the two Adams and their worlds are indiscernible yet completely different, and each one seems to repeat the other without either one being identifiable as the original or true world that the other copies.[14] Their relation is thus a relation of disjunction. What connects incompossible worlds in this disjunctive relation is a difference that is not part of either one. Or, rather, it is a difference that, while being unrepresentable in either universe, remains immanent to both of them, lying at the margins of each. 'Adam' could be the name given to such a differenciator in so far as he no longer has any fixed identity once his presence across incompossible worlds is admitted. The different worlds imply Adams that are the same and yet completely different. For Deleuze, this connecting difference cannot serve as a common identity for the worlds it relates because it has no identity itself, and thus it also cannot be a common origin (*DR* 105). It is thus a difference that neither divides up a general category into species and individuals nor reconciles differences into some higher unity. Rather than constituting identity, it constitutes only difference. In this way it is a 'difference in itself'.

Virtual and actual; differentiation and differenciation

'Phenomenology' is literally the science of phenomena or appearances. Hegel's *Phenomenology of Spirit* begins with a dialectical analysis of appearances as they are given to an individual consciousness. It examines them specifically to determine the conditions that endow these appearances with truth. This 'Dialectic of Consciousness' comprises three main stages. The first, called 'sense certainty', presents the immediate sensuous experience of an external thing appearing to consciousness. Hegel argues here that the assertion that truth is found in the thing's immediate appearance is self-negating. 'A truth', he maintains, 'cannot lose anything by being written down, any more than it can lose anything through our preserving of it' (Hegel 1977: §95). Yet in typing, for example, 'here and now it is exactly 5:55 pm and my laptop computer is in front of me', the statement becomes false even as it is being set down. What remains true, however, even in this immediate self-contradiction, is that immediate experiences are always framed by the concepts of time, space, subject and object: whether it is 5:55 pm, midnight, or 8:30 am, and no matter where I am and what is in front of me, my conscious experience always takes the form of an object appearing in a here and a now before a subject. The negation within sense certainty is thereby negated in the realization that every seemingly immediate experience is mediated by categories of 'perception'. This marks the next stage of Hegel's analysis, and the dialectical process begins anew.

If one asserts that the truth of a perception is found immediately within its conceptual object, this again is self-contradictory, as the object is paradoxically a unified, independent entity and a multiplicity of relations. An object independent of consciousness might, for example, be green, but this property is relational on two fronts, first in being green for a subject that perceives this colour – it is green *for me* – and second in being green as opposed to all other possible colours and to being colourless. In this way, stating what an object is necessarily invokes what it is not. For an object to be what it is, it must negate others by not being those others, but this also relates it to others and makes its identity dependent on them. This self-contradiction in the object of perception can only be overcome through a new concept that encompasses both a moment of unity and a moment of relation-to-others. Hegel posits such a concept as 'force', which is introduced as the third stage of the Dialectic of Consciousness.

An inert or powerless force, one that lacked efficacy and could not influence others, would not be a force at all. Hence the nature of force, in contrast to the thing of sense certainty and the object of perception, is that it is essentially in dynamic relations with others. Furthermore, these others must also be forces, into which the self-contradictory things and objects of the earlier stages of the dialectic have dissolved. Force, Hegel argues, determines and is determined by another force in a relation of opposition: 'The interplay of the two Forces thus consists in their being determined as mutually opposed' (Hegel 1977: §139). In accordance with dialectical thinking, this opposition entails both a separation of forces and their synthesis in a higher identity. This forceful dynamic of negative separation and reunification, Hegel maintains, provides the pivot to transition out of the Dialectic of Consciousness and into the next stage in the *Phenomenology of Spirit*, the Dialectic of Self-Consciousness. This shift is made possible by the recognition that not only does the object of perception dissolve into a network of force relations, but the subject as well: a subject gains its identity through its negative relations to objects, and this amounts to a dialectical relation wherein subject and object are united in a higher identity. The subject thereby rediscovers itself in its object, and this is precisely the definition of self-consciousness: to be self-conscious is to be immersed in the world, but to pass through a dialectical movement in which one separates oneself from this world in order to sense and perceive it as something external, and then overcomes this difference and the contradictions it entails. This dialectical separation and unity of self-consciousness is the condition for the truth of force relations: since these relations do not refer to anything beyond them, neither subject nor object transcending the network, they account fully for themselves, and so form a totality that for Hegel expresses the nature of the Absolute.[15]

Thus Hegel shows that the condition for the truth of an immediate experience is that the things that appear to consciousness are perceived as objects whose identities are constituted by a forceful dynamic of negative and reciprocal relations, with the conscious subject being absorbed into these relations. Conversely, the network of force relations revealed by this dialectical progression, by providing the mediating link for these appearances and constituting the identities of both subject and object, allows experience to 'make sense'. Now we certainly experience actual differences among things and between ourselves and things – we sense differences in colour, size, time, place and so forth. But the forceful relations that underpin the sense of these differences are not explicitly present in sensuous experience itself. They are not seen, touched or heard, but instead are presupposed by experienced identities and differences as the immanent condition of their meaningfulness. This is precisely what Deleuze calls the virtual: an immanent network of relations that constitutes the sense of actual experience. The term virtual comes from the Latin *virtus*, which means power. It is invoked by Duns Scotus, who maintains that a univocal sense of substantial being 'virtually includes' the heterogeneous senses of qualitative being, quantitative being and so forth, because quantities, qualities and other attributes depend on substance, which has the *virtus* to give them being.[16] But Deleuze's use of the term is most directly indebted to Bergson's conception of time as duration. Bergson maintains that past time does not simply disappear but instead remains embedded in the present as something real but virtual; the endurance of this virtual past in the present makes possible remembrance and recall, but also propels time and things existing in time creatively into the future. Bergson opposes duration to the linear chronological conception of time, which he associates with mechanistic conceptions of causality. To Bergson, these conceptions hold that worldly things and events follow universal laws, so that the future is predictable on the basis of present facts and circumstances. This linear time is a neutral medium that only measures becoming without having any effect on it. Against this, Bergson holds that duration's retention and reflux of the past back into the present compels time and things existing in time into an open and unpredictable future. The virtual nature of the past thus refers to both its continuing reality and its potency.

Deleuze refers to this virtual multiplicity of relations as 'microscopic' or 'molecular', in that it is hidden but constitutive of the actuality given to experience. Contra Hegel, he holds these virtual relations to be not dialectical or oppositional but disjunctive, and contra Bergson, he holds the domain of the virtual to be more extensive than that of a past retained within the present. For Deleuze, virtual relations fold heterogeneous differences in such a way that they express a 'power of the false'. This is a power that 'poses the simultaneity of incompossible presents, or the coexistence of not-necessarily true pasts. . . . [It] poses inexplicable differences to the present and alternatives which are undecidable between true and false to the past' (*C2* 131). The sense of Adam the sinner, to return to that example, is linked to the way Adam the non-sinner and his alternative, incompossible world are folded virtually into it. In this way, the virtual is an immanent excess that enframes actual experience, so that 'around each object that I perceive or each idea that I think there is the organization of a marginal world, a mantle or background, where other objects and other ideas may come forth in accordance with laws of transition which regulate the passage from one to another' (*LS* 305). What connects these virtual and incompossible events and worlds is a 'difference in itself' or differenciator, an Otherness that is unrepresentable and that serves as a conduit across which differences resonate.

Deleuze holds the virtual to be real but not actual. The virtual and actual form a pair that must be distinguished from the possible and the real: 'The possible is opposed to the real; the process undergone by the possible is therefore a "realisation". By contrast, the virtual is not opposed to the real; it possesses a full reality by itself. The process it undergoes is that of actualisation' (*DR* 211). The possible is normally considered a realm of multiple scenarios – Adam could possibly sin or possibly not sin – only some of which will become real. Conversely, a possibility that cannot ever be realized is not a possibility at all: it is impossible. However, Deleuze adds to this that the possible and real are related in terms of identity or similitude. Possibilities, indeed, are simply abstractions of the real that are made indeterminate – it is an abstract image of the real Adam who without contradiction may or may not have the act of sin attributed to him. In this respect, 'to the extent that the possible is open to "realisation", it is understood as an image of the real, while the real is supposed to resemble the possible' (212). In contrast, the virtual is a realm not of possibilities or impossibilities but of incompossibles, some of which are actualized. The actual and the virtual, Deleuze maintains, never resemble each other, and in this way the actualization of the virtual 'is always a genuine creation' (212).

The reason creation is found in actualization has to do with the way virtual and actual are distinct but interconnected types of expressive multiplicity, one characterized by involvement and the other by explication. The differenciator that relates differences through disjunction is itself virtual, both in the sense of inhering and in the sense of powering. But the virtual as a whole is a domain of differentiation: its relations are the infinitely small differentials of Leibnizian calculus, which 'vice-dict' and are involved in one another, although for Deleuze, contra Leibniz, these differentials are not limited by any principle of continuity or convergence and so relate incompossible individuals, events and worlds. Conversely, the actualization of this virtual, which also involves the virtual differenciator, explicates virtual differences into a domain of differenciation, actual differences being susceptible to conceptualization and organization into species, genera, categories and specific and individual differentiae.[17] Actually experienced differences are certainly conceptualized and categorized in this way – otherwise representation would not be possible – but this organization cannot be final because a virtual excess remains immanent to the ideas and objects of actual experience, referring them to a 'marginal world' that serves as their background. Thus, on the one hand, Deleuze maintains, the virtual combines 'the greatest power of being differentiated with an inability to be differenciated' (*DR* 187); while on the other hand, though actual differences may seem to be negatively related to one another, this is 'only in so far as these are cut off from the virtuality which they actualise, and from the movement of actualisation' (207). The actual and the virtual are related through this process of actualization, but this is another disjunctive synthesis, as the two domains of difference never correspond to or resemble each other. Thus, while it is possible to move from virtual force relations to the actual states of affairs they engender, 'if we go back up in the opposite direction, from states of affairs to the virtual, the line is not the same because it is not the same virtual' (WIP 156).

The question of how the virtual is actualized is a difficult one, and Deleuze's own explanations often seem figurative or metaphorical. Sometimes he refers to the process in terms of problem and solution: the virtual is an open, problematic structure of differences and actualization sets out a solution or response to this problematic, but as actual solutions cannot do away with the problematic that gives them meaning and sense, the virtual continues within these solutions as the field that both generates them and exposes their incompleteness (see DR 207–8). At other times Deleuze speaks of actualizations as 'dramatisations' of the virtual's dynamism, which 'create or trace a space' (216) and set down roles that act out particular situations corresponding to differentials of the virtual domain, though as with any dramatization certain incompossibles must remain unactualized (see 216–21). In general, however, actualization involves the constitution not of subjects or objects, but of perspectives or points of view, from which various organizations and classifications of differences can occur. Perspectives, of course, are always limited, and while there is always a multitude of actual albeit divergent and incompatible perspectives, it is impossible for all perspectives to be actualized at once. Moreover, perspectives express a sense in the classifications they make possible, and in this way they are assertive and never neutral: as will become clear in the next chapter when examining Deleuze's analysis of Nietzsche's master and slave moralities, perspectives emerge from forceful relations and are expressions of force. Finally, perspectives are always accompanied by semblances or illusions, which nevertheless have their own reality. From the perspective of standing on the earth's surface, for example, the sun and moon appear to be approximately the same size, and while this does not mean they *really* are the same size, it is still the case that they *really* appear this way and cannot, from this perspective, appear otherwise. Perspectives and their illusions thus have a truth status different from traditional philosophy's notion of universal and unchanging truth. However, this does not mean they can be denigrated as relativism. The latter term is usually dismissed as a self-contradictory subjectivism, amounting to the claim that 'truth is what I decide it is'. But perspectives are not chosen by subjects; rather, they condition the emergence of subjectivities. It is, among other things, the perspective we have viewing the cosmos from the earth's surface that makes us who and what we are. A perspective is therefore 'not a variation of truth according to the subject, but the condition in which the truth of a variation appears to the subject' (*FLB* 20). Deleuze holds perspectivism to be 'a truth of relativity (and not a relativity of what is true)' (21).

Repetition and the event

Deleuze declares: '[R]epetition is, for itself, difference in itself' (*DR* 94). In Hegel's terms, being-in-itself is a one-sided abstraction designating an isolated and independent thing. This thing-in-itself always negates itself and relates to another, thereby becoming a being-for-another. Finding itself in this other, however, this thing returns to itself and thus is 'for-itself' *through* this other. Being-for-itself in Hegel is therefore a dialectical synthesis of identity and difference. For Deleuze, the 'for itself' of difference also takes difference beyond itself, but as difference is not a thing-in-itself but a 'difference in itself' outside the scope of representation and identity, it cannot return to itself in the form of identity. The 'for itself' of difference thus speaks to the way difference in itself, functioning as a differenciator, expresses itself by involving and explicating itself, differentiating and differenciating itself. The mode of this involvement and explication, Deleuze holds, is repetition, but like the concept of difference, traditional philosophy regularly misunderstands repetition. A new concept of repetition, however, must be dual, since, like the virtual and actual themselves, the repetition of actualized differences is of a different order than that of virtual differences, and differs also from the repetition by which the differenciator repeats itself by going beyond itself.[18]

Representation, Deleuze argues, subsumes repetition within an order of resemblance. A thing, event or series is said to repeat another to the extent that the two are similar: the student repeats the music teacher by playing the notes to reproduce a tune, one house repeats another when they follow the same design, a court decision repeats another by following the same precedent or applying the same law and so forth. Repetitions differ in time and space, in the materials used and perhaps even in the way these materials are put together. Indeed, there must be such differences between an original thing and what repeats it or the latter could not be distinguished as a repetition. But these differences are held not to affect the fundamental sameness underlying them, and in this way, repetition obtains only to the degree that the differences between repetitions are treated with indifference, in so far as they are not held to matter: 'Repetition thus appears as a difference, but a difference absolutely without concept; in this sense, an indifferent difference' (*DR* 15). Conversely, when the student improvises rather than follows the teacher, or when a judge or jury breaks with precedent, repetition can perhaps be replaced by novelty or creativity. This indicates, however, that in cases where differences matter, there is no repetition. All this, for Deleuze, implies that repetition is linked to a kind of failure: a failure to differentiate, and in some cases a failure of memory, as when one says that those who forget the mistakes of history are doomed to repeat them.[19] Repetition is thus treated as something that occurs by default or error.

Deleuze therefore insists on another account of repetition. On the one hand, 'Modern life is such that, confronted with the most mechanical, the most stereotypical repetitions, inside and outside ourselves, we endlessly extract from them little differences, variations and modifications' (*DR* xix). The fact that these differences can be treated only with indifference is enough to show that 'repetition cannot be explained by the form of identity in concepts or representations. . .it demands a superior "positive" principle' (19). An alternative conception of repetition must therefore focus not on the similarities among repetitions but on their differences, showing how these can amount to genuine novelty or creation: repetition essentially repeats difference, and difference brings with it the new. On the other hand, repetition must be more than a difference

DELEUZE'S ONTOLOGY

or novelty occurring within time conceived as a linear chronological order. This chronological or 'clock time' conception is the time within which the traditional concept places repetitions, and it does nothing more than measure an indifferent temporal distance between them, as when one says 'this is the same thing we did yesterday afternoon', or 'we are repeating the same economic mistakes of the Great Depression of the 1930s'. It is what Heidegger calls the everyday or 'vulgar' concept of time, which treats time as a continuum of instants that when counted off can be used to calculate rates of change, and which privileges the present moment as a conduit that connects a past that no longer exists to a future that is yet to exist. Time is certainly experienced in this vulgar form, but it is necessary, as Heidegger argues when announcing his own project in *Being and Time*, to give this form 'its rightful due' (Heidegger 1962: 39). This requires showing how vulgar time springs from a more primordial *temporality* – that is to say, from time's fundamental structure, which for Heidegger delineates the horizon of our understanding of being.[20] Deleuze's project shares with Heidegger's this aim not of denying the linear aspect of experienced time but of providing it with a more comprehensive ontological elaboration.

Deleuzian repetition challenges and displaces the ordinary conception of time in two ways. First, it presents more complex, nonlinear relations between past, present and future. Bergson executes a similar move by conceiving duration in terms of an embeddedness and continuation of the past in the present, which compels time into an open and unpredictable future. So too does the early Heidegger by treating the future, and specifically the event of death, not as something that is 'not yet' in chronological time but as something ever present but seemingly coming from nowhere, structuring both the present and the past as they create a new future. Repetition, for Deleuze, takes place within the ways in which past, present and future fold into one another through another kind of synthesis. Second – and this too can be attributed in different ways to Bergson and Heidegger – without denying that time is experienced as a passage of instants that can be counted in order to measure changing things within it, Deleuzian repetition treats time not as a flow of moments but as an unchanging form. Deleuze takes this idea from Kant, maintaining that if time itself moved or changed, it would imply that it changed within another time, but should this other time also be considered as a flow, this thinking would ultimately lead to an infinite regress.[21] 'Time', in this respect, names not a flow or passage but the structure of that which passes or changes: 'time is the most radical form of change, but the form of change does not change' (*DR* 89). For Deleuze, there is a temporal structure that conditions the movement or change of things in time, and this structure is one that puts things 'out of sync' with themselves. Things move or change because they are never synchronous with themselves, because the way past, present and future are embedded in them does not allow them to endure as the same. The structure of that which changes in time is thus a structure that repeats difference.

Even the vulgar notion of time, for Deleuze, involves a synthesis structured as a repetition. If this ordinary conception treats the past in terms of the recall of a former present and the future in terms of an expectation of a present still to come, it still presupposes a connection of the instants that comprise this continuum: 'Time is constituted only in the originary synthesis which operates on the repetition of instants. This synthesis contracts the successive independent instants into one another, thereby constituting the lived, or living, present' (*DR* 70). This synthesis, which is carried out by consciousness as a necessary condition for change to be perceived, is the first and most basic of three syntheses of time that Deleuze outlines in *Difference and Repetition*.[22] Expectation and recall both occur in the present, with an image of a childhood event, for example, appearing to consciousness here and now. But consciousness also places such images at specific distances from the present – the childhood event happened at an exact moment in time, at 12:25 pm on my third birthday, for instance – and this requires that past and future are established as dimensions of the present, extending away from it. As a consequence, the character of this synthesis already takes time beyond the vulgar conception, since while they may indeed be marked punctually, the connection of this time's distinct moments means they can never be isolated instants-in-themselves. Every instant is a synthesis that connects it to its past and its future, and as such it is a difference. Deleuze refers to this first synthesis as the empirical foundation of time.

DELEUZE'S ONTOLOGY

Nevertheless, the first synthesis creates only a static line of time, which is inconsistent with the ontological structure of the present. That the first synthesis organizes instants into future and past indicates that the present itself cannot persist, but the first synthesis cannot account for the passage of the present and so another synthesis is required to structure it. The present can pass only if it could become different from what it is (Williams 2011: 13). Yet, on the one hand, this engenders the paradoxes of a present that must constitute the past in order to pass into it, that seems unable to constitute anything as it must pass away at the same time it carries out this function, and that in any event would alter the past it is meant to constitute by passing away into it (53). On the other hand, if there were some delay in the present's passing – if, for example, it would have first to constitute the past and afterwards merge with it – it is unclear how a future present could ever be in a position to replace it, and a new paradox of a present that extended into the future would be created (53–4). The only way out of this impasse would be for the present to be both present and past at once.

Here Deleuze is most directly and heavily indebted to Bergson, and to his idea that the present can be virtually past while it is actually present. Bergson distinguishes two forms of the past and memory. The first, which can be considered psychological, reduces the past to the present by embedding it either unconsciously in present habits (as when one follows the same path to work every day, having filtered out and left behind the previous mistake-filled attempts to learn the route) or consciously in the images of past events brought to presence in recollection. The second, however, is ontological, and involves the automatic, complete and ordered recording of the present as it passes, such that it endures and never simply passes into nothingness. There is nothing specifically human or psychological about this recording; on the contrary, human or psychological memory presupposes and depends upon this second memory, which Deleuze treats as a synthesis that includes the entirety of the past within it. Ontologically, then, each present is also immediately recorded and as such it both is virtually past and contains the entire past virtually within it.

The virtual past of one present is also a layer within each subsequent one, making the structure of duration one in which the past persists in the present and repeats itself within the structure of time. This virtual past also gives the actual present its sense and direction, each present being what it is because of all that came before it and being driven in this way into the time of an open future, where repetition repeats difference. Thus, even though Bergson portrays the relation between present and past as one in which 'our perceptions are undoubtedly interlaced with memories, and, inversely, a memory...only becomes actual by borrowing the body of some perception into which it slips' (Bergson 1991: 67), this reciprocity is not symmetrical. The past has priority over the present, because even though the past needs the present to become actual (in the sense of being an actively recalled and firm image of a past event), as something virtual the past is already both complete and fully real. The actual present, conversely, is nothing more than the entirety of this virtual past compressed to the point where it becomes actualized as a force of creative evolution and becoming.[23] Deleuze thus presents the Bergsonian synthesis of time through the images of sheets or layers of the past and peaks of the present (*C2* 98–125). It is a virtual synthesis of the past and of memory, where present and future are dimensions of the past, and while the first synthesis provides the empirical foundation of time, the second is a 'transcendental synthesis' (*DR* 81) that grounds its passage and unfolding: 'It is memory that grounds time' (79). 'Transcendental' here should not be confused with transcendence. The latter refers to what is above, beyond or outside, whereas the former refers to that which is presupposed as a condition of possibility, and which may be transcendent or immanent.

Bergson is often considered Deleuze's chief inspiration, yet Deleuze clearly turns away from him in linking the third synthesis of time to Nietzsche. The reasons for this are varied, and include a subtle suggestion by Deleuze that the transcendental ground Bergson establishes for time's passage invokes a form of transcendence.[24] More than this, however, Bergsonian duration ultimately falls not on the side of difference but on the side of identity, continuity and coherence. Within the layers of past preserved and repeated in successive presents there are 'non-localisable connections, actions at a distance, systems of replay, resonance and echoes, objective chances, signs, signals and roles which transcend spatial locations and temporal successions' (*DR* 83). Nevertheless, 'however strong the incoherence or possible opposition between successive presents, we have the impression that each of them plays out "the same life" at different levels' (83). This impression accords with Bergson's explicit intention to maintain the idea of a coherent ego that lives duration.[25] This ego does not take the form of an essential self or identity that remains static over time; rather, it is an entity that changes without passing away – in other words, it *endures*. Nonetheless, this dynamic ego remains a unity and a centre of action through the way it channels its past into its present and future. The difference that duration repeats is thereby limited in much the same way that Leibniz limited difference for the sake of a single best possible world. In Bergson, it excludes incompossibles and undecidabilities from the self and its past, denying a 'power of the false' in order to preserve the self as a subject.

The third synthesis of time, on the contrary, fractures the subject; it is the time of the 'aborted cogito' (*DR* 110).[26] Deleuze links this time to Nietzsche's eternal return, conceived as a disjunctive synthesis of incompossibles related and folded into one another through a differenciator; he holds the differenciator's power to come from it being neither past, present nor future but *untimely*.[27] Deleuze illustrates the structure of this third synthesis through a revised version of Freud's story of the Oedipal complex. For Freud, the Oedipal trauma, in which the father intervenes in the relationship between the boy and the mother with the threat of castration, is an event subjected to primary repression, and as such it can never be brought fully to consciousness and represented. It functions, however, to complete psychic development, establishing an order of desire and a body image centred around genital sexuality, and founding a superego and a sense of guilty conscience that internalize the paternal Law and civilization's fundamental prohibitions against incest and patricide. In this way, the trauma also establishes a radical break between an infantile pre-Oedipal self and an adult post-Oedipal self within an order of chronological time. Crucially, Freud almost always holds the childhood event to have been real, maintaining that the memories and desires that return in adulthood in the form of various neurotic behaviours cannot have been simply imagined or fantasized, or that, if they are fictitious, they must still result from real past experiences. Adult neurosis is understood in terms of a delayed effect in chronological time, and the role of psychoanalysis is to trace this effect to its real origin and, where possible, to remove the repression that is its cause. Deleuze holds that 'a decisive moment in psychoanalysis occurred when Freud gave up, in certain respects, the hypothesis of real childhood events, which would have played the part of ultimate disguised terms' (*DR* 17). In the 'solipsistic unconscious' (124) that Freud usually presupposes, it is clear that the time of the childhood self and the trauma it suffers precedes that of the adult who represses it, and from this 'the question then arises how to explain the phenomenon of "delay" which is involved in the time it takes for the supposedly original infantile scene to produce its effect at a distance, in an adult scene which resembles it and which we call "derived"' (124). But this succession is inapplicable on Freud's own terms in so far as he holds the unconscious to have no conception of linear time.[28] Within the unconscious, then, these two discontinuous selves, with their distinct memories of the past and expectations of the future, are not successive but coexistent. For Deleuze, the unconscious houses a resonance between these and other selves, each 'living' a different time series, so that the adults one knew or expected to be in childhood interact with the adult one thinks oneself to be among other adults and children, and so forth. These selves *repeat* one another, without any particular self being distinguished as the 'real' or 'original' self that the others copy. They are incompossible, presupposing entirely different timelines and entirely different worlds, yet they also lie at infinitely small and vanishing distances from one another. In this way, the unconscious becomes the site of a virtual intersubjectivity, the different temporal series of childhood and adult selves being such that they 'are not distributed within the same subject' (124). They remain connected by a common Oedipal trauma, but this event's presence does not establish an identity among these different subjectivities. Instead, remaining unrepresentable to all of them and viewed from a different perspective by each, its commonality is that of a univocal enigma. The event thus functions as a differenciator, a difference in itself with its own impenetrability, sustaining 'the resonance of the two independent and temporally disjointed series' (*LS* 226). And as the event need not be a real one from childhood, it takes on an untimely character: it has already happened, yet is still to come, and yet perhaps never happens at all. As such, it does not mark a chronological moment when the self becomes broken into multiple subjectivities, but instead indicates a fundamental discontinuity whereby the self is always already cracked.

To be out of sync with myself thus means to be caught up in diverse lines of time that refer to different subjectivities. The 'I' is a multiplicity of subjects living different temporalities within the same, not so unified being, resonating and repeating one another across an untimely and enigmatic conduit. It is this temporal multiplicity and discontinuity that structures the way the self changes 'in time', with the sense of any change being inseparable from incompossible and undecidable pasts, presents, futures and subjectivities, and with any actual repetition unfolding in chronological time being inseparable from the way incompossible subjects, times and worlds repeat each other in a virtual domain. Actualized events unfold in time similarly. A long relationship breaks down with each partner seeming to have changed and grown apart from the other; yet in another sense the breakdown occurs with neither one having changed, what made each person ultimately incompatible with the other having been there from the start. Both of these realities are true, even though they are incompossible, presupposing completely different individuals and worlds. The sense of the event itself as it comes to pass and as it is interpreted and reinterpreted afterwards must include these incompossibilities, which is why it takes such a long time – if such a time is ever reached – for the event to have a settled meaning. When Deleuze links the third synthesis to eternal return, he therefore assigns several meanings to Nietzsche's doctrine. Against standard interpretations that see it as the return of identical events over an infinite time, he holds it to be a return of difference, or a return of the untimely, which always throws the settled identities and meanings of individuals, collectives and events out of joint. These unfoldings of difference and untimeliness, however, still occur within time. As the structure of time in which coextensive temporalities resonate with and repeat one another, however, it does something more: against the grounding of movement carried out by the second synthesis of time, the eternal return *ungrounds* movement, releasing it from a past that conditions it or a future that imposes a telos or destiny on it. Deleuze holds that the eternal return poses a *'false movement'*

(*C2* 143), which, as such, is not really a movement at all. It is thereby linked to what Deleuze calls a 'line of flight' or 'deterritorialization' that need not 'move' anywhere, to transformations that involve 'a curious stationary journey' (*D* 127). Each of these formulations of eternal return introduces a kind of newness into becoming: the differences in each repetition reveal the inadequacy of any concept of repetition that conceives it through principles of identity and similarity, treating difference with indifference; the untimeliness engendered by the eternal return is always new by virtue of never being located and fixed in time; and the eternal return as the structure of time is the guarantor of novelty, constituting 'the intrinsic quality of that which becomes in time' (*C2* 275).

This quality marks the character of time's structure as 'Event'. Considered historically or empirically, an event is an occurrence at a specific time and place that marks a moment of change. As opposed to the banal or the everyday, things after an event are no longer the same, and in this respect, events are rare. But in so far as their sense exceeds the time, place and background causes that condition but do not necessarily determine their emergence, events refer to a virtual Event that they actualize. Deleuze offers as illustration the event of battle, which 'is not an example of an event among others, but rather the Event in its essence. . .because it is actualized in diverse manners at once, and because each participant may grasp it at a different level of actualization within its variable present' (*LS* 100). The battle is a virtual problematic with multiple incompossible senses, hovering over the entire battlefield and indifferent to the individual combatants who live it. It is experienced and holds significance in completely different and incommensurable ways for the soldier who flees, the one who lies gravely wounded, the one who manages to overcome both his courage and his cowardice through the course of the conflict and so on (100–1). Similarly, as the out-of-sync or cracked structure of time, the Event provides a univocal sense for the diverse events that occur in time: 'the war, the financial crash, a certain growing older, the depression, illness, the flight of talent. But all these noisy accidents already have their outright effects; and they would not be sufficient in themselves had they not dug their way down to something of a wholly different nature which, on the contrary, they reveal only at a distance and when it is too late – the silent crack' (154–5). In contrast to the rarity of the empirical event, then, the ontological Event, as the condition for change and becoming, is ubiquitous. Whether spectacular or banal, extraordinary or everyday, things and events have, by virtue of the way they have being in time, an event-ness that ensures they are never the same as anything else, that they are always repetitions of difference.

Yet at this point a difficulty arises that, ironically, concerns the ability to make a *real* difference. For if the structure of time ensures only that no two events, like drops of rain or grains of sand, are ever exactly the same, this hardly makes it the guarantor of genuine novelty or creativity. And even if time can engender such novelty, it still seems to offer no criteria for differentiating a banal from an extraordinary change.[29] Of course, this lack of criteria ought to be expected if, as was discussed in respect to White's 'weak ontology' thesis in the previous chapter, Deleuze's thought does not derive political imperatives from an ontological base, and indeed proposes an ontology of uncertainty that rules out such a direct connection to politics. Nevertheless, it seems to be with this lack of criteria in mind that certain critics of Deleuze hold that his philosophy of the univocal Event, along with his refusal to sanction the ideas of lack and negativity that would establish fundamental breaks or ruptures in relation to identity, makes any form of genuine novelty, of radical or revolutionary change, impossible.[30] The conclusion that seems inevitably to follow this line of critique is that Deleuze's philosophy is either politically incoherent or simply apolitical.[31]

In many respects, however, these criticisms of the political implications of Deleuze's ontology foist on him a conception of politics that simply is not his own. Deleuze does not deny either the historical reality of past revolutions or the possibility of a revolutionary present or future. But, on the one hand, he rejects the view that the sense of any revolution can be subsumed in the idea that it breaks with the mundane, the everyday or the established powers. As Deleuze says of Nietzsche, he 'does not believe in resounding "great events", but in the silent plurality of senses of each event' (*NP* 4). And, on the other hand, he holds that a politics calling for radical or revolutionary change frequently remains too restricted in both its breadth and its depth. It remains limited in breadth because, as with the sense of all events, there are multiple forms of novel becoming whose political significance is often lost because they are treated by this politics as being merely personal or aesthetic. And it remains limited in depth in so far as any revolutionary politics that depends on the consolidation of a revolutionary identity ultimately refers to a micropolitical domain of becoming that is no less 'revolutionary' but is not based on identity formation. Most understandings of revolutionary politics, Deleuze holds, focus on the historical factors that precede and might seem to cause its emergence, such as conditions of inequality and exploitation, holding these to lead to the formation of a collective identity that opposes them. These historical contexts, however, only provide the background for another kind of revolutionary experimentation that is neither historical nor oppositional, but rather untimely and creative.[32] Politics, like time and becoming, consists of multiple dispersed layers that are interwoven and folded into one another, and where it might seem like a mundane and repetitive 'politics as usual' dominates one level, important transformations and repetitions of difference may take place on another. Indeed, in the ontology Deleuze advances, such combinations of apparent stasis and fundamental change are to be expected – hence the complexity of his and Guattari's attitude towards the events of May 1968.[33]

As for the question of being able to grasp the difference between changes, it is certainly the case that Deleuze does not offer a set of hard criteria, normative or otherwise, either to identify genuinely creative changes or to distinguish what might be seen as positive or valuable versus negative or destructive change. He and Guattari speak of experiments that can be botched or that can end up being cancerous, fascist or self-destructive, but this seems only to lead them to raise the question of 'whether we have it within our means to make the selection' (ATP 165) without providing any answer. We will return in greater detail to this issue later, but can note here that Deleuze holds this selection to be a matter of ethics, understood as an *ethos* or a way of life, albeit one that is political in nature. It is, in this respect, a question of 'another sensibility, another way of feeling' (NP 64), and this makes it less a question of knowing or cognitively grasping different possibilities for change and more a matter of a sense 'that allows one to 'see' them. Deleuze considers Foucault to have been a 'seer' who grasped the intolerable in what was known to all but nevertheless invisible. Foucault's establishment of the Prison

Information Group (*Groupe d'Information sur les Prisons*, or GIP) came from the fact that 'what he saw was actually intolerable. . . . It was intolerable, not because it was unjust, but because no one saw it, because it was imperceptible. But everyone knew it. It was no secret. Everyone knew about this prison in the prison, but no one saw it. Foucault *saw* it' (*TRM* 274–5). To see in this way is to take up a perspective, and to be taken up by it; it is to go through 'a curious stationary journey'. It engenders certain profound changes even where little or nothing seems to have occurred: after the GIP, Deleuze maintains, even though the status of prisons had not altered, a new form of political utterance was created by both inmates and non-inmates (279–80). Politics, for Deleuze, emerges from becomings in which what changes first and foremost is not our world but our own selves, without which no worldly change can be accomplished.[34] These changes, in turn, are a matter of repetition.

The simulacrum and the simulation of identity

Deleuze's ontology, then, is an ontology of sense in which an immanent and forceful 'difference in itself' involves and explicates itself at multiple levels, generating both virtual and actual disjunctive syntheses of difference that are structured by and unfold via repetition. Deleuze and Guattari refer to these networks of difference as 'multiplicities' that do not reduce to any form of unity, thus exceeding the dialectical opposition between the One and the Many. And they also call them 'rhizomes', in reference to underground fleshy plants such as ginger that grow horizontally, sending out roots and shoots, without a fixed centre or limit.[35] Deleuze and Guattari distinguish rhizomatic pluralisms from arboreal or tree-like ones in which differences emerge like roots and branches from a central trunk. Arboreal pluralisms submit difference to principles of identity and unity, wherein they are different only in relation to a more encompassing sameness. It is in relation to these two images that they declare: 'We're tired of trees. We should stop believing in trees, roots, and radicles. They've made us suffer too much' (*ATP* 15).

In his early works, however, Deleuze uses the term 'simulacra' to designate 'systems in which different relates to different through difference itself' (*DR* 277). He later rejects this terminology, writing in a 1990 letter to Jean-Clet Martin that by the time of *A Thousand Plateaus* he had 'totally abandoned the notion' and that it 'is all but worthless' (*TRM* 362). In their last collaborative work, Deleuze and Guattari declare: 'Philosophy has not remained unaffected by the general movement that replaced Critique with sales promotion. The simulacrum, the simulation of a packet of noodles, has become the true concept; and the one who packages the product, commodity, or work of art has become the philosopher, conceptual persona, or artist' (*WIP* 10). This statement accords with the dominant contemporary uses of the concept of simulacra, which retain its Platonist reference to a false difference that is detached from and merely simulates reality. Ironically, this idea of simulacra as a 'difference without a real status' (Badiou 2000: 25) is also attributed to Deleuze by interpreters who hold him not to be a thinker of multiplicity at all. It is not surprising that Deleuze would eventually distance himself from the vocabulary of simulacra and simulation, given the misunderstandings that came to surround interpretations of his use of these terms.

Nevertheless, Deleuze's early deployment of this language is directed precisely against this Platonist dismissal of simulacra, attacking a central ambiguity in Plato's treatment of this difference. On the one hand, Plato holds simulacra – including art, illusion, simulation and the human figures who embody these, such as the artist, the actor and the sophist – to be mere copies of copies. In the *Republic*, for example, the Idea or Form of a couch is distinguished from the physical couch that copies it and that is manufactured by the craftsman who grasps the Form intellectually, and from the painting of the couch created by the artist who simply plays with images. Form, copy and simulacrum are in this way each assigned different degrees of reality and truth (Plato 1961: *Republic*, 596b–599), with Plato treating simulacra as weak imitations inhabiting the lowest regions of the order of reality he calls the 'divided line'. On the other hand, however, Plato worries that simulacra have a deceptive nature that allows them to masquerade as truth. Thus, although he holds that, in accordance with the principle that everyone has a single skill that allows him or her to do one thing best, no actor can play different

DELEUZE'S ONTOLOGY

roles such as tragedy and comedy equally well (396a–b), he declares that the ideal city will ban any actor 'who was capable by his cunning of assuming every kind of shape and imitating all things' (398a). The problem Plato encounters is that the deceptiveness of simulacra is inconsistent with the view that they are copies of true reality twice removed. If one takes an original document and photocopies of it, and then takes the photocopy and copies it, and then continues the procedure, the successive copies become more faded and obviously imperfect. What characterizes a good simulation, however, is that *it seems to be as real as what it is said to copy*. In this way, it is *neither* an original *nor* a copy, putting the distinction between the two into question.

Deleuze argues that this quandary forces Plato to treat simulacra as not merely degraded copies but false or illegitimate ones: unlike the genuine copy that participates and thereby resembles its Form, the simulacrum is a pretender that 'produces an *effect* of resemblance' (*LS* 258). The real aim of Plato's thought, then, is to establish the difference between copies and simulacra. The distinction between the Form of Beauty and the beautiful thing, for example, ultimately serves to distinguish what genuinely partakes of Beauty and what feigns participation. This capacity to deceive, however, also gives simulacra a power to exceed their place that challenges the very hierarchy of Form, copy and simulation that Plato employs in the effort to contain them. As copies are repetitions that resemble the Forms serving as their models, this separation of copy from simulacrum, Deleuze maintains, requires 'subordinating difference to instances of the Same, the Similar, the Analogous and the Opposed' (*DR* 265). This subordination, however, lacks any ontological basis, having 'no motivation apart from the moral' (265).

Legitimate copies change and become in accordance with the Form that acts upon them, their likeness to eternal models resulting from an internal connection to these exemplars. In contrast, simulacra elude the Form's power, so that their false likeness to the Form must be an effect 'completely external and produced by totally different means than those at work within the model' (*LS* 258). Simulacra thereby elude the orders of identity and resemblance while still mimicking their effects, and so they too are repetitions, but repetitions of difference. In this sense they follow 'a model of the Other' (258), but this indicates that they really follow no model at all. In contrast to the unidirectional becoming of copies governed by Forms, simulacra are characterized by a 'pure becoming' that moves in two divergent directions (or senses) at once. Plato speaks of such a paradoxical becoming in several dialogues, particularly *Parmenides*,[36] though he often also dismisses it. Deleuze, however, holds that this dual valence is the positive character that simulacra display when they are no longer denigrated as copies of copies. 'The simulacrum is built upon a disparity or upon a difference. It internalizes a dissimilarity' (258). And in this way simulacra are disjunctive syntheses of difference. The affirmation of simulacra, which, Deleuze holds, executes a 'reversal of Platonism' (256), is thus an affirmation of difference, divergence and a repetition that forever eludes identity and the present.

This repetition of difference, however, also engenders the appearance of identity, stability and continuity: 'an identity would be found to be necessarily projected, or rather retojected, on to the originary difference and a resemblance interiorised within the divergent series. We should say of this identity and this resemblance that they are "simulated". . . .The same and the similar are fictions engendered by the eternal return' (*DR* 126). This is most certainly not a simulation of reality, as the dismissive view of simulacra would contend. Rather, it demonstrates that identity and its correlate concepts, which are often taken to be the basis for conceiving reality, are simulations or surface effects created by the simulacrum's multiplicity. Nevertheless, it would be incorrect to say that stability, continuity and identity are simply unreal; rather, it is the foundational position and the substantiality they seem to hold that are untrue. In this respect it comes down to an error of perspective, the stability and endurance of identity being similar to the way the wave patterns formed in the wake of a ship moving through water may appear fixed when seen from a distance: identity, in short, is an appearance that arises from becoming without this becoming ever actually ceasing to change. Consider, for example, an individual who has a seemingly stable personality characterized by generosity, a sarcastic sense of humour and a short temper. Since no one remains the same over time either physically (our bodies constantly change) or 'spiritually' (evermore layers of our past accumulate in us, our comportment towards the future shifts in different ways, we having changing relationships to different people and so forth), the individual who retains these traits over time cannot have them for the same reasons because he or she is not actually the same person. These constants are only the somewhat regular results of the varying syntheses that make the individual who he or she is at particular moments and in particular contexts. The stability, which is certainly real, exists in the effect, it is a surface effect of processes of becoming and repetition, but through an illusion of perspective it appears to be the individual's enduring base or character, persisting through all changes. A reversal of this perspective is what Deleuze has in mind when he speaks of identity as a principle that must now revolve around difference (40).

Plato relies on the really existing partial stabilities of the physical world to posit a distinction between appearance and unchanging essence, allowing him to indicate the existence of Forms and thereby introduce transcendence into philosophy. Ironically, it is essence that is only apparent, and this appearance is generated by the very simulacra Plato disparages. Even after replacing the terminology of simulacra with that of rhizomes and multiplicities, Deleuze retains the idea that difference generates the illusory appearance or simulation of identity. He and Guattari note that the multiplicity they call the plane of immanence 'is surrounded by illusions. These are not abstract misinterpretations or just external pressures but rather thought's mirages' (*WIP* 49). The persistence of these mirages accords with Deleuze's central ontological tenets concerning difference and sense. The enigmatic Deleuzian differenciator, as a difference in itself, must be characterized in such a way that it 'is always missing from its place, from its own identity and from its representation' (*DR* 105). Implicating and explicating itself across various syntheses of difference, it expresses itself in the strange way in which incompossibilities are somehow connected and resonating with one another. Returning a final time to the example of Leibniz's theodicy, if the differenciator can be named 'Adam' it is because it generates an illusion by which it hides its own character as a difference, presenting itself instead as a common identity across differences: there is no single and fixed identity for Adam, who sins in one world and does not sin in another, but there is nevertheless the appearance of one. In that case, however, the real illusion is that underneath all possible illusions, disguises and differences, there is a fixed identity: 'The only illusion is that of unmasking something or someone' (106). This, indeed, was the starting point of Deleuze's ontology of sense: appearances present the illusion of there being an essence beneath them, when there is actually nothing – or, rather, there is only difference – underneath.

* * *

In those strands of contemporary political theory where Deleuze has been most influential, the account of the virtual and actual, the dynamic and vitalist conception of becoming, the role of the past and memory in the structure and unfolding of time and the multiplicity of time itself are obvious sources of inspiration. In all these respects, it is a Bergsonian Deleuze who seems to be the primary inspiration for this theory, although Deleuze's debts to Spinoza, Nietzsche and others have also been appreciated.[37] But what has frequently been ignored is the thesis on identity as a simulation or optical effect, various theorists indebted to Deleuze perhaps assuming it is germane only to the language of simulacra that Deleuze himself abandoned. This neglect is perhaps also the result of a continuing focus on identity that many 'political theories of abundance' retain despite taking their cue from Deleuze's thought. And it may further be due to a concern that if identity were epiphenomenal it would also be inconsequential, although as we will see, Deleuze sees the categories of identity still playing an important and inescapable role in structuring many aspects of social and political life. Regardless, these theorists tend to converge with a reading commonly offered by Deleuze's critics, a reading that, while treating both virtual and actual as realms of difference, holds the actual to be a domain of relative fixity, as though actualization were a coagulation and individuation of the virtual's energetic becoming.[38] While such a view may accord with a Bergsonian understanding of the virtual and actual, as Bergson himself in *Creative Evolution* distinguishes spirit and matter in terms of the former being a virtual energetic force or *élan vital* and the latter being a condensation and settling down of this impulse,[39] it is not Deleuze's position. Identity certainly pertains to Deleuze's actual, as its differenciation allows for categories and resemblances to be established, but it does not define it. Rather, coagulation, identity, subjects and objects that seem to endure over time, the negative separation of things from what they are not and so forth are simply appearances that characterize actual entities and events when viewed from a certain macro-level perspective. As will be seen, the status of identity as a simulation is central to the micropolitics that Deleuze articulates. On the one hand, it provides a space for a politics that leaves identity behind; on the other hand, however, the appearance of identity is crucial for such a politics to be instigated. The same dynamics of becoming that generate the appearances of stability and identity also provide the mechanisms by which they are dissolved.

3

Deleuze's Nietzsche

As noted at the end of the previous chapter, it is primarily a Bergsonian Deleuze who has been presented in the recent political theory that has drawn on his work. This trend accords with a more general one found in many circles of Deleuze scholarship that foregrounds Deleuze's relation to Bergson and often treats Bergson as his chief inspiration.[1] There is certainly an irony in this interpretation, given the role Nietzsche plays in many of the key lines of thought that unfold in Deleuze's writings. It is Nietzsche who replaces Bergson in the move from the second to the third synthesis of time in *Difference and Repetition* and in the turn to the 'Powers of the False' in the sixth chapter of *Cinema 2*. It is Nietzsche too with whom the thesis of univocal being, which holds that all beings are compelled by an immanent excess towards their self-overcoming, culminates in 'nomadic distribution and crowned anarchy' (*DR* 37; see also 41). Many of the key ontological theses Deleuze tries to develop through Bergson, particularly in his early essay 'Bergson's Conception of Difference' (*DI* 32–51) and his *Bergsonism*, seem clearly to find their real home only in Nietzsche.[2] And the ethical themes developed throughout Deleuze's work are certainly indebted far more to Nietzsche (and Spinoza, who is very close to Nietzsche here) than Bergson, with Nietzsche's genealogy of bad conscience, for example, providing the key signposts for Deleuze and Guattari's genealogy of social machines in *Anti-Oedipus*. But Deleuze also explicitly identifies Nietzsche as the figure who transitioned his approach from one that took other thinkers 'from behind' in order to make them say something that broke with the traditional readings of the history of philosophy to one that brought his own voice into works of original philosophy. And, interestingly, Deleuze identifies his Bergson book as an exemplar of the earlier approach, suggesting that Bergson's thought was more a kind of fertile soil for experimentation than the key influence on the way Deleuze read others or approached philosophy generally.[3]

In broader political theory and philosophy circles, Deleuze is best known for his seminal work on Nietzsche. This is no doubt due to the way Nietzsche gained prominence in Anglo-American debates in the late 1970s and early 1980s, and also to the way Deleuze's *Nietzsche and Philosophy*, originally published in 1962, played an important role in the French-led Nietzsche revival of the time. For many who criticize the recent use of Nietzsche, particularly in the kind of 'radical democracy' debates discussed in the first chapter, Deleuze is held responsible for inaccurately portraying a 'softer' Nietzsche who can be made into an ally of pluralism only by conveniently forgetting his antagonism to liberal democracy,[4] or for using Nietzsche to valorize an incoherent relativism unable to make the normative judgements on which liberal political theory depends.[5] Others less antagonistic to Nietzsche and more sympathetic to Deleuze's reading focus their criticisms on his use of Nietzsche to attack Hegelian dialectics, holding that Hegel cannot be separated from Nietzsche and dismissed in the easy way Deleuze makes out. Deleuze directs a harsh polemic against Hegel in his Nietzsche book, and declares in its conclusion: 'There is no possible compromise between Hegel and Nietzsche. Nietzsche's philosophy...forms an absolute anti-dialectics and sets out to expose all the mystifications that find a final refuge in the dialectic' (*NP* 195). To many, Deleuze's text betrays a profound ignorance of Hegel, and stages a naive opposition to dialectics that, in a quite dialectical fashion, remains dependent on its Hegelian adversary.[6] Those who are critical of Deleuze on these points usually seem unaware of the role Hyppolite's reading of Hegel plays in his early work, and of the engagements Deleuze has with Hegel that go beyond those found in *Nietzsche and Philosophy*.[7]

If the idea of an ontology of sense, which the early Deleuze identifies in Hegel, is kept in mind, it can be seen that despite the strong rhetoric in *Nietzsche and Philosophy*, in this text and elsewhere Deleuze uses Nietzsche's thought to present a subtle and sophisticated critique of and alternative to dialectics. The key source Deleuze uses to develop the ontology underpinning his reading is Nietzsche's unpublished notebooks, the *Nachlass*, which are only partially available in English in the collection published as *The Will to Power* (1968), although enough is there to support Deleuze's reading. The reliance on Nietzsche's unpublished writings is not without controversy, although also not without precedent: it is central to Heidegger's reading of Nietzsche, for example. Deleuze acknowledges that 'we cannot make use of the posthumous notes, except in directions confirmed by Nietzsche's published works, since these notes are reserved material, as it were, put aside for future elaboration' (*DR* 297). The issue for interpreters, then, is the extent to which the ontology of difference Deleuze draws from Nietzsche's notes carries forward the attacks on identity that are well established in the writings he approved for publication. In Deleuze's hands, Nietzsche's conceptions of quantity, quality, force and will to power, found primarily in the notebooks, are directed against Hegel's dialectical understanding of reconcilable difference, while Nietzsche's published and unpublished writings on the eternal return are brought together to articulate a structure of time that underpins an ethics of overcoming, which Deleuze deploys against a Hegelian ethics of reciprocal recognition. In the Preface to *Difference and Repetition*, Deleuze attributes a wide range of recent philosophical developments to 'a generalized anti-Hegelianism' (xix), and it is unsurprising that his readings of Bergson, Spinoza, Leibniz and many other figures form part of his own project against Hegelian dialectics.[8] But it is through Nietzsche that this project reaches its fulfilment and inaugurates another: the search for a new form of philosophical expression.[9] This second project is inseparable from a transmutation of thinking and being, which is underpinned by Nietzsche's view that 'the point of critique is not justification but a different way of feeling: another sensibility' (*NP* 94).

A new ontology of sense and force and a new method of critique

Deleuze opens his seminal work on Nietzsche with the statement that 'Nietzsche's most general project is the introduction of the concepts of sense and value into philosophy' (*NP* 1). Sense, as was discussed in the previous chapter, is part of an expressivist ontology that opposes essentialist and humanist conceptions of being. These latter ontologies take human being to be the being of a subject, and treat values as the foundational principles this subject uses to judge and evaluate. Deleuze, however, contends that Nietzsche's philosophy executes 'a *critical* reversal' wherein values emerge from *evaluations* – that is, from '"perspectives of appraisal". . . .Evaluations, in essence, are not values but ways of being, modes of existence of those who judge and evaluate, serving as principles for the values on the basis of which they judge' (1). Nietzsche himself certainly does not limit evaluation and judgement to human being, holding these instead to be components of the sense expressed by being as such.[10] When the focus is placed on our own being, however, it becomes clear that 'we always have the beliefs, feelings and thoughts that we deserve given our way of being or our style of life' (1). Our values, judgements and sense of things follow quite naturally from our position in the world, and from the way the world constitutes us and conditions the emergence of our subjectivity. But perspectives are necessarily limited, and therefore multiple, so that what matters above all is the 'differential element' (2) that sense and values express and from which they arise.

Nietzsche's method of 'genealogy', Deleuze contends, aims precisely to excavate this differential element, which is ultimately a 'difference in itself' that implicates and unfolds itself in actual relations of difference. In everyday language 'genealogy' denotes a family tree, a record of ancestry and origin, and Nietzsche's genealogy of morality is certainly a study of the historical origins of our moral values, as well as a study of their psychological origins. But for Deleuze it is above all an exploration of ontological origins, and of the sense and value of these origins.[11] Genealogy investigates the senses and values that can emerge from a constitutive ontological difference in itself.

Genealogical analysis proceeds through an association between sense and force: 'We will never find the sense of something (of a human, a biological or even a physical phenomenon) if we do not know the force which appropriates the thing, which exploits it, which takes possession of it or is expressed in it' (*NP* 3). Meaning, sense and the perspectives from which they follow are products of a struggle among forces, and, though Deleuze does not use the term in *Nietzsche and Philosophy*, we can add that these are virtual forces of the type discussed in the previous chapter. This formulation is incomplete, however, as perspectival sense is never related to an independent thing or object; rather, 'the object itself is force, expression of a force' (6). Nietzsche, Deleuze argues, holds that the concepts of thing and object, whether physical (as in the idea of the atom) or psychological (as in the idea of the ego), cannot account for their necessary relations to others, and thus only become coherent when replaced with the concept of force (6–8). In this way, 'every force is. . .essentially related to another force' (6). The broad similarities to the concept of force that emerges in Hegel's Dialectic of Consciousness is no doubt behind Deleuze's warning that Nietzsche's theory of forces should not be confused with Hegel's (8–10). Hegel, as we saw in the last chapter, argues that the thing of sense certainty and the object of perception are ultimately subsumed by a notion of relational forces, which oppose or negate one another in such a way that an identity of opposites obtains. Against this, Deleuze maintains, 'in Nietzsche the essential relation of one force to another is never conceived of as a negative element in the essence' (8). Rather than a dialectical relationship, Nietzsche's forces are related through another kind of difference: 'For the speculative element of negation, opposition or contradiction Nietzsche substitutes the practical element of *difference*, the object of affirmation and enjoyment' (9). Instead of a dialectical synthesis, then, Nietzsche presents the synthesis of forces as one of disjunction.

Nevertheless, Deleuze's claim that the Nietzschean account of force is aimed at the Hegelian conception seems to be weakened by the rather unphilosophical language he uses to present it. He states that 'all force is appropriation, domination, exploitation of a quantity of reality' (*NP* 3); that 'a new force can only appear and appropriate an object by first of all putting on the mask of the forces which are already in possession of the object' (5); and that 'the force which makes itself obeyed. . .affirms its own difference and enjoys this difference' (8–9). The idea of force is also stretched to the point where any form of body, 'whether it is chemical, biological, social, or political' (40), is said to be constituted by unequal force relations, and organic action and thought are explained in terms of forceful instincts or drives. This metaphorical and vitalist approach seems too far removed from that of the *Phenomenology* to have any substantive connection to Hegel. However, this is precisely where Deleuze directs it. Despite the apparent philosophical sloppiness in his personification of forces, Deleuze maintains that it is Hegel's language of opposition, contradiction and negation that is inadequate to the task of grasping the nature of force relations. Hegel's account remains one-sided and incomplete because his stolid and seemingly more analytical and philosophical language removes the *forcefulness* that makes forces what they are.

> Hegel...proposes an abstract movement of concepts instead of a movement of the *Physis* and the *Psyche*. Hegel substitutes the abstract relation of the particular to the concept in general for the true relation of the singular and the universal in the Idea. He thus remains in the reflected element of 'representation', within simple generality. He represents concepts instead of dramatizing Ideas. (*DR* 10)

In contrast, Deleuze argues, Nietzsche's approach reflects a rigorous 'method of *dramatisation*' (*NP* 78) that goes beyond abstract representations of force. Terms such as 'active', 'reactive', 'dominating' and 'submissive' express the nature of force concretely. They denote an asymmetry and agonism that for Deleuze underpins the sense of things, concepts and events, making them obstinately resistant to mediation. And they allow Nietzsche to establish a typology of forces and force relations that can determine the perspectival origin of different senses and values: certain values must derive from a noble perspective engendered by active and dominant forces; others must follow from a base one engendered by reactive and weak forces.

Underpinning this portrayal of agonistic force relations is Nietzsche's rethinking of quantity and quality, which Deleuze draws primarily from the *Nachlass*. There is a subtle relation between quantity and quality that, for Deleuze, makes genealogy an interpretive art: '[T]he problem of measuring forces will be delicate because it brings the art of qualitative interpretations into play' (*NP* 42). Nietzsche himself explicitly opposes his conceptions to those of mechanistic world views that reduce qualities to quantities – that treat the colour red, for example, as nothing more than light waves vibrating within a certain frequency band – but Deleuze holds them also to be applicable to a critique of dialectics. First to mechanism. Nietzsche declares that 'everything for which the word "knowledge" makes any sense refers to the domain of reckoning, weighing, measuring, to the domain of quantity' (Nietzsche 1968: §565); but he also maintains that 'we need "unities" in order to be able to reckon: that does not mean we must suppose that such unities exist' (§635). Mechanism begins with unities that can be quantified or counted, but the idea of unity applies to abstract things and objects, not to forces. On a more concrete level, where there are no unities or things pre-existing their relations but only incongruent relations of force, quantity cannot be a number but only a relation: as Deleuze argues, there is no 'quantity in itself', but rather 'difference in quantity', a relation of more and less, but one that cannot be placed on a fixed numerical scale. Forces are determined quantitatively – 'Nietzsche always believed that forces were quantitative and had to be defined quantitatively' (*NP* 43) – and this determination takes the form of relative strength and weakness.[12] But this difference does not entail fixed numerical values being assigned to each force, as this can only be done in abstraction, when, for example, two forces are isolated in a closed system, as mechanism does when it examines the world. A quantitative difference between forces is therefore on the order of an intensive difference à la Leibniz, an intensive quantity in which forces vice-dict rather than contradict one another.

Hegel too is critical of the independent unities posited by mechanism, as unity always negates itself and relates to what it is not. However, far from keeping quantitative difference, numerical value and quality separate, he seeks to synthesize them in such a way that they pass into one another. In Hegel's logic (1975: §§89–111), quantity and quality are opposites synthesized in the concept of 'measure' through the idea that a sufficient change in quantity yields a change in quality: when water reaches 100 degrees Celsius it boils. It follows that diverse quantitative changes can be treated equally, which, for Deleuze, amounts again to an abstraction, in so far as it ignores the singularity of changes and relations in order to organize them according to a higher sameness. Quality, in the form of the idea of equality, is thereby imposed on quantity in a way that annuls the intensive difference germane to it. Although it is certainly true that different pots of water, under analogous conditions, will boil at 100 degrees, there are still ontological differences within any repetition of identity, and while these remain outside the order of representation and may be treated with indifference by science and dialectics, they are indispensable to the sense of these phenomena.

Nietzsche himself frequently criticizes the assumption of identical cases in logic, science and judgement.[13] 'What interests him primarily, from the standpoint of quantity itself', Deleuze states, 'is the fact that differences in quantity cannot be reduced to equality' (*NP* 43). Deleuze thus holds that for Nietzsche forces can *never* be equal, and so their differences cannot be dialectically resolved: 'To dream of two equal forces, even if they are said to be of opposite senses is a coarse and approximate dream, a statistical dream in which the living is submerged but which chemistry dispels' (43).[14] Being related through disjunction, Nietzschean forces are in relations of inequality, but an inequality in flux: they are relations of *disequilibrium*. When forces clash one is necessarily superior and so dominates an inferior force that submits to it, though the latter force does not cease to be a force (40) and, for this reason, force relations can be inverted or reversed. Physical, psychological, vital and social regularities can certainly emerge from these changing force relations and preserve themselves over time. But as Nietzsche says of the supposed instinct for self-preservation in living things, this 'is only one of the indirect and most frequent *results*' (Nietzsche 1989: §13).

Quality here arises from quantity. There is always a quantitative difference between forces, but as forces are nothing beyond their relations to other forces, this difference in quantity between forces is constitutive of what each force is, and therefore the qualities each one has.[15] Relative strength entails domination, and therefore the quality of being 'active', so that powerful forces command, create, transform and overcome; weakness, conversely, entails a quality of being 'reactive', which manifests itself in submission, but also adaptation, compromise and utilitarian calculation (*NP* 40–4). The active or reactive quality of each force thereby indicates the tactics or means by which it exercises its power (54). When weak or inferior forces become dominant – when their sense and valuations of things becomes hegemonic – it is not because they form a greater force than what had dominated them (56–8). Rather, the 'triumph of reactive forces' (145) is a matter of qualities that allow weak forces to overcome their quantitative inferiority and cause strong forces to lose their grip on dominance: 'inferior forces can prevail without ceasing to be inferior in quantity and reactive in quality, without ceasing to be slaves in this sense' (58).

The final aspect of Nietzsche's ontology of forces is the 'will to power'. Once mechanism's abstractions of unity and numerical quantity are eliminated, 'no things remain but only dynamic quanta, in a relation of tension to all other dynamic quanta: their essence lies in their relation to all other quanta, in their "effect" upon the same' (Nietzsche 1968: §635). But if the connection between the quantitative differences among related forces and the distinct qualities of each force is accepted, then the will to power must be acknowledged, Nietzsche maintains, simply because 'mere variations of power could not feel themselves to be such: there must be present something that wants to grow and interprets the value of whatever else wants to grow' (§643). Nietzsche holds the will to power to be the drive that must be imputed to forces to make them what they are: no force, whether active or reactive, could be or become without a non-subjective compulsion to discharge its strength against whatever might resist it. He thus declares that 'it expresses the characteristic that cannot be thought out of the mechanistic order without thinking away this order itself' (§634), as without the will to power everything in mechanism's 'purely quantitative world. . .would be dead, stiff, motionless' (§564). Nietzsche defines the will to power 'as an insatiable desire to manifest power; or as the employment and exercise of power, as a creative drive, etc.' (§619). But he also holds that it is not a will in the ordinary sense: 'the will of psychology hitherto is an unjustified generalization. . .this will *does not exist at all*' (§692). Deleuze maintains that the will to power has dual aspects as a supplement to force and a factor internal or immanent to force, as a differential and a genetic element of force relations, and as a product of force relations and a determinant of these relations (*NP*

49–52). He also holds it to be the principle of the quality of force and the signification of the sense of related forces – that is to say, it is what the configuration of active and reactive forces expresses (83, 85). This expression, Deleuze holds, can be either affirmative or negative: 'What a will wants, depending on its quality, is to affirm its difference or to deny what differs' (78). It thereby embodies a perspective – as Nietzsche states, 'every center of force adopts a perspective toward the entire remainder, i.e., its own particular valuation, mode of action, and mode of resistance' (Nietzsche 1968: §567). Affirmative and negative wills to power are closely related to the active and reactive qualities of forces, but they are not identical to them. Rather, Deleuze explains, affirmation expresses active forces in their becoming dominant, while negation expresses forces in their becoming reactive.[16]

From all this, Deleuze says, Nietzsche derives his critical genealogical method: 'Any given concept, feeling or belief will be treated as symptoms of a will that wills something. What does *the one that* says this, that thinks or feels that, will? It is a matter of showing that he could not say, think or feel this particular thing if he did not have a particular will, particular forces, a particular way of being' (*NP* 78). This will, again, is not a human or psychological will. It is rather a dimension of being that must be imputed to it once it is understood as expressive. In *Difference and Repetition*, Deleuze links Nietzsche's will to power to the differenciator, holding it to be 'a difference which is originary, pure, synthetic, and in-itself' (*DR* 125). In this regard, willing is the virtual aspect of force by which it differentiates and differenciates itself, involving and explicating itself in a repetition of difference. The will to power 'makes the difference' between diverse and incommensurable perspectives, differenciating forces into distinct actual types from a virtual level of intensive and differential relations of mutual imbrication and tension. There is no resolution or reconciliation among these perspectives or the wills to power that express them. For Deleuze, this is the basis for Nietzsche's pluralism – 'Nietzsche's philosophy cannot be understood without taking his essential pluralism into account' (*NP* 4) – and ultimately where his anti-Hegelianism resides: 'Anti-Hegelianism runs through Nietzsche's work as its cutting edge. We can already feel it in the theory of forces' (8).

Nietzschean and Hegelian masters and slaves

For Deleuze, Nietzsche's affirmative and negative wills to power affirm or deny difference. The denial of difference is its reduction to opposition and negation, which is why, Deleuze argues, a dialectical negation of negation that returns difference to identity presents only a semblance of affirmation. In Hegel's social and political thought, this pseudo-affirmation takes the form of reciprocal recognition among self-conscious beings. The parameters of this idea are set out in Hegel's Dialectic of Lordship and Bondage, also known as the Master–Slave Dialectic. Deleuze is not the first to counterpoise Nietzsche's genealogy of noble and slave moralities to Hegel's dialectical analysis. But where others treat the Nietzschean version as a kind of inverted dialectic in which the roles Hegel assigns to master and slave figures are reversed, Deleuze holds that Nietzsche's genealogy challenges and overturns dialectics as such. The entire dialectic, Deleuze contends, conceives difference from the perspective of weak and inferior forces, a perspective that can only see it as opposition: 'There *is* a standpoint from which opposition appears as the genetic element of force – the standpoint of reactive forces' (*NP* 159). Once opposition is treated as foundational, its synthesis amounts to one where identity is recognized through it, according to an abstract paradigm of representation: 'The famous dialectical aspect of the master-slave relationship depends on the fact that power is conceived not as will to power but as representation of power, representation of superiority, recognition by "the one" of the superiority of "the other". What the wills in Hegel want is to have their power *recognised*, to *represent* their power' (10).

The Dialectic of Lordship and Bondage is part of the Dialectic of Self-Consciousness, which comprises the fourth chapter of the *Phenomenology of Spirit*. Analogous to the Dialectic of Consciousness that precedes it, the aim of this dialectic is to determine the conditions under which self-consciousness has truth – that is to say, the conditions in which its subjective self-certainty accords with objective reality. On a basic level, self-consciousness for Hegel is a process of negation in which a conscious being detaches itself from the world in order to experience and perceive it as if from outside, and then negates this negation by realizing that it is immersed in the world, thereby overcoming the initial alienation. In being aware that it carries out this process, self-consciousness recognizes itself as an agent that makes a difference in its world. Now the second negation, by which consciousness both exercises its agency and connects back to its world, can take two forms: consciousness can negate the independence of an external thing by possessing, consuming or destroying it, or it can negate itself in such a way that it gives itself over to some other in the world. Both of these forms are expressions of desire – and Hegel, in the pages preceding the Dialectic of Lordship and Bondage, defines self-consciousness as '*Desire* in general' (Hegel 1977: §167) – but only the second can secure the certainty and truth that the dialectic seeks. And this second form of desire is only possible in relation to another self-conscious being. Put simply, I cannot secure my own self-consciousness simply by seeking objects that I desire and negating their independence from me, since this is an activity also performed by many other beings that lack self-consciousness;[17] if my self-consciousness is valuable, this can be confirmed only by my being *recognized* as an object of desire for another, but this other must be a valuable self-conscious being too. If my dog or cat seems to value me, this is not enough to validate my sense of human worth, and I would not seek to negate my subjectivity in order to become an object of my pet's desire anyway. Recognition must therefore be reciprocal, as my self-consciousness and self-worth depend upon being valued by another in whom I can perceive the same kind of self-awareness or relation-to-self that I seek to confirm in myself. As Hegel says: 'A self-consciousness exists *for a self-consciousness*. Only so is it in fact self-consciousness; for only in this way does the unity of itself in its otherness become explicit for it' (§177). The social attainment of reciprocal recognition is the realization of the Identity of identity and difference in a community, and Hegel places this achievement at the culmination of human history. This is a community in which each member, no matter how different and alien the others may seem, can recognize himself in the self-consciousness of others, so that they are opposed to him and yet also the same. The later chapters of the *Phenomenology* trace out this human history, which reaches its conclusion in 'Absolute Knowing, or Spirit that knows itself as Spirit' (§808).

The Dialectic of Lordship and Bondage outlines the first stages of this process at a personal level, and while reciprocal recognition is not achieved in it, this condition is revealed as its ultimate necessity. It begins with two individuals, each seeking recognition from the other of his value as a self-conscious being while refusing to recognize the other in turn, and thus refusing to take the necessary step of self-negation. In this way each one opposes and frustrates his own and the other's desire. Because they understand self-consciousness as a demonstrable independence from the world and all its constraints, each is compelled to establish his freedom and mastery by engaging in a life-and-death struggle. Only by risking life can one demonstrate that life has no hold on one's freedom, making one's mastery manifest and securing one's value as a desirable being. This struggle can end with one or both combatants dying, or with both giving up before reaching a final resolution, but these results cannot advance the dialectic. However, if one capitulates in the face of the possibility of death – the ultimate negation – then the dialectic can commence with the victor assuming the role of the master and the loser the role of the slave.

It would seem initially that the master's self-consciousness is now validated by virtue of the slave's recognition of his superiority. But this is quickly revealed to be an empty and valueless acknowledgement, as it comes from an inferior and therefore lacks significance. The lord's strategy of obtaining recognition by force is thus self-defeating, leading to the negation of his freedom and sense of worth. Indeed, despite being the victor, the master ends up becoming dependent on the slave's providing for his needs, thereby losing the capacity to care for himself. Meanwhile, the bondsman, whose self-consciousness appears initially to have been negated, sees this negation reversed through the fear of death and the compulsion to work. Experiencing the possibility of death negates the bondsman's initial view that life and freedom oppose each other, and compels him to find meaning in his life against the meaninglessness death poses to him. Being compelled to work by his master, the bondsman learns to hold his desire in check in order to carry out tasks, and to design and execute a plan to complete his projects. He thereby achieves a sense of autonomy and mastery even in the absence of recognition (Hegel 1977: §§194–6). This amounts to the 'rediscovery of himself by himself' as 'the bondsman realizes that it is precisely in his work wherein he seemed to have only an alienated existence that he acquires a mind of his own' (§196). While lack of recognition keeps the bondsman from achieving genuine self-consciousness, where subjective certainty and objective truth correspond, it is from his inferior position that the dialectical negations necessary to achieve it emerge. Ultimately, the sense and direction of Hegel's history are found in the working out of the Master–Slave Dialectic, which is driven by the bondsman and which ends when the hierarchy and alienation embodied in the relationship of lordship and bondage are replaced by equality.

As already seen, however, such equality and reconciliation are anathema to Nietzsche. Genealogy begins from the premise that relations are not oppositional and cannot be equalized, but instead are agonistic and in flux. If equality, opposition and the identity of opposites are treated as values, the question becomes: what is the nature of the will to power that wills them, and what is the perspective from which they appear to be real? Once this analytical shift is made, it becomes clear that the master's and slave's perspectives, even while constituted only through each other, remain irreducible and irreconcilable. The pretence of recognition amounts to a denial and disrespect of difference, demonstrating that recognition issues from a negative will to power that, for Nietzsche, has become the dominant expression of values. The dialectic as a whole reflects a slave perspective, and, as such, so too does its presentation of the master: there is nothing more inaccurate, for Nietzsche, than the portrayal of the master as one who seeks to dominate the weak in order to secure his identity and sense of self. As Deleuze states: 'Underneath the Hegelian image of the master we always find the slave' (NP 10).

Inferior forces do not cease being forces, but their submissive relation to more powerful forces means they must discharge themselves in a qualitatively different way. To be a slave is to be compelled into passivity, and the slavish will to power must therefore express itself indirectly. Unable to act in a world of agonism and strife, the slave judges action from the perspective of the recipient: what benefits me, what seems to be selfless on the part of the actor, is good; what is harmful to me, and can be attributed to the actor's selfishness, is evil. In a creative moment, inferior forces invent the moral concept of evil as intentional harm and attribute it to the powerful. Since those who can only be the recipients of others' actions are by nature too impotent to be harmful, this invention also enables the slaves to secure their identity as good through contradistinction: they are evil; we are not like them; therefore we are good. This constitutes 'the slave revolt in morality' (Nietzsche 1967: 1.10).

Central to the so-called self-consciousness and interiority conceived of by the slave is this false separation of doer and deed, by which nobles and slaves are said to choose their actions. 'To demand of strength that it should *not* express itself as strength', Nietzsche proclaims, 'is just as absurd as to demand of weakness that it should express itself as strength' (1967: 1.13). Despite the fact that the strong and weak both have the values they ought to have and act in the way they should be expected to act given their position in relations of strife, 'popular morality. . .separates strength from expressions of strength, as if there were a neutral substratum behind the strong man, which was *free* to express strength or not to do so' (1.13). The will to power that wills this moral opposition between good and evil thus condemns the strife and conflict that characterize force relations, positing instead, alongside its invention of a self-conscious subject, ideals of purity, harmony and truthfulness that separate good and evil subjects. These ideals are associated with the slaves themselves, who make virtues out of the very passivity forced upon them. They celebrate their own purity, humility and obedience as signs of their strength, suggesting that those who choose to harm others lack the strength of will to prevent themselves from acting otherwise.[18] The slavish will to power demands that there be a purpose to suffering, and it suffers much because it is a will to power of weakness. It demands justice from 'a moral world order' (Nietzsche 1974: §357), and this leads the slaves to invent a transcendent God who embodies their ideals and who guarantees the ultimate punishment of evildoers.

Nietzsche attributes the creations of slave morality to *ressentiment*, the French word for 'resentment', which is a spirit that arises in 'natures that are denied the true reaction, that of deeds, and compensate themselves with an imaginary revenge' (Nietzsche 1967: 1.10). For Deleuze, *ressentiment* emerges when inferior reactive forces lose their place in the hierarchical schema of forces, the result being that they no longer obey the superior forces that normally compel them to coordinate 're-actions'. Within the healthy organism, reactive forces play the roles of receiving stimuli in order to prepare for active responses and of ruminating on the traces of past experiences in the unconscious (*NP* 112–13). The slave is one in whom the divide between consciousness and the unconscious is breached, so that past traces invade consciousness without a reaction or response being acted out. The slave is thus one who can neither react nor forget, and in whom old offenses and injuries fester like poison. In this way, 'it is their [reactive forces'] change of place, their displacement which constitutes *ressentiment*' (114). Once *ressentiment* emerges, weakness comes to the fore in such a way that power is exercised without action: 'In Nietzsche "passive" does not mean "non-active"; "non-active" means "reactive"; but "passive" means "non-acted". The only thing that is passive is reaction insofar as it is not acted. The term "passive" stands for the triumph of reaction, the moment when, ceasing to be acted, it becomes a *ressentiment*' (118). The slaves' passivity, this 'non-acted reaction', thus serves as a cover for an aggression far more dangerous, precisely because it is far more impotent, than anything the active master could produce.[19]

Clearly the perspective of the strong who act must be of a different order to that of the weak. Ironically, if unsurprisingly, they will hardly fit the slaves' portrayal, even though the reasons behind this portrayal are easy to comprehend.[20] Active forces express themselves immediately, imposing themselves on resistances that struggle against them. But this requires that resisting forces offer a genuine challenge: they must be active and powerful in order for active forces to express their strength. For the active or noble man, therefore, 'good' names his action, the agonistic context in which his strength is expressed and, crucially, the opponents against whom he struggles. In contrast, what is unable to measure up – essentially what is inferior and slavish – is called 'bad' rather than 'evil'. Now it is certainly the case that this noble morality opposes good and bad. But, as both Nietzsche and Deleuze make clear, good is not defined in opposition to bad: there is no sense in which one is good simply by virtue of not being bad. Deleuze asks: 'who is it that *begins* by saying: "I am good"? It is certainly not the one who compares himself to others, nor the one who compares his actions and his works to superior and transcendent values. . . .The one who says: "I am good", does not wait to be called good' (*NP* 119). The noble conception of good thus differs from its slavish counterpart not only in the judgements it expresses – affirming active aggression over passivity, conflict over peace, and so forth – but in its valuation of identity. While slaves use opposition to secure their identity as good, nobles *seek to transcend their limits and overcome themselves*. This is why the nobles largely ignore the slaves: they cannot be bothered to harm them, there being no challenge in it, which only fuels the slaves' *ressentiment* towards them. If the nobles do injure the slaves, it is out of carelessness rather than maliciousness. Their restraint, however, does not come from any idea that dominating the weak is evil or immoral; rather it is because it is useless and, ultimately, dishonourable – the noble can only endure an opponent or enemy 'in whom there is nothing to despise and *very much* to honor!' (Nietzsche 1967: 1.10).

Two points concerning the relationship between noble and slave figures must be noted. First, even though slave morality invents a false opposition in relation to the nobles and noble morality affirms itself without reference to the slaves, there remains a constitutive relation between them, and between the active and reactive forces whose becoming is expressed in their respective wills to power. The slaves, of course, could not develop their morality without being compelled into passivity by the strong. But the nobles too relate to the weak through what Nietzsche calls the 'pathos of distance', a sense of their difference or distance from what they stand above, which is necessary for their perspective and indispensable to developing a sense of internal or intensive difference that drives them to new possibilities.[21] This distance, which is an irreducible relation of disjunction, is the 'differenciator' that establishes the respective places of the divergent noble and slavish perspectives. While noble morality affirms this difference, slave morality denies it and reduces it to a simple opposition. Thus, even while Nietzsche acknowledges that the noble perspective misunderstands its counterpart, largely because of the oppositional dimension that admittedly resides in its morality, its 'sin against reality' is far less serious than that committed by the slaves.[22]

Second, as already mentioned, Nietzschean force relations can be reversed and inferior forces can become dominant without, however, ceasing to be weak. Deleuze argues that reactive forces triumph not by overpowering active forces but by separating the latter from their strength: reactive forces 'do not form a greater force, one that would be active. They proceed in an entirely different way – they decompose; *they separate active force from what it can do*; they take away a part or almost all of its power. In this way reactive forces do not become active but, on the contrary, they make active forces join them and become reactive in a new sense' (*NP* 57). The passive, adaptive, resentful and cunning qualities of reactive forces, which emerge from the quantitative difference that puts them in an inferior position, enable their victory over powerful but unreflective active forces. Indeed, when Nietzsche outlines the slave tactics that ultimately overturn the dominance of noble morality, they are all familiar ploys of a cunning and disabling passive aggression: separating the doer from the deed and asserting that the strong have a choice in acting while the weak choose to endure ('Oh, go ahead and don't worry about me; if I must suffer, I will'),[23] laying a guilt trip through the idea of bad conscience, which reaches its height with the image of God on the cross ('He died for all our sins, you know, yours and mine'),[24] invoking pity simply by displaying their own sickliness and helplessness,[25] and, ultimately, making action, affirmation and overcoming shameful.[26] 'In each case', Deleuze maintains, 'this separation rests on a fiction, on a mystification or a falsification' (57). These fictions all revolve around an assertion of identity: the subject that stands apart from its actions and qualities in order to choose what to do or be; the transcendent divinity who embodies purity; and the ideal of purity – the ascetic ideal – from which this world is judged to be dirty and imperfect. In each case, something is exempted from the world of becoming, which allows becoming to be condemned as unworthy. For Nietzsche, these valuations continue into a modern liberal and scientific age because the denigration of becoming and the elevation of identity can survive even in the absence of a God who in the past served as an ontological guarantee for them – although not without nihilistic consequences.

It would be wrong to treat Nietzsche's genealogical account as primarily historical (and the same can be said of Hegel's Master–Slave Dialectic). Certainly he refers to real historical individuals and groups and tells the story of how a Judeo-Christian morality came to replace an ancient one he associates with the Greeks, Romans, Vikings and others. But, as Deleuze says, this is part of the method of dramatization. Nietzsche also speaks of the struggle between the two moralities continuing to take place within the modern self (Nietzsche 1967: 1.16), and of the slavish usurpation of morality being not a historical event but the foundation of history and culture as such: 'the *meaning of all culture* is the reduction of the beast of prey "man" to a tame and civilized animal, a *domestic animal*' (1.11). In these respects genealogy is also a psychological and, as Deleuze argues, an ontological critique: it explores, with respect to human being, the perspectival origin of our values. The reason we have our morality is not simply the weakness of individuals or groups that might perpetuate it, nor simply its having been habituated into us, but above all because of weakness itself: it is our own weakness, the perspective we assume in our most petty and resentful moments, when our reactive drives are in ascendency and our active power is disabled, that has come to dominate us. Our history and our individual and collective psychologies follow therefrom.

The will to truth and nihilism; the Overman and eternal return

Slave morality, Nietzsche maintains, expresses a 'will to truth'. This will does not demand truth – as Deleuze notes, '[i]t is well known that in fact man rarely seeks after truth: our interests and also our stupidity separate us from truth even more than our errors do' (*NP* 95). Instead, it demands that the world conform to an ideal that links truth to purity, goodness, beauty, universality and utility, and links falsity to the opposite values. In philosophy, the will to truth treats truth as something to which thought is entitled 'by right' (95). The will to truth issues from a perspective of weakness that cannot act affirmatively and directly in relations of strife and conflict. It consequently condemns this world by comparing it to some higher standard, often invoking another world in which this standard is realized. Neither Nietzsche nor Deleuze denies the existence of truth. On the contrary, there are many different kinds of truth, including scientific (water boils at 100 degrees), historical (the Nazis committed genocide), moral (murder is wrong) and personal (this is the right thing for me), but the validity of each must be assessed according to very different rules and their status is almost if not always contingent (even water boils at 100 degrees only under certain conditions).

The problem of the will to truth comes from its conviction 'that truth is more important than any other thing, including every other conviction' (Nietzsche 1974: §344). When Nietzsche examines whether this conviction means 'I will not allow myself to be deceived' or 'I will not deceive, not even myself', he holds the first to be consistent with a 'long-range prudence' that could accept that sometimes it is better not to know the truth at all. He thus settles on the second as the proper expression of science's absolute belief in truth's value. But given that such a view should never have come into being 'if both truth and untruth constantly proved to be useful, which is the case' (§344), he concludes that the foundation of this will does not relate to truth at all, but instead rests on other values: 'Consequently, "will to truth" does *not* mean "I will not allow myself to be deceived" but – there is no alternative – "I will not deceive, not even myself"; *and with that we stand on moral ground*' (§344). A genealogy of morality must therefore challenge the established will to truth, as it is an expression of dominant values and evaluations that go beyond those narrowly associated with the search for truth. The value this will gives to truth 'must for once be experimentally *called into question*' (Nietzsche 1967: 3.24).

The will to truth is also a form of nihilism. 'In the word nihilism', Deleuze writes, '*nihil* does not signify non-being but primarily a value of nil. Life takes on a value of nil insofar as it is denied and depreciated' (*NP* 147). For Nietzsche, nihilism emerges because morality is 'a system of evaluations that partially coincides with the conditions of a creature's life' (Nietzsche 1968: §256), these evaluations necessarily being 'always behind the times; they express conditions of preservation and growth that belong to times long gone by; they resist new conditions of existence with which they cannot cope and which they necessarily misunderstand' (§110). This disjunction between life and the values that condition it and are meant to preserve it is found equally in the modern scientific will to truth as in its Platonic and Christian predecessors. Even though it differs from its forerunners in refusing to juxtapose this world to another deemed more worthy, science has retained the same moral valuation of truth and simply transposed it onto the idea of objective scientific method used to approach this world. Consequently, it is no better adapted to the conditions of life – and particularly life's relation to simulacra – than the theological and metaphysical views it replaces.

For you only have to ask yourself carefully, 'Why do you not want to deceive?' especially if it should seem – and it does seem! – as if life aimed at semblance, meaning error, deception, simulation, delusion, self-delusion, and when the great sweep of life has actually always shown itself to be on the side of the most unscrupulous *polytropoi*. . . . Thus the question 'Why science?' leads back to the moral problem: *Why have morality at all* when life, nature, and history are 'not moral'? (Nietzsche 1974: §344)

Modern science reduces religion to a mere belief that can be held or rejected as one sees fit because truth lies elsewhere. Yet ultimately it cannot raise itself above the level of mere belief because the link it makes between truth, purity and universality implicitly invokes a transcendent guarantee. Thus, 'it is still a *metaphysical faith* upon which our faith in science rests' (§344). And this faith continues not just in science's approach to truth, but in morality more generally, in so far as modern moral values continue to idealize purity and universality, and to condemn impurity, deception and simulation, according to the slavish opposition of good and evil.

The disjunction between values and life, however, is genealogical and ontological as well as historical, and so the event of nihilism has many senses, in accordance with Nietzsche's pluralism (*NP* 4). The historical aspects are outlined in Nietzsche's parable of the madman and related aphorisms in *The Gay Science* (1974). A madman lights a lantern in the bright morning hours, enters the marketplace and declares he is seeking God.[27] This provokes laughter from the many non-believers there, and the madman responds by declaring that God is dead and we have killed him. He continues that we have 'wipe[d] away the entire horizon', 'unchained this earth from its sun' and sent ourselves 'plunging continually. . . . Backward, sideward, forward, in all directions. . . . Is there still any up or down?' (§125). But when he notices the crowd simply staring at him in astonishment and disbelief, the madman throws down his lantern and concludes: 'my time is not yet. This tremendous event is still on its way, still wandering; it has not yet reached the ears of men. . . . .This deed is still more distant from them than the most distant stars – *and yet they have done it themselves*' (§125). In this regard, as Nietzsche says later, the advent of nihilism, 'the greatest recent event', has created an interregnum period in which the value of old ideals has become null but new ones have not yet been created because it is still not appreciated 'how much must collapse now that this faith has been undermined because it was built upon this faith, propped up by it, grown into it; for example, the whole of our European morality' (§343). Nihilism has become necessary 'because the values we have had hitherto thus draw their final consequence; because nihilism represents the ultimate logical conclusion of our great values and ideals – because we must experience nihilism before we can find out what value these "values" really had' (Nietzsche 1968: Preface, §4).

Ontologically and genealogically, however, nihilism is hardly limited to the developments of the late nineteenth century. Genealogically, nihilism, being the triumph of reactive forces, is found at the origin, where it is constitutive of (slavish) human being: '*Ressentiment* and bad conscience are constitutive of the humanity of man, nihilism is the *a priori* concept of universal history' (*NP* 166). In this respect, the modern death of God is not the advent of nihilism, because it was a nihilistic will to truth that invented the fiction of a transcendent being in the first place. But the event of nihilism is also untimely, as the madman indicates when he says it has already occurred yet he has still come too early. Ontologically, nihilism has many senses, which correspond to the different configurations that can exist between reactive forces and the negative will to power. When working together, the negative will to power is a will to nothingness that allows reactive forces to defeat active forces (148). This complicity takes the form of pity – 'Pity, in Nietzsche's symbolism, always designates this complex of will to nothingness and reactive forces, this affinity or tolerance of one for the other' (150) – and expresses a 'negative nihilism' that invents a supersensible world in order to depreciate this world, culminating in a universal Christian God who watches over humanity. When reactive forces turn against the negative will to power, having become 'less and less tolerant of this leader and witness' (149), the consequence is 'reactive nihilism', which 'finds its principle in the reactive life completely solitary and naked, in reactive forces reduced to themselves' (148). This corresponds to God's death at the hands of man, out of *ressentiment* towards the God whose pity and unending love became unbearable (154), but also to the death of the Christian God at the hands of Christianity's own morality and will to truth.[28] Man replaces God and science replaces religion, but various attempts to assert secular values in place of higher ones ultimately lead to 'passive nihilism', a resignation in the face of nothingness. This is dramatized by the figure of the last man, who embodies 'the exhausted life which prefers to not will, to fade away passively, rather than being animated by a will which goes beyond it' (151), and it becomes the final variant of nihilism's depreciation of life. Nihilism's various ontological senses thus follow an order corresponding to its historical development, but they are not exclusive stages; rather, they also coexist and intermingle with one another. As Nietzsche says about his contemporary condition, for example, 'God is dead; but given the way of men, there may still be caves for thousands of years in which his shadow will be shown' (Nietzsche 1974: §108).

Nietzsche claims that it is necessary to work through nihilism in order to overcome it and carry out a revaluation of values or a 'transvaluation'. And Deleuze maintains that the start of this transmutation is found within the nihilistic condition itself. For Nietzsche, nihilism expresses the fundamental fact of the human will, that it would 'rather will *nothingness* than *not* will' (Nietzsche 1967: 3.1), while for Deleuze, the last man is the figure who prefers to fade away passively, without even willing nothingness. In the last man, reactive forces and the will to power have fallen asunder. But in this final form, the reactive man who has long ago turned against the negative will to power finds the will to power turned against him, with the result that the will is actively transformed.

Reactive forces owe their triumph to the will to nothingness: once this triumph is established they break off their alliance with it, they want to assert their own values on their own account. *This* is the great resounding event: the reactive man in place of God. We know what the result of this is – the last man, the one who

> prefers a nothingness of will, who prefers to fade away passively, rather than a will to nothingness. But this result is a result for the reactive man, not for the will to nothingness itself. The will to nothingness continues its enterprise, this time in silence, beyond the reactive man. *Reactive forces break their alliance with the will to nothingness, the will to nothingness, in turn, breaks its alliance with reactive forces.* It inspires in man a new inclination: for destroying himself, but destroying himself actively. (*NP* 173–4)

This 'active destruction' inverts the entire nature of man's being, but into something that is no longer human. Deleuze maintains that the nature of man is essentially reactive, and this is the case even with the 'higher man' who might emerge from a dialectical movement of negative forces (166–71). But reaction is not the essential nature of force, nor is negation the essential nature of the will to power. Negation, and therefore nihilism, is indeed the ground for knowledge of the will to power – it is 'the *ratio cognoscendi of the will to power in general*' (172) – and thus only the negative will to power, along with its sense and values, is known and knowable to us. But negation only exists in relation to affirmation, just as reactive forces have their quality only through their relation to active forces. Affirmation, the becoming active of forces, is thus the ground for the existence of negation – 'it is the *ratio essendi of the will to power in general*' (173). The affirmative will to power, which in many respects Nietzsche associates with the noble and his morality, is realized in the idea of the Overman, who, Deleuze argues, must not be confused with the higher man: 'We must reject every interpretation which would have the Overman succeed where the higher man fails. The Overman is not a man who surpasses *himself* and succeeds in surpassing himself. The Overman and the higher man differ in nature; both in the instances which produce them and in the goals that they attain' (168). Active destruction overcomes man, giving birth to a qualitatively different type.

However, this internal negation and destruction of nihilism – a negation that, according to Deleuze, ends with affirmation, and, indeed, is followed as well by another negation (*NP* 177) – would appear to be the epitome of dialectical reversal. Deleuze counters this conclusion in part by accepting the appearance's reality. He notes that Nietzsche gives to the character of Zarathustra, who announces the coming of the Overman, an 'ape' or 'buffoon' with whom he will always be confused (*NP* xviii, 179). Moreover, he cites Nietzsche's rejection both of the idea that negation could exist as an independent ontological force – 'affirmation does not let negation remain *as an autonomous power or primary quality*' (178) – and of the idea that affirmation could contain no negation in it – the problem with the yea-saying ass is that 'it always says yes, *but does not know how to say no*' (178). There is thus a back-and-forth movement between affirmation and negation, but, for Deleuze, this is not enough to establish a dialectic, because 'everything depends on the role of the negative in this relation' (8). In this respect, 'the concept of the Overman is directed against the dialectical conception of man, and transvaluation is directed against the dialectic of appropriation or the suppression of alienation' (8). Where dialectical negation ends in the affirmation and reconciliation of identity through opposition, Nietzschean transvaluation, Deleuze argues, ends in an affirmation of difference, and, as such, it negates and destroys all established identity-oriented bases of values and evaluations. It is not a negation of negation, but of negation's apparently foundational status, and of the concepts and values related to it. For this reason, 'if we understand affirmation and negation as qualities of the will to power we see that they do not have a univocal relation. Negation is *opposed* to affirmation but affirmation *differs* from negation. We cannot think of affirmation as "being opposed" to negation: this would be to place the negative within it' (188).

Transvaluation, for Deleuze, is 'not a change of values, but a change in the element from which the value of values derives' (*NP* 171). It is therefore a change in the perspective from which evaluations arise, and in the forces that constitute this perspective. In many respects new values will undoubtedly affirm and condemn the same actions as the old values: as Nietzsche writes, '[i]t goes without saying that I do not deny – unless I am a fool – that many actions called immoral ought to be avoided and resisted, or that many called moral ought to be done and encouraged – but I think the one should be encouraged and the other avoided *for other reasons than hitherto*' (Nietzsche 1982: §103). Here, for Deleuze, the key difference between overcoming and the dialectic lies in the difference between securing values through the reciprocal recognition of a subject and overcoming the *ressentiment* that would demand that the subject be the ground of values, responsible for both values and actions. To affirm difference is to negate dialectical opposition, and to negate the demand for identity that accompanies it. This affirmation, Deleuze argues, is the affirmation of eternal return, and it is linked to Zarathustra's death or going under.[29]

As discussed in the last chapter, the eternal return for Deleuze implies a temporal structure of disjunction in which the self is cracked into dispersed subjectivities. It is through this structure that genuine creativity emerges. Nietzsche's most well-known formulations of the doctrine, however, suggest that it affirms simply that in an infinite chronological time identical individuals and events will recur endlessly.[30] Affirming such a return would seem to accord with his view of *amor fati* or 'love of fate'. But Deleuze (*DR* 6) points to evidence of another doctrine, implied, for example, when Zarathustra rejects the dwarf's proclamation that time is a circle ('You spirit of gravity. . .do not make things too easy for yourself!' [Nietzsche 1966: 'On the Vision and the Riddle', 158]), and later when he scoffs at his animals' rendition of the same thesis ('The Convalescent', 215–20). The circular eternal return, Deleuze argues, is 'the eternal return of the mean, small, reactive man' (*NP* 65). It is a scientific and nihilistic eternal return (see Nietzsche 1968: §55) that must be overcome. Nevertheless, for both Deleuze and Nietzsche, this overcoming also presents the appearance of both a circular time and a linear progression.

When Zarathustra is asked to teach his doctrine of overcoming to cripples, he rejects the idea of removing their burdens or healing their disabilities. Instead, he states his preference for those missing an eye or limb to the men of *ressentiment*, 'inverse cripples', who remain so attached to their identities and to themselves that they cannot overcome past wounds. The man of *ressentiment* cannot let go of past sufferings or of himself: he demands an answer to the question, 'why has this shit happened *to me*?' In response, Zarathustra first demands that the will take responsibility for these events, 'to recreate all "it was" into a "thus I willed it"' (Nietzsche 1966: 'On Redemption', 139). But he then adds that this move is just one more form of *ressentiment*. It answers the slavish man's question by making him assume responsibility and guilt for it, holding the past to be his punishment (140). Accepting this burden may reconcile the will with the past, but, Zarathustra proclaims, 'that will which is the will to power must will something higher than any reconciliation' (141). Genuine overcoming thus requires that 'the creative will says to it, "But thus I will it; thus shall I will it"' (141), that is to say, that the past's eternal recurrence is also willed. The transmutation here comes in expunging *ressentiment*, but in this way it is the self that is expunged – what is overcome is not the past itself but the ego that demands justification for its suffering, a meaning for its existence. The self and its world are completely transformed in this 'curious stationary journey'. This is not a denial of suffering or of past injustices – the shit isn't any less shitty, so to speak – but rather an overcoming of the 'me' that defines itself and its world in relation to this suffering. In this way, willing the eternal return brings about the new through an affirmation of what was and what will come. But this affirmation of eternal recurrence is also an affirmation of all of time, and the relations of strife and disjunction that structure it. 'If we affirm one single moment', Nietzsche writes, 'we thus affirm not only ourselves but all existence. For nothing is self-sufficient, neither in us ourselves nor in things; and if our soul has trembled with happiness and sounded like a harp string just once, all eternity was needed to produce this one event – and in this single moment of affirmation all eternity was called good, redeemed, justified, and affirmed' (1968: §1032). Affirmation of oneself comes through the dissolution of the self's ideal of itself as a unified subject, without the promise of some later reconciliation or recognition. This is the non-dialectical form of Nietzschean overcoming.[31]

When Deleuze conceives of the eternal return in terms of an action that realizes the third synthesis of time, he argues that within it 'the present is no more than an actor, an author, an agent destined to be effaced; while the past is no more than a condition operating by default' (*DR* 94). Past sufferings and injuries provide the default condition for overcoming through the affirmation of eternal return. Yet from this initial perspective the act appears impossible, too great for the wounded ego that would have to carry it out. Action depends on a unity in the present, which is achieved, Deleuze says, through the consolidation of the self around an ego ideal (110–11, 115), an image – or, rather, a simulation – of the actor it wants to be. Only through this semblance of unity can the self attain a moment of subjectivity that makes it equal to its task. But while overcoming finds its origin in this apparent unification, 'the event and the act possess a secret coherence which excludes that of the self;. . .they turn back against the self which has become their equal and smash it to pieces, as though the bearer of the new world were carried away and dispersed by the shock of the multiplicity to which it gives birth: what the self has become equal to is the unequal in itself (89–90). Overcoming is thus the event in which the self uses identity to press beyond it, its ego being dissolved and thereby opened to multiplicity. To overcome is to become *different*, where difference does not determine or return to identity. In this way, for Deleuze, overcoming institutes a kind of creativity, realized in thinking and the thought of the eternal return, that breaks with the past and with the self that would be defined by it. This opening towards multiplicity affirms a self that is out of joint with itself, one that is a complex of differences related through a 'difference in itself'. And in this way the act of affirming the eternal return makes 'repetition, not that from which one "draws off" a difference, nor that which includes difference as a variant, but making it the thought and the production of the "absolutely different"; making it so that repetition is, for itself, difference in itself' (94).

For Nietzsche, the process of overcoming is first and foremost an ethical one, in the sense of an ethos or way of life. This is particularly clear when he counsels 'giving style' to one's character through a strategic assessment and reworking of the material that makes one what one is, this material including one's past, character traits, habits and more.[32] The imperative, he writes, is 'that a human being should *attain* satisfaction with himself, whether it be by means of this or that poetry and art. . . .Whoever is dissatisfied with himself is continually ready for revenge, and we others will be his victims, if only by having to endure his ugly sight' (Nietzsche 1974: §290). This task is ethical for Deleuze too, but he adds that it is also micropolitical – indeed, it marks an important point where the ethical and the political meet. As we will see, micropolitics is an engagement with the constitutive elements of our being, but these constituents include the semblance of identity that arises and that, in our weaker and resentful moments, seems to define fully what we are.

4

Desire and desiring-machines

Michel Foucault's analytic of power relations is certainly one of the most important contributions to recent political theory, and indeed to work across the social sciences and humanities. His thesis, with respect to modern and contemporary forms of disciplinary and normalizing power, is that various shifts related to the emergence of the modern age problematize the dominance of established forms of power structured around a transcendent sovereign and relying on threats of physical punishment and death to those who would resist them. Social and economic changes linked to new capitalist modes of production and exchange, the rise of social contract understandings of sovereignty, and liberal ideas of individual freedom all require a new form of 'governmentality' able to constitute individuals in ways that counterbalance new economic and political freedoms. This does not mean that individuals must all become 'the same' as each other or made passive and 'docile',[1] but it does mean they must be constituted against a norm that measures them. New power relations must therefore, among other things, constitute these norms and map out a whole series of deviant categories that stand in opposition to them.

Modernity thus sees the rise of standards of normality, the identification of forms of deviance falling away from these norms, and the birth across the new human sciences of various 'experts' who develop these categories and study the individuals who are classified according to them. Within various institutions such as the family, schools, hospitals, prisons, factories and the military, individuals have these standards held over them and are rewarded or disciplined to the extent to which they conform to the norms expected of them. This is hardly a top-down situation, however, because even while disciplinary and normalizing structures entail hierarchies of authority and subordination, their various techniques of implementation – the most important being observation, testing, classification and confession – all involve the subordinate's participation in his own subjection. The most recognizable sites of discipline are found in spaces of confinement, but this is not a necessary condition: 'Discipline sometimes requires *enclosure*, the specification of a place heterogeneous to all others and closed in upon itself' (Foucault 1979: 141).[2] Although disciplinary society is historically recent, Foucault notes that its methods of discipline are actually quite old. What marks modern society as disciplinary society is thus not the techniques it employs but the centrality it gives to constituting individuals and collectives in ways that can be seen to make the body politic more prosperous and efficient. Sovereign force and punishments remain, and are often still wielded, but they no longer express the most important and defining operations of power in today's societies. Modern society's disciplinary character is confirmed by the way its failures to create an efficient and well-organized population always lead to calls to strengthen its disciplinary institutions: 'for the past 150 years the proclamation of the failure of the prison [to reduce criminality] has always been accompanied by its maintenance' (272).

Disciplinary power differs from its sovereign-based counterparts in its focus on the 'microscopic' realm of power relations. 'Micro' in this context does not mean individual or tiny, but rather constitutive: 'micropower' relations function at the level where individual and collective standards of normality and deviance, authority and subordination, are constituted. Micropower relations are force relations that, in the Hegelian as well as the Nietzschean sense, give meaning and direction to power regimes. Foucault calls them 'the moving substrate of force relations which, by virtue of their inequality, constantly engender states of power, but the latter are always local and unstable' (Foucault 1990: 93). States of power, in turn, comprise a macroscopic domain that is 'the over-all effect that emerges from all these mobilities, the concatenation that rests on each of them and

DESIRE AND DESIRING-MACHINES 91

seeks in turn to arrest their movement' (93). These states comprise the commonly recognized types of power, such as legal, economic and institutional power. Foucault holds that liberal and Marxist theories recognize power only at this macroscopic level, where it can be considered a possession, and thereby miss the more subtle dynamics of a modern society that 'has gradually been penetrated by quite new mechanisms of power that are probably irreducible to the representation of the law' (89). A police officer on the street, a teacher in school and a judge in a courtroom all possess powers that they can choose to use or not to use – the teacher can fail the student, the police officer can arrest the citizen and so on. But these seemingly stable powers, linked to their authoritative positions, depend on networks of discourses, practices and power relations to establish the social meanings and subject positions that allow these individuals to exercise them. Micropower relations construct the meaningful truths and identities necessary for macro-level powers to operate.

Exceeding the individuals whose roles are constituted by them, and remaining 'constantly in tension, in activity' (Foucault 1979: 26), micropower relations are diffused throughout society and its institutions. They cannot, for Foucault, be centred in the State, as their breadth, depth and heterogeneity surpass any such localization. Unlike the powers of the policeman or the judge, which might at least appear to be derived from state institutions and laws, micropower relations are not governed by any individual or collective subject, operating instead in a way that is 'both intentional and nonsubjective' (Foucault 1990: 94).[3] Moreover, they are inherently porous and unstable, as they are always accompanied by relations of resistance that can use the very rules and strategies that power relations engender to mutate and overturn them. Micro and macro levels are immanent to each other but related by way of a 'double conditioning' (99–100), whereby micropower relations can sustain or subvert the power of authority figures, and these authorities can exercise their powers in ways that strengthen or undermine the microscopic hierarchies on which they depend. The exercise of power at either level often has multiple and conflicting effects in this regard: the use of police force to maintain police authority, for example, often fortifies and undercuts it at the same time.

Foucault is frequently held to place power and resistance in opposition, treating power as a force that imposes identities on individuals and collectives and resistance as a force that dissolves or deconstructs power's identity formations. There is certainly much to dispute in this reading of Foucault's thought. If anything, his genealogies of power relations reveal not only that power consistently fails to create 'normal' individuals, but that its actual goal is to produce relatively harmless and generally manageable forms of deviance, individuals who need not have well-constituted and well-understood identities but who can be continually subjected to discipline.[4] Moreover, he is quite explicit in criticizing 'juridico-discursive' models of power for understanding power in terms of law, restriction and an opposition between licit and illicit, and for mistakenly assuming that power operates in an oppositional way at all levels, micro and macro.[5] Resistance, Foucault says, takes various forms as 'adversary, target, support, or handle in power relations' (Foucault 1990: 95) and is 'the odd term in relations of power' (96), indicating that power and resistance are more accurately seen to be folded into each other in a relation of disjunction.[6] At a macroscopic level there are, occasionally, 'great radical ruptures, massive binary divisions' (96). But such binaries are really only partial and imperfect integrations that distribute relations of power and resistance into separate camps: 'hence one should not assume a massive and primal condition of domination, a binary structure with "dominators" on one side and "dominated" on the other, but rather a multiform production of relations of domination which are partially susceptible of integration into overall strategies' (Foucault 1980: 142).

Nevertheless, Deleuze also attributes this sort of opposition between power and resistance to Foucault, holding that he thereby misses the important revolutionary role played by desire. In *A Thousand Plateaus*, Deleuze and Guattari state their disagreements with Foucault as follows: '(1) to us assemblages seem fundamentally to be assemblages not of power but of desire (desire is always assembled), and power seems to be a stratified dimension of the assemblage; (2) the diagram and the abstract machine have lines of flight that are primary, which are not phenomena of resistance or counterattack in an assemblage, but cutting edges of creation and deterritorialization' (*ATP* 531n. 39). And in 'Desire and Pleasure' (*TRM*

122–34), Deleuze contends that Foucauldian power relations, rather than being partially integrated into overall strategies, are nothing other than strategies of integration, and that resistance, therefore, is merely a counter-strategy (127–9), whereas desire has the capacity to execute deterritorializations surpassing those of strategic resistance. 'Desire', Deleuze maintains, 'is wholly a part of a functioning heterogeneous assemblage' (130), structured by disjunction, and as such is more fundamental than the opposition between power and resistance. And he holds that by proceeding in this way, he is able to ask the question that eludes Foucault: 'How can power be desired?' (125). Holding that his central question concerns the articulation of truth (Foucault 1988a: 32–3), Foucault responds that for him desire remains caught up in relations of power and knowledge that, in a modern context, constitute desire as a hidden source of truth about the individual, who is then examined, judged and normalized on this basis. Foucault therefore turns to pleasure as a way to contest the connection Western society draws between desire and truth – a connection that is filled with tensions and knots of resistance precisely because desire and truth do not necessarily correspond. Deleuze answers that he considers pleasure to be 'on the side of strata and organization' (*TRM* 131) and to amount to a subordination of desire to law and regulation.

Whether these distinctions between desire and power and between desire and pleasure are really, as Deleuze thinks, 'more than a matter of vocabulary' (*TRM* 130), or whether equivalences can be drawn between Foucault's and Deleuze's thought on these points, it is notable that these issues are not raised in Deleuze's monograph on Foucault. Nor is Foucault portrayed as opposing power and resistance, even if only as a temporary position he might have held before his final turn to the care of the self. Instead, the thinker who emerges in Deleuze's *Foucault* is one who demonstrates that power and knowledge are structured by a fundamental disjunction between the visible and the sayable, and who turns resistance into a folding of power back onto itself. Perhaps Deleuze's statements that, in contrast to his previous commentaries, he was in his book 'trying to see Foucault's thought as a whole', and that others 'didn't really understand these transitions, this pushing forward, this logic in Foucault' (*N* 84), were a subtle criticism of his own earlier views.

In any event, even in their disagreements, Foucault and Deleuze have a common target in their formulations of power and of desire: psychoanalysis, which, while recognizing a domain that is microscopic in Foucault's sense and molecular in Deleuze and Guattari's sense, consistently introduces lack, negation and transcendence into it. On a philosophical level, as Foucault writes in his introduction to *Anti-Oedipus*, psychoanalysis maintains allegiance to 'the old categories of the Negative (law, limit, castration, lack, lacuna), which Western thought has so long held sacred as a form of power and an access to reality' (Foucault in *AO* xiii). And on a political level it becomes complicit with either the forces of modern liberal capitalism or forces of resistance that are ultimately reactionary. Foucault's ethics of care for the self and Deleuze and Guattari's 'schizoanalysis' both aim to replace this negation with a multiplicity that can be linked to overcoming. This is certainly an ethical task – and Foucault says of *Anti-Oedipus* that it 'is a book of ethics, the first book of ethics to be written in France in quite a long time' (xiii) – but one that ultimately passes into politics. Moreover, it is a task that is carried out at the micropolitical level. Politics is inseparable from ethics, and it necessarily begins as micropolitics.

Desire as lack and the subject of lack

Hegel defines self-consciousness as '*Desire* in general' (Hegel 1977: §167) because of the way desire establishes negative relations to others. Natural desire, being the desire of appetite, seeks to negate external objects by possessing, consuming or destroying them; human desire for recognition is the desire to negate oneself as a subject in order to become a desired object for another, though this negation of subjectivity brings with it the promise of confirming self-consciousness's value, so that subjectivity is ultimately recuperated. In both cases, desire refers to something that self-consciousness finds lacking in itself, indicating that the attainment of what is desired will bring with it a sense of fulfilment and completeness. In defining desire in terms of a lack to be filled, Hegel follows a well-established philosophical tradition usually traced back to Plato.[7] The promise of the Hegelian dialectic is that fulfilment will be achieved in a society of reciprocal recognition, which not only meets the economic and material needs of every member but also overcomes the inequality, dissonance, and alienation of the Master–Slave relation. Even if material desires are satisfied, a lack of recognition means that one cannot attain a sense of self-worth; but recognition must come from another who is also recognized and valued as a self-conscious being or it becomes valueless in turn. If self-consciousness cannot be secured through the recognition of a self-conscious other, the individual cannot confirm his status as an autonomous, self-reflective agent who makes a difference in the world. Reconciliation through reciprocal recognition is thus a way for self-consciousness to secure its identity and subjectivity.

In contrast to Hegel's two forms, Lacan conceives of desire as an irresolvable lack. Its negativity surpasses both that of appetite or material need and that of recognition demanded from another, but is nevertheless also generated by the interplay of these dialectical forms. Lacan also links this non-dialectical negation to language, whose structure is crucial to subjectivity, since a language user becomes a subject by assuming the position of an 'I' who states facts, articulates concepts or expresses feelings and beliefs. In the first place, he maintains, there is 'a deviation of man's needs due to the fact that he speaks: to the extent that his needs are subjected to demand, they come back to him in an alienated form' (Lacan 2006: 579). When an infant cries out to be fed, or when an adult states his needs in language, there is not only a call for these needs to be met, but a simultaneous demand for love or recognition from the other who would respond to them. In this way, 'demand in itself bears on something other than the satisfactions it calls for' (579). While need is particular, the demand that splits off from it is universal as a consequence of the fact that language expresses meaning through signifiers, which are general or universal and which the infant must take from others, since he does not invent language himself: 'This is not the effect of his real dependence . . . but rather of their [the needs] being put into signifying form as such and of the fact that it is from the Other's locus that his message is emitted' (579). The demand for love is also unconditional, and in this sense too it surpasses need's particularity. The Other's response to demand, in turn, has categorical import: the mother confirms her unqualified love by answering to the infant's needs, or her contempt by ignoring them, in either case expressing something that transcends the situation itself, as her response does not convey love or hate at *only* this moment. 'In this way,' Lacan argues, 'demand annuls (*aufhebt*) the particularity of everything that can be granted, by transmuting it into a proof of love, and the very satisfactions demand obtains for need are debased (*sich erniedrigt*) to the point of being no more than the crushing brought on by the demand for love' (580). Demand 'constitutes the Other as having the "privilege" of satisfying needs, that is, the power to deprive them of what alone can satisfy them. The Other's privilege here thus outlines the radical form of the gift which the Other does not have – namely, what is known as its love' (580). Demand thus directs itself at a 'phantom of Omnipotence' (689) in the form of an Other who can provide or withhold love, and who must consequently be 'bridled by the Law' (689) so that its caprice can be controlled.

But the seemingly cancelled particularity of need returns as a residue of desire '*beyond* demand' (Lacan 2006: 580) because, Lacan argues, no particular gift of love can meet demand's requirement for unconditionality. Even when the subject receives everything it needs and demands, it continues to feel lacking, which indicates to it that something has been withheld. But this something, this *objet a*, must remain nameless – and in this way it is more than a *particular* thing – since the subject has already voiced everything it could articulate. Desire thus points to something that, unable to be expressed in language, must have been primordially excluded from it: 'What is thus alienated in needs constitutes an *Urverdrängung* [primal repression], as it cannot, hypothetically, be articulated in demand' (579). As the object that could quench desire's thirst cannot be identified, desire itself cannot attain fulfilment, and in this way it is rendered infinite. But the effect of this quandary is not simply to leave the subject incomplete: the place of its constitution is also subverted. That an *objet a* is withheld from the subject implies that it is desired and enjoyed by another. This is not the Other to whom demands are made but instead an Other who exercises a power of prohibition, so that the terrain on which the infant finds itself shifts from that of the mother who provides love to that of the father who intervenes in the mother–child relationship. In this way, Lacan says, the infant's subjectivity is constituted on the alien terrain of an Other who bars it from accessing the Other's desire. This prohibition, this paternal Law, subverts the recognition that would give the subject the validation it seeks.

By a reversal that is not simply a negation of the negation, the power of pure loss emerges from the residue of an obliteration. For the unconditionality of demand, desire substitutes the 'absolute' condition: this condition in fact dissolves the element in the proof of love that rebels against the satisfaction of need. This is why desire is neither the appetite for satisfaction nor the demand for love, but the difference that results from the subtraction of the first from the second, the very phenomenon of their splitting (*Spaltung*). (580)

Desire thereby introduces an indispensable but irreconcilable element into the subject's composition. In so far as it depends on its relations to others, the subject is necessarily constituted as an incomplete and lacking being. But while a dialectical reconciliation between the subject and its others would be conceivable, leading to 'a subject finalized in his self-identity' (Lacan 2006: 675), this possibility is foreclosed by a further relation to an enigmatic Other, 'an alterity raised to the second power' (436), to whom the subject attributes an enjoyment (*jouissance*) proscribed to it, and who, not recognizing the subject, remains alien to the subject in turn. In language too signifiers are constituted by a dialectical and an extra-dialectical relation. A signifier attains its meaning through relations of opposition, finding its place by not occupying the space of any other signifier; but language itself is founded through a metaphorical substitution in which a particular signifier comes to stand in for a lost and nameless something that must be excluded from language in order for language to function. The same primal repression that follows from the split between need and demand thus arises in the language taken up by the subject to voice its needs to others. And just as this repression points to a missing object, it also implies an equally mysterious authority of prohibition, which Lacan associates with the phallus. The phallus is the 'Master Signifier' that connotes the power of a transcendent Other, a power that makes itself felt in all the signifiers that designate the identities of subjects and objects, marking them with a lack that goes beyond the dependence of each signifier on all the others.

To be a subject, to be able to say 'I', is thus to carry an inexpressible and inescapable sense of loss. Lacan links this sense of loss to the idea of trauma, the traumatic experience of denial being the event that makes the subject come truly into being.[8] As with Deleuze's account of Oedipal trauma outlined in the second chapter, this event for Lacan need not have really happened in chronological time, as it speaks rather to the way in which the subject always already finds itself fractured. Trauma implies an original unity that has been broken, which suggests that the subject once had something now lost to it. But since any such unity is imaginary and never actually existed, the missing object that would return the subject to its former wholeness is unrecoverable. The subject of trauma is thus compelled to seek this impossible lost object of desire beyond every demand, or to appeal to the authority that seems to take this object as its own desire. The result is a series of repetitions in which the subject tries to secure its identity: repetitions of love, where the subject seeks another who can complete it, but this fails each time because no particular other can substitute for 'the part of himself, lost forever, that is constituted by the fact that he is only a sexed living being, and that he is no longer immortal' (Lacan 1981: 205); and repetitions of self-negation, which are linked to a sado-masochistic drive (185), where the subject prostrates itself before the Other in the hope of receiving acknowledgement and recognition, of becoming the *objet a* for the Other.

As noted in Chapter 1, Lacan's thesis on the subject inspires many radical democratic theories of lack. A central focus of these theories is the struggle of individual and collective subjects to secure their identities by identifying and fixing various others, a process that can be successful only in so far as the subject can repress its relation to an excessive object of desire and a mysterious Other. The *objet a* that would complete the subject and the Other who would block fulfilment must thereby be reduced to identifiable objects and others – in short, what must be repressed or excluded is precisely the lack that cannot be filled. But as the subject remains related to something indefinite, these reductions inevitably fail, leading to a 'return of the repressed'. These political theories treat lack as foundational, as a 'primordial lack', an 'ontological lack', or a 'kernel of the Real' conceived as a radical negativity or impossibility.[9] Ontological here does not indicate something that straightforwardly pre-exists the subject. Rather, because the subject comes into being with a sense of loss, a memory of something that never was, it must invoke or presuppose lack *as if* it were primordial. And because the terms by which this lack is invoked make it impossible to symbolize, it cannot be given positive form – or, rather, any positive form assigned to it can only amount to a temporary substitution of the lack for a thing that would occupy its place. Lack is therefore ontological and foundational inasmuch as it always transcends the attempt to identify something else that is sufficient to its place. In this respect it has a truth value, albeit as an impossibility. Any further attempt to give lack a positive form, to *say* what would precede the subject and language, thus amounts to an illicit attempt to leap outside the boundaries that allow subjectivity and meaning to exist.

But Lacan himself is hardly straightforward on these points. In the first place, as already seen, non-dialectical lack is introduced only through a detour made through language, or what Lacan calls the Symbolic, and the way this domain is established by seeming to exclude something that cannot be given positive status. On the one hand, to be excluded implies also an excessiveness in relation to signification, which gives the lack its ambiguous status: as many theorists of lack are quick to point out, this lack is at the same time a foundational excess, as it indicates something beyond the Symbolic. But in that case, it is still excessive only with the establishment of the Symbolic – otherwise, it is rightly considered *neither* excessive *nor* lacking. On the other hand, however, and perhaps more profoundly, desire, the impossible *objet a*, and the Law all emerge not with the establishment of the Symbolic but rather with a subsequent event: the response the subject receives to its needs and demands. This response is clearly extraneous to both the Symbolic's structure and the subject's founding within it, since neither of these *requires* a response from the Other. They only oblige the subject to exclude something of the particularity of its needs when it enters language to articulate them, and the subject's constitutive passage into language is completed simply by this articulation, irrespective of any response. The Symbolic structure may determine that any response will be lacking. But that is another matter. Desire as lack may begin with the establishment of the Symbolic, but it does not arise from it.

In the second place, there is desire's relation to drives, which Lacan, even while associating them with an extra-linguistic Real, certainly does not treat as something unapproachable.[10] It should be noted that the agency implied by the two concepts is completely different: with desire, agency lies in the subject – '*I* desire a lost object'; but with the drives this is inverted – 'I *was driven* to the object, *driven to desire it*'. But there is more. As Lacan frequently points out, the usual translation of Freud's *Trieb* as 'instinct' gives it the misleading sense of being purposeful.[11] 'Drive' is not 'thrust' (Lacan 1981: 162), although thrust, understood as 'a mere tendency to discharge' (163) is a central quality of drive. But thrust is not kinetic – 'it is not a question of something that will be regulated with movement' (165) – as this would imply a temporary phenomenon, an energy that is used up, whereas drive's force remains constant. Against all this, Lacan maintains that Freudian drives operate on a plane of 'potential energy' (164) and that through their discharges they invest themselves onto objects. Tendencies to discharge are engendered by the way transmissions across this plane create quantitative potential differences in energy, which function as stimuli or excitations (163). As these stimuli are immanent to the energetic plane, they do not refer to the objects that receive investment and so are not linked to need: 'there is absolutely no question in *Trieb* of the pressure of a need such as *Hunger* or *Durst*, thirst' (164). Freud defines pleasure as the decrease in tension brought about by the discharges that bind drives to objects, meaning the pleasure principle operates simply when drives invest themselves, irrespective of whether they attain their objects or achieve their aims.[12] As Lacan states: 'Even when you stuff the mouth – the mouth that opens in the register of the drive – it is not the food that satisfies it, it is, as one says, the pleasure of the mouth' (Lacan 1981: 167). Although investment is not kinetic, it does involve the drive's energy following the path of a circuit, a 'movement outwards and back in which it is structured' (177). A drive's thrust takes it around its object and 'plays a trick' on its object,[13] which it does not necessarily absorb or capture.

The subject's drives, Lacan notes, achieve satisfaction simply in discharge, but the subject himself does not. Through this paradox, 'something new comes into play – the category of the impossible' (Lacan 1981: 166). This impossible, Lacan maintains, 'is so present in it [the pleasure principle] that it is never recognized in it as such' (167), but it accounts for why the drive remains indifferent to the objects of its investments and why these investments shift. Impossibility indicates that the object is not actually an object of need – 'its function as object . . . is to be revised in its entirety' (168). The drive's indifference is thus explained by the fact that it discharges itself in relation to the '*objet a* cause of desire', which thereby takes 'its place in the satisfaction of the drive' (168). A drive is satisfied to the extent that any object, whatever it is, successfully substitutes for the impossible object, with the drive thereby circling around and 'tricking' both its object and itself: 'The *objet petit a* is not the origin of the oral drive. It is not introduced as the original food, it is introduced from the fact that no food will ever satisfy the oral drive, except by circumventing the eternally lacking object' (180). Desire, however, *must* attain its object to be fulfilled, and so even while drives are successfully discharged, the desiring subject remains lacking. Desire is forced to shift accordingly, and the drives follow these shifts. At every stage in their development – from the oral to the anal and finally to the genital phase, an order that for Freud governs the emergence of sexuality as an independent drive – the drives are directed by the subject's relation to the Other's prohibitions: they are oriented 'by the intervention of something that does not belong to the field of the drive – by the intervention, the overthrow, of the demand of the Other' (180).

Clearly the drives' indifference to their objects need not be explained in this way. All that is implied by the idea of drives as discharges on a field of potential energy is that when a discharge occurs it must be onto some object, just as when lightning discharges it must go somewhere, such as from cloud to ground or to another cloud. Moreover, the lost object, as already noted, arises only after the subject's entry onto language – which is, effectively, its entry into subjecthood – and this is clearly extraneous to the drives' general operation. The vicissitudes or vacillations of the drives therefore have no necessary relation to the desiring subject. Lacan himself admits as much when he says that the drive manifests itself in 'the mode of a headless subject, for everything is articulated in it in terms of tension, and has no relation to the subject other than one of topological community' (Lacan 1981: 181). This exteriority of the drives to the subject, however, indicates how drives and desire are related. *Desire is a configuration of the drives, introduced by a linguistic and thus a social structure; Lacanian desire organizes drives around a non-dialectical lack in accordance with a subject constituted by its search for a lost object.* Through desire, the drive 'is given the task of seeking something that, each time, responds in the Other' (196). While drives remain indifferent to how, if at all, they are organized, the subject, as an 'I' who desires, would fall apart without this arrangement. It is thus necessary for the drives to circulate in accordance with the structure of the unconscious, which is 'situated in the gaps that the distribution of the signifying investments sets up in the subject' (181). As unnameable lacks populate any signifying structure, the subject's unconscious, which is founded alongside its articulation of need, 'has the radical structure of language . . . a material operates in the unconscious according to certain laws, which are the same laws as those discovered in the study of natural languages' (Lacan 2006: 496). Drives thus flow around the lacks that structure the subject's unconscious, and the subject is thereby driven to that which it desires.[14] Nevertheless, this correspondence cannot be anything more than a contingent arrangement.

That Lacan still insists on such a correspondence thus reveals his continuing commitment to a classical conception of the subject, and to an understanding of language and signification that accords with it. He does modify this subject from being a self-conscious agent aware of its decisions and actions, validated either through a solipsistic reflection à la the Cartesian 'I think therefore I am' or a dialectic that establishes self-consciousness through otherness. And he inverts the relation between the subject and language, putting language on the side of the Other and beyond the subject's control. Yet at the same time, he holds that 'Freud's discovery was to demonstrate that this verifying process authentically reaches the subject only by decentering him from self-consciousness, to which he was confined by Hegel's reconstruction of the phenomenology of mind' (Lacan 2006: 241). That Lacan aims to decentre but still retain this subject upon a broader foundation is clear when he states that his use of the term designates 'the Cartesian subject, who appears at the moment when doubt is recognized as certainty – except that, through my approach, the bases of this subject prove to be wider, but at the same time much more amenable to the certainty that eludes it. This is what the unconscious is' (Lacan 1981: 126). The conditions under which subjectivity is constituted require that desire organizes drives around a lack treated as though it were foundational. And it requires that both language and subjectivity are structured so as to retain a sense of a transcendence that organizes them from above.

Deleuze and Guattari acknowledge the existence of lack, but they insist that it is an effect, not a foundation: 'Lack . . . is created, planned, and organized in and through social production. . . . It is never primary; production is never organized on the basis of a pre-existing need or lack' (AO 28). Desire as lack, they argue, does not even emerge from the negative experience of need. Rather, need is experienced in this way only after desire has been manoeuvred by social and economic forces into a search for lost fullness: 'The deliberate creation of lack as a function of market economy is the art of a dominant class. This involves deliberately organizing wants and needs . . . amid an abundance of production; making all of desire teeter and fall victim to the great fear of not having one's needs satisfied' (28). On the one hand, psychoanalysis errs by conceiving desire as lack – as though this was not already a manipulation of both desire and drives – and reading all psychoanalytic symptoms through this lens (23–4). This error is carried forward by linking the analysis of desire to a familial sphere presumed to be structured by the triangular scheme of the Oedipus complex, where the child is placed between a mother who answers demand and a father who intervenes to prohibit. Not only does this interpretation, which is often highly forced,[15] purport to represent desire's most fundamental state – and representation is already an abstraction and thus a misinterpretation of desire's fundamental multiplicity – but it also holds the family structure to inform social life, when it is really a reflection of social structures and powers. On the other hand, then, psychoanalysis errs by failing to relate itself to its outside – 'We dream of entering their [psychoanalysts'] offices, opening the windows and saying, "It smells stuffy in here – some relation with the outside, if you please"' (357) – and thus to recognize the historical specificity of the connection between an Oedipal orientation of desire around an unnameable lack and a distinctly modern social form. In this way it becomes complicit in the replication of this form, which it purports to criticize: 'psychoanalysts are bent on producing man abstractly, that is to say ideologically, for culture' (108). It is not Oedipus and the family that explain the social, but the reverse.[16] *Anti-Oedipus* is an anti-Lacanian work, but it most certainly is not anti-Lacan. Deleuze and Guattari contend throughout that Lacan himself pushes psychoanalysis away from the Oedipus complex and de-oedipalizes the unconscious, but his acolytes misunderstand this.[17] They maintain that he acknowledges the historical specificity of Oedipus (*AO* 83) and takes psychoanalysis to the point of autocritique by revealing, beyond a Symbolic structure that is supported by the fantasies of an unconscious Imaginary, the domain of the Real. Rather than being an impossible that eludes symbolization, the Real, they argue, is the 'reverse side' of the Oedipal structure: it is 'the real production of desire . . . the "real inorganization" of the molecular elements [of the unconscious]' (309). One can certainly question this view, as the Oedipus complex remains prominent in Lacan, and he extends its role beyond the historical specificities of capitalism, holding it 'to mark the limits our discipline assigns to subjectivity: namely, what the subject can know of his unconscious participation in the movement of the complex structures of marriage ties, by verifying the symbolic effects in his individual existence of the tangential movement toward incest that has manifested itself ever since the advent of a universal community' (Lacan 2006: 229). Regardless, Deleuze and Guattari also declare that Lacan 'saved psychoanalysis from the frenzied oedipalization to which it was linking its fate' only at the cost of 'a regression' that kept the unconscious under the power of 'the Law, and the signifier – phallus and castration, yes! Oedipus, no!' (*AO* 217). Lacan certainly links what he considers a growing contemporary 'barbarism' to 'an ever greater realization of man as an individual' and 'the increasing absence of all the saturations of the superego and the ego-ideal that occurs in all kinds of organic forms in traditional societies' (Lacan 2006: 99). And he clearly demands a renewed priority of the Law in response to this condition. When assessing the 'faith so difficult to sustain' that allows Spinoza to detach himself from human desire, for example, he simply concludes: 'Experience shows us that Kant is more true, and I have proved that his theory of consciousness . . . is sustained only by giving a specification of the moral law which, looked at more closely, is simply desire in its pure state, that very desire that culminates in the sacrifice, strictly speaking, of everything that is the object of love in one's human tenderness' (Lacan 1981: 275). Faced with a choice between a Spinozist ethic of affirmation and Kantian moral law, Lacan sides consistently with the latter. For Deleuze and Guattari, Law is not absent in contemporary society, but, like Foucault's thesis on the continuation of sovereign forms of power in modern disciplinary society, it takes on a supporting function and no longer defines society's central features. Both Law and Oedipus are social forms that repress desire, although they emerge from desire's own social investments. There is a genealogy of desire that traces the shifts in its investments to the point where it desires its own repression. But there is also a process of desire that goes unnoticed when repression and law are read back onto its nature. As Deleuze, Guattari and Foucault note, the psychoanalytic idea of prohibition raises the question of whether the offending desire pre-exists its prohibition or whether it is constituted through it: essentially, did the child desire his mother before she was forbidden to him, or did the interdiction create the desire to transgress the law? Foucault maintains that the whole question is 'beside the point' as desire is conceived in either case in relation to law and negation.[18] Similarly, Deleuze and Guattari maintain that it rests on 'a strange sort of reasoning [that] leads one to conclude that, since *it* is forbidden, *that very thing* was desired' (*AO* 70). The fallacy is to assume from the prohibition itself the nature of what is prohibited (114–15). Desire, for Deleuze and Guattari, is not in the first instance a desire for an object, lost or otherwise.

Desiring-machines; social machines

Deleuze and Guattari identify a Platonist logic that places desire on the side of acquisition rather than production. Once this happens, desire's productivity can be portrayed only as the invention of fantasies needed to compensate for something missing in reality (*AO* 25). But this image of desire misses desire's real productive capacity, its power to create, among other things, really existing social forms. Against this, Deleuze and Guattari insist on desire's productive and *machinic* character. Desire is a machine – that is, an assemblage of heterogeneous parts that function. Production is the immanent principle of desire (5) and desiring-production is 'primary production' or 'the production of production' (7), where no distinction is made between producing and its product. To produce in this respect is 'to rearrange fragments continually in new and different patterns or configurations; and as a consequence, [to have] an indifference toward the act of producing and toward the product, toward the set of instruments to be used and toward the over-all result to be achieved' (7). Desiring-production is a schizophrenic process, not in the sense of being an escape from reality – the clinical diagnosis of schizophrenia as a mental disorder, and Deleuze and Guattari make clear that they are not glorifying schizophrenia as a mental illness, even if they take issue with psychoanalytic interpretations and treatments of the condition – but in its continual integration of seemingly incompatible elements. Understood simply as a drive to connect and synthesize, 'desire "needs" very few things' (27), and thus experiences no lack. Indeed, lack only characterizes the state of a subject that, having withdrawn from itself, has lost its desire (27). Schizoanalysis examines the workings of these non-subjective 'desiring-machines', its central question being not what desire seeks or means (the psychoanalyst's question), nor what function it serves (the ethnologist's question), but simply how it works (180–1).

Desiring-machines are microscopic or molecular assemblages of heterogeneous drives, flows and partial objects, which populate the unconscious and 'are by nature fragmentary and fragmented' (*AO* 5). They also connect to other fragmentary desiring-machines in such a way that 'every machine functions as a break in the flow in relation to the machine to which it is connected, but at the same time is also a flow itself, or the production of a flow, in relation to the machine connected to it' (36). Deleuze and Guattari adapt the terminology of partial objects and flows from post-Freudian child psychoanalyst Melanie Klein's concept of part-objects. Klein holds the infant psyche to be constituted through object-relations, but these are not in the first instance relations to whole objects, the infant not yet having developed firm boundaries between inside and outside, or between real objects and objects of phantasy, and not yet having achieved a sense of itself or its parents as distinct individuals. Kleinian part-objects are irreducibly bivocal, appearing to be both good and bad, benevolent and persecutory, thereby becoming objects of both love and hate. The breast is the paradigmatic part-object since it contains nourishment but does not guarantee its presence when the child wants it. Klein traces the pre-Oedipal development of the psyche through a 'paranoid–schizoid' position where the infant seeks desperately and aggressively to separate good and bad part-objects, a task that consistently fails as the objects switch from good to bad and so forth; followed by a 'manic–depressive' position in which the infant's ego is unified enough to be able to see its mother as a complete and loving object, but one it has injured through its earlier violent acts and consequently lost. These changes pave the way for the onset of the Oedipus complex, which begins when the boy lovingly tries to repair the damaged object of desire and regain its love, thereby substituting himself for the father. With the normal resolution of the complex, psychic development, for Klein, culminates with a stable ego whose psychic images of individuals and objects correspond to the real complete individuals and objects they represent. Deleuze and Guattari criticize Klein for aiming at this solution, thereby imposing 'the point of view of the whole, of global persons, and of complete objects' (45) onto the unconscious. Desire, they maintain, does not refer to whole objects or persons in this way (72, 324). The unconscious is thus not a realm of part-objects that refer to wholes, but rather partial objects that remain disjointed.[19]

Constructed with fragments and flows whose relations are replete with strife and tension, 'desiring-machines work only when they break down, and by continually breaking down' (AO 8). Deleuze and Guattari identify three syntheses that constitute machinic desire: connective, disjunctive and conjunctive.[20] The first synthesis joins heterogeneities, constituting the machine and its functioning. But 'produced, at a certain place and a certain time in the connective synthesis' (8) is a 'body without organs' or BwO,[21] which carries out the second synthesis. The BwO is a differenciator engendered in the synthesis that constructs the desiring-machine, and in so far as production is defined by connection, it emerges as 'an element of antiproduction' (8) within the productive process. It expresses a friction, a knot of resistance within the desiring-machine, the way it 'suffers from being organized in this way, from not having some other sort of organization, or no organization at all' (8). The BwO thus repels the connected fragments, and in this way effects their disjoining. In doing so, 'it is not the proof of an original nothingness, nor is it what remains of a lost totality' (8) but rather an immanent Otherness that folds the desiring-machine's partial objects together in such a way that they neither correspond to nor oppose one another. Deleuze and Guattari maintain that the BwO and its fragments are not opposed to each other, but instead 'are opposed conjointly to the organism' (326) – that is, to any synthesis that would wrap them into a whole. Desiring-machines can operate only because of this tension between the BwO and partial objects: 'Repulsion is the condition of the machine's functioning, but attraction is the functioning itself. That the functioning depends on repulsion is clear to us, inasmuch as it all works only by breaking down' (329–30).

The disjunctive synthesis is also a 'recording synthesis'. Machines function on the basis of their connections, but they are explained in terms of their disjunctions (*AO* 15). In repelling various fragments and flows, the BwO establishes separations among them that serve as a primitive or molecular code, in this way becoming a 'surface of inscription' for them. Here the BwO bears a general resemblance to Lacan's Master Signifier, seeming to occupy a transcendent position and establishing the distinct meanings of partial objects as so many differentially related signifiers. But this code is not a meaningful structure; instead, it is an 'assignifying' regime whose signs do not signify anything because 'they are under the order of the included disjunctions where *everything is possible*' (328). Put differently, and precisely because desiring-machines can be assessed only in terms of how they work rather than what they mean, this molecular recording synthesis expresses the *sense*, rather than the identity, of the machine's partial objects and flows. As discussed in Chapter 2, sense for Deleuze is a disjunctive synthesis in which differences relate to one another through a difference in itself or differenciator.[22]

Finally the third, conjunctive synthesis gives rise to a form of the subject. This is not a subject of lack, nor one with a resolved identity, but a schizophrenic and *nomadic* subject that is 'out of sync' with itself. Deleuze and Guattari maintain that the strife between desire's connectivity and the BwO's force of repulsion is reconciled in the unconscious through the production of 'intensive quantities' that the subject 'consumes'. If we recall from the previous chapter that intensive quantity for Nietzsche is a forceful difference in quantity that implies both an active or reactive quality and an affirmative or negative expression of will to power, then these intensive quantities can be considered expressive zones on the plane of differential forces that is the unconscious. As Deleuze and Guattari state: '[T]he opposition of the forces of attraction and repulsion produces an open series of intensive elements, all of them positive, that are never an expression of the final equilibrium of a system, but consist, rather, of an unlimited number of stationary, metastable states through which the subject passes' (AO 19). These states can be associated with 'personages', which include historical figures and parents (there certainly are parental figures in the unconscious[23]), but these 'exist only as fragments' (97) rather than complete individuals.[24] Or, rather, they are *dramatizations* of the unconscious's expressive intensities, in the same way as Nietzsche's nobles and slaves dramatize different wills to power. The subject appears and is consummated by way of a becoming – a becoming-noble or becoming-slave, or, in the case of Judge Schreber,[25] a becoming-woman – and this is the way both reconciliation and consumption are realized. These states are in no way chosen by the subject; rather, the subject is *driven* to them, and is constituted by being so driven. The subject emerges as an 'I' that always recognizes itself and its desires retrospectively, by way of the intensities through which it passes. It takes the form of a declaration, 'so *that's* what it was' or 'so *that's* what I desired'. Through this schizophrenic process, the subject passes through a series of incompossible intensive states that resonate and repeat one another.

There is no Nietzsche-the-self, professor of philology, who suddenly loses his mind and supposedly identifies with all sorts of strange people; rather, there is the Nietzschean subject who passes through a series of states, and who identifies these states with the names of history: "*every name in history is I* . . . " The subject spreads itself out along the entire circumference of the circle, the center of which has been abandoned by the ego. At the center is the desiring-machine, the celibate machine of the Eternal Return. . . . . It is not a matter of identifying with various historical personages, but rather identifying the names of history with zones of intensity on the body without organs; and each time Nietzsche-as-subject exclaims: "They're *me*! So it's *me*!" (21)

What characterizes all these syntheses at the molecular level is that they are inclusive, not by virtue of bringing differences into unity but rather by incorporating incompossibles that vice-dict rather than contradict one another. The unconscious, in short, is a realm of virtual differentiation rather than the actualizing differenciation into distinct types that can, to some degree, be organized by the principles of identity, negation and contradiction. Psychoanalysis, on the other hand, consistently applies exclusive forms of these same syntheses to the unconscious, in this way introducing specific types and meanings into a realm that is properly evaluated only in terms of the way it works. Unconscious personages, for example, are taken to be representations of the parents, and desire is interpreted accordingly: 'So it was your father, so it was your mother' (*AO* 101). Desire's drive to establish connections, for example, is construed as incestuous desire for the mother, even though in this realm 'one would look in vain for persons or even functions discernible as father, mother, son, sister, etc., since these names only designate intensive variations' (162). In this way the unconscious is reconfigured according to the kind of meaningful signifiers that imply an excessive lack, giving birth to the subject of desire as lack. Ironically, psychoanalysis discovers an Oedipal desire that must be repressed in order to constitute the subject only by first repressing the productivity of desiring-machines through 'the illegitimate use of the syntheses of the unconscious' (75).

Differenciation into distinct and exclusive objects and persons certainly occurs – and hence representation is possible – but this process takes place in the realm of social production. Deleuze and Guattari maintain that desiring-production and social production have the same natures – both are machinic – but inhabit different regimes, one molecular and the other 'molar'. In chemistry, a mole – also known as Avogadro's number, which is approximately 6.022×10^{23} – is the number of atoms or molecules of a substance needed for the aggregate mass in grams to equal the substance's atomic mass. For example, a mole of carbon, whose atomic mass is 12, will be 12 grams, while a mole of oxygen, whose atomic mass is 16, will be 16 grams. Among its many applications in nineteenth-century science, the mole was used to establish constants that emerge from large statistical aggregates. Thus, to demonstrate the ideal gas law, which holds that equal volumes of different gases, under the same conditions of pressure and temperature, will contain an equal number of molecules, one simply needs to establish the mass of different gases held in containers of equal size and placed under the same conditions of temperature and pressure, since this will determine the number of molecules in each in accordance with the Avogadro constant.[26] For Deleuze and Guattari, the molar is a domain where desiring-production is configured *'according to the laws of large numbers'* (*AO* 287). At a molecular level, the nature of gas molecules is random and dynamic, and individually they have no temperature or pressure, as these are functions of the average kinetic energy of a mass. But large samples of these molecules display stable properties of this sort simply because individual variations do not affect overall statistical traits, just as individual random coin flips do not substantially affect the overall 50/50 split between heads and tails when the aggregate number of flips becomes sufficiently large. Similarly, as a mass phenomenon desire can display characteristics of structural unity even though at a microphysical level it resolves into 'waves and corpuscles, flows and partial objects that are no longer dependent upon the large numbers; infinitesimal lines of escape, instead of the perspectives of the large aggregates' (280). Exclusive differences emerge only at this level of overall structural unity.

None of this means that the molecular is individual and the molar is collective. Individuals are themselves molar, and the molecular is no less complex and collective than the molar domain (*AO* 280). Like Foucault's micropower realm, molecular desire is diffused throughout social formations, and the latter are its overall effects.[27] In addition to its role in the disjunctive synthesis of molecular desiring-machines, the BwO also functions 'as a pivot, as a frontier between the molar and the molecular' (281), since, as a differenciator, it both differentiates in the virtual and differenciates in the actual. In this way, however, the molecular and the molar are mutually imbricated – 'everywhere there exist the molecular *and* the molar: their disjunction is a relation of included disjunction' (340) – and thus are in a relation of double conditioning. On the one hand, social machines are determined directly by the investments of desiring-machines – Deleuze and Guattari reject Freud's idea that desire is only invested in the social after it is repressed and then sublimated – such that *'social production is purely and simply desiring-production itself under determinate conditions'* (29). On the other hand, the molar social forms that emerge from desiring-production react back upon this molecular domain, bringing themselves to bear on and appropriating and directing the latter's productive flows. In this respect, the analogy to large aggregates of random coin flips does not capture the full relationship between the two realms. A more appropriate image would be that of currents of air, water and heat that interact in never fully predictable ways to engender a cyclonic circulation, which in turn appropriates the wind, water and heat energies to create a hurricane. At a microscopic level these currents are no less chaotic and random even after they are caught and wrapped up in the hurricane's macroscopic structure and dynamics, which determine the distribution of singular points of force alongside overall trajectories, thresholds and the necessary intensities of triggers that can prompt sudden changes. By the same token, molecular variations can only rarely destabilize these system-level properties once they are established in their full force.[28]

Deleuze and Guattari contend that through the molar differentiations that desiring-machines engender, desire comes to repress itself. More than this, as the social is a direct result of investments of molecular desire, this process amounts to desire desiring its own repression. It is important to make clear what repression means in this context. It is certainly not that desiring-production is somehow arrested, even if this might on some level appear to be what molar structures accomplish. Indeed, Deleuze consistently rejects the portrayal of society as an architecture that encloses desire or anything else, saying instead that 'for me, a society is something that is constantly escaping in every direction . . . society is a fluid, or even worse, a gas' (*TRM* 280). Instead, repression is a matter of funnelling flows, controlling their circulation, and thus reconfiguring desire's dynamic and direction: 'Repression cannot act without displacing desire, without giving rise to a *consequent desire*, all ready, all warm for punishment, and without putting this desire in the place of the *antecedent desire* on which repression comes to bear in principle or in reality' (*AO* 115). Social repression thus involves, for example, channelling drives into circulation around lacks and lost objects, thereby introducing them to a pattern of neurosis; or tying desire to subjectivity, to an 'I' who desires, by wrapping it into 'collective and personal ends, goals, and intentions' (342). In such cases desire is lured into positions where it can be managed: 'Oedipus is the baited image with which desire allows itself to be caught (*That's* what you wanted! The decoded flows were incest!)' (166); but at the same time the lure itself is a form of desire – 'desire is that, too: a trap' (166). In this way, desire leads itself down 'a path of resignation' (60), to 'resignation-desires' (62). But it thus always *remains* desire, even if it assumes a negative and reactive form.

If 'the sign of desire is never a sign of the law, it is a sign of strength' (*AO* 111), and if the forces of desire are 'essentially active, aggressive, artistic, productive, and triumphant' (122), then the Nietzschean answer to the question of how desire comes to desire its repression becomes clear: it is a matter of the triumph of reactive forces, the displacement of weak drives, which engenders a becoming-negative that separates the active forces of desiring-production from what they can do, leading them to resignation. In their genealogy of social forms, which culminates with the Oedipal repression of desire in modern capitalism, Deleuze and Guattari associate each stage with a moment in Nietzsche's genealogy of the emergence of bad conscience or guilt. As Nietzsche demonstrates, guilt is a condition where desire delights in self-torture.[29] Any social formation refers back to the desiring-machines that would desire or will it. The genealogical task is therefore to determine the configurations of desire that will these social forms and the difference they make in being so configured. It is further to show how under these conditions desire could not desire otherwise than as it does. In this respect the social form is always only a symptom, never a cause: psychoanalysis is not the reason we are neurotic, even if it works to make us so.

If psychoanalysis comes to take over the role of the priest after the death of God, continuing to peddle guilt in the contemporary secular age,[30] it is because, as Nietzsche demonstrates, the advent of nihilism does not dissolve old slavish values in the wake of the collapse of their divine guarantor, but continues and even intensifies them. Just as the slaves infect the nobles by inducing pity through their own display of sickliness, so neurosis, 'the only illness consisting in making others ill' (*AO* 269), becomes a vehicle to infect desiring-production. When molar social formations react back upon the molecular flows of desire that engender them, they are able to penetrate the molecular realm because there is something within it that can serve as their support. Deleuze and Guattari identify a 'primary repression' (9) in the BwO's repulsion of partial objects, holding it to be the hook on which the exclusive disjunctions of social production find a hold (339). But there would be no way the priestly psychoanalyst could successfully 'teach us resignation' (59) if *ressentiment* could not emerge off the displacement of reactive forces in the unconscious. It is only through *ressentiment*, unfolded as a molar form and then turned back onto the unconscious, that the latter's inclusive differentiations can become the support for exclusive negations and contradictions.

Territorial, despotic and capitalist social machines

As their nature is identical to that of desiring-machines, social machines too are constituted by connective, disjunctive and conjunctive syntheses. They organize productive flows at a molar level, including flows of individuals, populations, technologies and goods, which are all ultimately flows of desire. Social machines also have an element corresponding to the BwO: 'the forms of social production, like those of desiring-production, involve an unengendered nonproductive attitude, an element of antiproduction coupled with the process, a full body that functions as a *socius*' (*AO* 10). The socius is a molar recording surface. It carries out the disjunctive syntheses that inscribe social production with meaning, while being unproductive and meaningless itself. It thereby assumes a role as a 'quasi cause' (11) of production, and productive forces appear to be 'miraculated' by it (10). As Marx demonstrates with capitalism, for example, money is valueless in itself, yet seems inexplicably to produce profit – and it is fetishized and desired precisely for this reason – while industrial capital seems responsible for producing relative surplus value while being objectively valuable itself. In both cases, 'what is specifically capitalist here is the role of money and the use of capital as a full body to constitute the recording or inscribing surface' (11). But other social forms have elements that perform the same role, some being immanent to the systems of production they organize, others assuming a transcendent status. Social machines thus associate flows with chains of connected signs, separate these through exclusive disjunctions and establish conjunctions among them. The form the resulting assemblages take delineates the type of social machine at work. In all cases social machines struggle to contain desire's schizophrenic process of inclusive connection, disjunction and conjunction, precisely because it poses the greatest threat to them: 'If desire is repressed, it is because every position of desire, no matter how small, is capable of calling into question the established order of a society . . . desire is revolutionary in its essence . . . and no society can tolerate a position of real desire without its structures of exploitation, servitude and hierarchy being compromised' (AO 116). Deleuze and Guattari analyze three types of social machine that form a genealogy of desire's molar repression: savage–territorial; barbarian–despotic; and civilized–capitalist. While they are linked in certain respects to a historical order, they are also wrapped up in one another: capitalism, for example, 'has haunted all forms of society' (140); conversely, 'modern capitalist and socialist States take on the characteristic features of the primordial despotic State' (220). Nevertheless, while they are never entirely distinct, the three machines can be distinguished by their respective orientations to desiring flows. Territorial and despotic machines submit desire to codes, the latter anchoring its code in a transcendent source. Capitalism, conversely, decodes flows, 'substituting for intrinsic codes an axiomatic of abstract quantities in the form of money' (139). Capitalism's mechanism is 'axiomatic' because, like the term's use in mathematics, it comprises formal rules or propositions whose application to the elements in its domain is indifferent to those elements' properties or qualities. Capitalist exchange abstracts away the distinct qualities of commodities so that numerical equivalences can be established between them, each commodity's use value being irrelevant once exchange value becomes dominant. Conversely, codes determine the qualitative differences between flows, which therefore retain their incommensurability and irreducibility to one another (247).

Territorial machines code desire by separating distinct lines of filiation and establishing conjunctions of alliance. Their unproductive recording socius is a system of physical cruelty that directly marks the body, and it includes 'tattooing, excising, incising, carving, scarifying, mutilating, encircling, and initiating' (*AO* 144). As Deleuze and Guattari note (144), this is the system identified by Nietzsche as the basis for conscience, which requires that a memory be 'burned into' men in order to give them the 'right to make promises' (Nietzsche 1967: 2.1–2.3). Psychoanalysis and certain strands of anthropology have long associated these structures in primitive societies with the incest taboo, and thus the Oedipus complex, marriage and alliance consequently being understood in terms of an exchange of women that wards off incest desire and ensures exogamy. But Deleuze and Guattari argue that there is no reason to accept these starting points: '[I]t is doubtful that incest was a real obstacle to the establishment of society, as the partisans of an *exchangist* conception claim' (*AO* 116). The primitive machine's coding expresses a generalized anxiety and fear of decoded flows of desire as such, and this is evident in the machine's exclusion of the market from its coded structure: 'The primitive machine is not ignorant of exchange, commerce, and industry; it exorcises them, localizes them, cordons them off, encastes them, and maintains the merchant and the blacksmith in a subordinate position, so that the flows of exchange and the flows of production do not manage to break the codes in favor of their abstract or fictional quantities' (153). Moreover, alliance marriage does not operate as an economic exchange, but instead links together stronger and weaker filial lines, thereby introducing non-exchangeable elements such as prestige that function as compensations (150). In so far as kinship alliances are determined by political and economic factors (147), it is not a matter of 'a kind of primary equilibrium of prices, a primary equivalence or equality in the underlying principles' (187). In this way, 'the essential process is not exchanging, but inscribing and marking' (186) – that is to say, establishing and maintaining the qualitative distinctions that characterize a code, organizing desire accordingly. Oedipal logics of incest, and capitalist logics of exchange and debt, are modern forms that have been read onto this primitive machine: 'We see no reason for believing in the universality of one and the same apparatus of sociocultural repression' (184).

Although it separates family groups rather than plots of land (the communities in question are frequently nomadic and thus have no connection to particular locations), the primitive machine is nevertheless territorial in so far as these segments are established immanently, the system of cruelty marking bodies that 'are the earth's products' (*AO* 144) and the whole process taking place 'on an indivisible earth where the connective, disjunctive, and conjunctive relations of each section are inscribed along with other relations' (145). In this regard the barbarian machine deterritorializes the primitive machine, even while it founds the territorial borders of a State structure by establishing the transcendent position of the despot, who 'imposes a new alliance system and places himself in direct filiation with the deity' (192). The new machine's socius is the despot himself: through his prescriptions and prohibitions he becomes 'the sole quasi cause, the source and fountainhead and estuary of the apparent objective movement' (194) even while being powerless without his army, along with the 'doctors, priests, scribes, and officials' (193) who are indispensable to the cult of personality surrounding him. The primitive codes remain, but they are 'overcoded by the transcendent unity' (196) of the State form. In this way an overarching imperial order of Law is established, replacing the cruelty of the old machine with a new terror: '[T]he system of terror has replaced the system of cruelty. The old cruelty persists, especially in the autonomous or quasi-autonomous sectors; but it is now bricked into the State apparatus, which at times organizes it and at other times tolerates or limits it, in order to make it serve the ends of the State, and to subsume it under the higher superimposed unity of a Law that is more terrible' (211–12).

The despot appropriates the primitive code by breaking it and standing above it – he *does* commit incest by marrying both his sister and his mother, but this 'royal barbarian incest is merely the means to overcode the flows of desire, certainly not a means to liberate them. O Caligula, O Heliogabalus, O mad memory of the vanished emperors!' (*AO* 201–2). Lacan's analysis of the transcendent Other who enjoys a desire he prohibits to others, of the Master Signifier that marks (overcodes) the signifying system, finds its proper application in the desiring investments that engender the despotic machine (208–9, 217). But this structure is still not Oedipal, even though the Oedipus would be impossible without the moment of transcendence established by the despotic machine.[31] The despotic machine instead expresses Klein's pre-Oedipal positions, being paranoid–schizoid in its partitioning and organization of society and manic–depressive in its positing an empty transcendence (33, 212). There is not yet the universalized and internalized sense of guilt that comes with the death of God, for even though despotic terror engenders *ressentiment* among its subjects, this has not been turned back on itself (214–17).[32] And like the primitive machine, the despotic machine shares a 'dread of decoded flows – flows of production, but also mercantile flows . . . of exchange and commerce that might escape the State monopoly' (197). Rather than exclude the decoded flows of the market, the State seeks to control them through a monopoly of power over its resources and the use of taxes to maintain its apparatus (197). Its role here is 'to recode as best it can, by means of regular or exceptional operations, the product of the decoded flows' (223).

Clearly capitalism does not arise simply because of the presence of decoded flows of the market, since these are known even to the savages, and they always to some degree escape the despotic machine's codes. Nor is it a matter of technological development, for then one could rightly ask 'why capitalism wasn't born in China in the thirteenth century, when all the necessary scientific and technical conditions nevertheless seemed to be present' (*AO* 197), and similar questions could be asked about the ancient Roman slave economy and the feudal serf economy (223). There must instead be a shift in desire itself, not to a decoded desire or a desire for decoding, both of which 'have always existed' (224), but to a completely different kind of machine: '[C]apitalism and its break are defined not solely by decoded flows, but by the generalized decoding of flows, the new massive deterritorialization, the conjunction of deterritorialized flows' (224). Capitalism's deterritorialization of the despotic State machine does not return desire to its savage condition, but instead takes it into another immanent organization, one in which the decoded flows are not excluded but brought into the machine's centre.

The capitalist machine conjoins flows, starting with the parallel flows of capital and labour, which come into force in Europe with the dissolution of feudalism (*AO* 225). Through conjunction, these

DESIRE AND DESIRING-MACHINES

flows are submitted to an axiomatic of abstract exchange, whereby their value is determined simply by what they can be bought and sold for on the market. This process reaches dominance as capital directly appropriates production, becoming a miraculous quasi cause (226–7). But capitalism also augments and intensifies this dynamic by producing both surplus value and a range of unproductive surpluses of unemployment and stagnation, all of which it plugs back into its productive process. It absorbs these into new forms of consumption and investment, drawing on the forces of advertising, media, large bureaucracies, military structures and imperialist ventures. In this way capitalism continually internalizes what had been the outer limits of its productivity, introducing 'the presence of antiproduction within production itself' (235). Its cynicism appears in its ability to invent new axioms to turn anything into a commodity and thus a source of profit (238). Even garbage becomes an opportunity for business ventures. Psychoanalysis too participates in this process – it 'constitutes for its part a gigantic enterprise of absorption of surplus value' (239). It is no surprise that in capitalist society therapy abounds.

On a superficial level it might seem that capitalism, by decoding desire and liberating its flows, is more aligned with it than previous social machines. Nevertheless, in the cruelty and terror of their codes, primitive and barbarian machines share a greater affinity with desire because they do not suppress its polyvocity, while capitalism seeks to erase it through axiomatization (*AO* 184–5, 336–7). Capitalism remains antagonistic to desire, because it executes only a partial deterritorialization, decoding desire only at a molar level. Hence 'it would be a serious error to consider *the capitalist flows and the schizophrenic flows* as identical, under the general theme of a decoding of the flows of desire' (245). Releasing desire at a molecular level, the schizophrenic process is an *absolute* as opposed to a relative deterritorialization; it does not follow decoding with axiomatization. It thus confronts capitalism as its '*exterior* limit . . . or the conclusion of its deepest tendency' (246), so that capitalism must find ways to displace, absorb, limit, discipline or otherwise put to use this schizophrenic excess. Capitalism is perpetually driven towards its limits – of surplus value (the tendency of the rate of profit to fall), of decoding and of axiomatization – which it struggles to displace and internalize. As a result, it becomes 'the *relative* limit of every society; it effects *relative* breaks, because it substitutes for the codes an extremely rigorous axiomatic that maintains the energy of the flows in a bound state on the body of capital as a socius that is deterritorialized, but also a socius that is even more pitiless than any other' (246).

Capitalism's decoding and deterritorialization are thus accompanied by 'factitious and artificial reterritorializations' (*AO* 303). Its tendency to decode always heading towards its limit, capitalism produces the very schizophrenic subjects that threaten it, and then 'institutes or restores all sorts of residual and artificial, imaginary, or symbolic territorialities, thereby attempting, as best it can, to recode, to rechannel persons who have been defined in terms of abstract quantities. Everything returns or recurs: States, nations, families' (34). Codes thus continue to exist, even if sometimes appearing anachronistic, as they are adapted to present conditions and put into continual variation (232). The State is similarly retained and updated, assuming immanent functions of absorbing antiproduction in its army and bureaucracy (235) and of regulating capitalism's axiomatic: '[T]he conjunction of the decoded flows, their differential relations, and their multiple schizzes or breaks require a whole apparatus of regulation whose principle organ is the State. The capitalist State is the regulator of decoded flows as such, insofar as they are caught up in the axiomatic of capital' (252). And the family assumes a new role as the vehicle to bring social repression directly into the unconscious: 'In short, Oedipus arrives' (265). For the liberation that is indeed achieved by capitalism would spin out of control were there not some way for it to discipline and reterritorialize desire at the molecular level. It is therefore necessary to constitute individuals in ways that make them manageable, and 'the Oedipal triangle is the personal and private territoriality that corresponds to all of capitalism's efforts at social reterritorialization' (266).

The family's mission under capitalist social production is thus 'to produce neurotics by means of its oedipalization, its system of impasses, its delegated psychic repression, without which social repression would never find docile and resigned subjects, and would not succeed in choking off the flows' lines of escape' (*AO* 361). Oedipus is the fiction that separates desire from its productive force of connection. Even in this, however, Oedipus is actually powerless to cause anything (115, 178). The neurotic is the politically harmless and occasionally useful form of deviance that capitalism succeeds extremely well in producing. Again, repression does not mean desire's arrest, but a reconfiguration of its flow that separates it from what it can do. And docility is not submissiveness, though it does indicate compliance to the requirements of capitalism, limiting forms of resistance to those that can be managed by the system. A resigned subject is one whose desire is structured around a nameless lack, and who can be manipulated in a perpetual search for fulfilment. This desire as lack also correlates with the capitalist search for endless profit, where, as Marx shows, money becomes a mystical and fetishized object. As Deleuze and Guattari maintain, capitalist cynicism is accompanied by a 'strange piety' that spiritualizes both the State and capital (225). But the capitalist subject is also one who has internalized a sense of guilt and consequently desires his own repression, welcoming it as something deserved. Thus, 'the law tells us: You will not marry your mother, and you will not kill your father. And we docile subjects say to ourselves: so *that's* what I wanted!' (114). But this law 'has an interest in discrediting and disgracing' (114), and psychoanalysis, in no way challenging the law's legitimacy, instead revives 'an age-old tendency to humble us, to demean us, and to make us feel guilty' (50). Capitalism produces schizophrenia, and its apparatuses of social and psychic repression work to turn schizophrenia into neurosis: 'Rather a society of neurotics than one successful schizophrenic who has not been made autistic' (102).

* * *

Desire restored to its genuine creative power, Deleuze and Guattari declare, is the one true threat to capitalism: '[W]e believe that capitalist society can endure many manifestations of interest, but not one manifestation of desire, which would be enough to make its fundamental structures explode, even at the kindergarten level' (*AO* 379). The schizophrenic process has the capacity to overturn capitalism not by opposing it but simply by doing something else: it is a-systematic rather than anti-system. It is therefore a matter of going further in the direction set by capitalism itself, 'for perhaps the flows are not yet deterritorialized enough, not decoded enough, from the viewpoint of a theory and a practice of a highly schizophrenic character' (239), and thus the operative rule must be 'that one can never go far enough in the direction of deterritorialization' (321). This task is a collective one, as desire is a collective phenomenon. Collective interests can also play a role, but they cannot be effective alone. On the one hand, people can only revolt if it is what they *desire*: 'Revolutionaries often forget, or do not like to recognize, that one wants and makes revolution out of desire, not duty' (344). On the other hand, however, a group's interests, which are preconscious, bear no direct relation to its unconscious investments of desire (347). Some collectives cling to interests aligned to the forces that repress and exploit them; but others whose interests are indeed revolutionary can still carry desires that are reactionary, desires of spitefulness and *ressentiment* that continue to judge the world through slavish categories of good and evil, friend and enemy.[33] The first case finds its extreme in the molar phenomenon of political fascism, which was used to mobilize the most hateful desires of the masses. But both cases express a molecular fascism, a 'fascism in us all, in our heads and in our everyday behaviour, the fascism that causes us to love power, to desire the very thing that dominates and exploits us' (Foucault in *AO* xiii). The ethical aim of *Anti-Oedipus*, as Foucault points out, is to discover how to 'keep from being fascist, even (especially) when one believes oneself to be a revolutionary militant' (xiii). It is here that we enter the micropolitical domain.

5

Micropolitics

The story behind the organization of the 2004 European Social Forum is useful for illustrating a ubiquitous political problem.[1] It begins with a proposal to hold the event in London, which was put forward at the European Preparatory Assembly in 2002 by members of Globalise Resistance, NGO War on Want and the Newcastle branch of Unison. The initiative surprised many UK activists, who felt they should have been consulted, and this feeling was reinforced when London Mayor Ken Livingstone and the Greater London Assembly were approached for support, some activists being wary of such government involvement. An early meeting meant to bring together interested parties was held on a working day, which hindered representatives from smaller organizations whose unpaid positions meant they had to hold other jobs, and little information was circulated ahead of time, seemingly because this was considered unnecessary by those managing the process. With larger organizations putting forward substantial funds and having significant leverage during negotiations, and with many aspects of the UK Organizing Committee's meeting agendas seemingly decided ahead of time by a small cabal, many felt excluded from the process, and objected in ways that led to their being labelled disruptive malcontents. Some who felt disenfranchized left the official organizing process and planned autonomous spaces to run alongside and independent of the ESF. The Organizing Committee did ultimately recognize these autonomous spaces as part of the official event and listed them in the programme, but the animosities that developed during this time were still evident when the ESF was finally held.

As one can imagine, those disenchanted with the official process turned to the internet. In January 2004, Stuart Hodkinson sent a message to the 'Democratize the ESF' email list making a distinction between 'Horizontals' and 'Verticals'. This may not have been its first usage, but regardless, after the email the binary opposition was quickly adopted by self-styled 'Horizontals,' who, wanting to distinguish themselves from those who in their minds were imposing strict hierarchies of governance and control, claimed to hold more egalitarian and open organizational principles. Those they called 'Verticals' certainly did not accept the label, and had their own rather condescending names for these 'Horizontals.' There was a decided absence of Nietzschean nobles on both sides of this divide.

There was certainly no necessity behind the adoption of this opposition – the email could simply have gone unnoticed. But once it became part of the political discourse among groups in the dispute, it had definite political effects. It organized different activists into two broad camps, setting at least in part the direction of future individual and collective statements and actions. As a form of discourse, it was obviously also a form of knowledge and power. But it was also enormously limited. Members of one group did not really share anything beyond a general antagonism towards those deemed to belong to the other, and they did not necessarily even share the same reasons for their antagonism. And nothing prevented those within one group from being at odds with one another, since they had distinct agendas, practices and perspectives beyond those that focused on their negative relation to the opposing side. Hence it is unsurprising that more than a few activists found the division unhelpful when it came to working through the issue of how to plan the forum collectively. And commentators had difficulty even defining the distinction, as these loose groupings did not identify a specific ideology or world view of politics, leaving little to the distinction beyond an apparent and vague contrast. At bottom there was only a clash among dispersed and heterogeneous individuals and organizations, each one having its own internal dynamics, including perspectives on the present, memories of the past and expectations of the future. Out of the dispute emerged oppositional categories of identity that failed to delineate what these clashing forces actually were, instead capturing and organizing them in the most superficial way.

Oppositions of this sort arise and persist across political and social life. They may have some initial benefits, but they generally become hindrances long before they take the form of the antagonistic friend/ enemy rifts that worried Foucault.[2] Assuming there are equally insidious implications of trying to diffuse these tensions through the appeal to moral or political principles deemed universally applicable or rational – the kind of appeals that, for example, keep Rawlsian liberal theory 'on the surface' politically and unable to engage in complex issues of power and desire – the question becomes whether this kind of politics is necessary or inevitable. It perhaps would be if, at the micro or molecular level, principles of identity meant that meaning and subjectivity could not emerge without negation and opposition playing a constitutive role, or if that level were really nothing more than a personal, aesthetic or in any event distinctly apolitical domain. However, if it is the case that not only is the personal necessarily political, but an aesthetic dimension of politics is inescapable – and Nietzsche's criticism that our sense of rationality and truth is at bottom grounded in moral and aesthetic perspectives would seem to vindicate this – then the molecular dimension of life takes a political centre stage. Politics begins with micropolitics, and so too does any new politics to which we might aspire.

Thought's dogmatic image

There is a dogmatic image of thought, Deleuze maintains, that ties it to identity and the subject. It operates on a model of recognition, and postulates a principle of 'good sense' and an ideal of 'common sense'. The principle is a moral conviction that natural thinking capacities are universally held, and that thought has a love of and an innate connection to truth. Its favourite assertions take the form of, 'everybody knows'. In the case of Descartes's 'I think therefore I am', for example, everybody knows (or 'nobody can deny') what thinking, being and the self are. While this crude universalism is certainly problematic, it allows philosophy to 'claim innocence' and side with pre-philosophical popular opinion, or *doxa* (*DR* 129–30).[3] The ideal expresses a faith that in its natural exercise thinking accords with both other faculties for cognition and the object that they collectively re-cognize. Recognition is thus 'the harmonious exercise of all the faculties upon a supposed same object: the same object may be seen, touched, remembered, imagined or conceived' (133). Together these elements establish an image that aligns thought with all the baggage of valuations attached to philosophy's will to truth (135–6). Grasping truth is taken to be the essence of thinking, and thoughtlessness is thereby linked to falsity, that is, to misrecognition or error. But the examples of error posed by philosophy – saying that 7 + 5 = 13 or greeting Theodorus when it is really Theaetetus who enters (150; also *NP* 105)[4] – reveal the wholly puerile nature of this approach to thought. Such errors certainly pose no real threat to thinking, and thinking is hardly vindicated by catching and avoiding them.[5] And isn't *that* what *everybody knows*?

If thinking is not natural – and, as Deleuze states, '"Everybody" knows very well that in fact men think rarely, and more often under the impulse of a shock than in the excitement of a taste for thinking' (*DR* 132) – then it is right to seek out the conditions that engender it. Deleuze declares: 'Something in the world forces us to think. This something is an object not of recognition but of a fundamental *encounter*. What is encountered may be Socrates, a temple or a demon. It may be grasped in a range of affective tones: wonder, love, hatred, suffering. In whichever tone, its primary characteristic is that it can only be sensed. In this sense it is opposed to recognition' (139). Within what we recognize we encounter something that is 'imperceptible precisely from the point of view of recognition', and thus 'from the point of view of an empirical exercise of the senses in which sensibility grasps only that which also could be grasped by other faculties' (140) – in other words, it is something that also cannot be remembered, imagined, conceived and so forth. There is a dimension of sense immanent to what is cognized that is not re-cognizable. Plato provides an analogue to this when he identifies a paradoxical duality encountered in the qualities of perceived things: 'Whereas a finger always calls for recognition and is never more than a finger, that which is hard is never hard without also being soft, since it is inseparable from a becoming or a relation which includes the opposite within it (the same is true of the large and the small, the one and the many)' (141).[6] Plato, however, treats this paradox of sense – and notably 'paradox' comes from the Greek *paradoxon*, what is 'against *doxa*' – as a spur to reminiscence, which takes thought not to an empirical past but to the soul's connection, outside chronological time, to eternal Forms. Reminiscence thus does no more than 'complicate the schema' of recognition by leading thought to bear 'upon another object, supposed to be associated with or rather enveloped within the first [perceived object], which demands to be recognised for itself independently of any distinct perception' (141–2). Moreover, Deleuze argues, by conceiving this duality in terms of the coexistence of contrary qualities, Plato domesticates the encounter that compels thinking by treating sensible qualities or the sensible realm (*aisthēton*, which Plato opposes to *noēton*, the intelligible realm) as though they were the being of the sensible (*aisthēteon*). The being of the sensible, sense itself, comprises not contraries or even contradictories, but disjoined and incompossible differences. It is a completely different kind of paradox. Encounters not with contrariety but with difference, Deleuze holds, are what force us to think, to press beyond recognition and the harmony of our faculties: 'For it is not figures already mediated and related to representation that are capable of carrying the faculties to their respective limits but, on the contrary, free or untamed states of difference in itself; not qualitative opposition within the sensible, but an element which is in itself difference, and creates at once both the quality in the sensible and the transcendent exercise within sensibility' (144).

Through such encounters thinking reaches its height in the thought of eternal return – that is, in the thought of a univocal difference in itself, a structure of time as becoming and as the guarantor of novelty, and a transvaluation that takes the self on a 'curious stationary journey'. Deleuze states: 'To think is to create – there is no other creation – but to create is first of all to engender "thinking" in thought' (*DR* 147). One could well ask why creation lies only in thought, why in this formulation neither politics nor art nor science seems to have its own creativity. In fact each of them is creative in ways irreducible to philosophy, which is not coextensive with thought – indeed, Deleuze acknowledges, 'no one needs philosophy to think' (*TRM* 313). Each domain finds its inventiveness in the ideas it creates, ideas that are never general but germane to its particular field: philosophy invents concepts, science invents functions, cinema invents 'blocks of movement/duration' and so on (312–16). These ideas can certainly be translated and adapted to other domains, but 'the rule of application is never one of resemblance' (*DI* 206). Every idea is an intervention on a field of differences that brings about a synthesis of these differences. In this way, an idea is always 'a rare event' (*TRM* 312). Above all, an idea is not a representation, which is why it 'is not on the order of communication' (320). Ideas are expressions distinct from the communication of information.

Action too is inventive – it would be ludicrous to suggest otherwise – but there is always a complex and subtle link between action and thought, or between praxis and theory. Whereas a certain kind of political theory understands practice to be the application of theory and theory to be inspired by practice, Deleuze maintains that when theory, which always develops within a local domain, encounters obstacles in its path, it needs praxis to create relays that connect it to the ideas and inventiveness of theories in heterogeneous domains. Theory, in turn, serves as relay to connect praxis to other, heterogeneous practices that help it overcome blockages (*DI* 206). In this way, the nexus of theory and political practice is one in which practice is used 'as an intensifier of thought, and analysis as a multiplier of the forms and domains for the intervention of political action' (Foucault in *AO* xiv). In each case, however, it is the encounter with a blockage, a problem, a *difference*, that presses thought and action to connect to an outside. And this blockage is not something recognized – if it were, how could it constitute a problem? – but rather something that can only be sensed. Foucault's encounter with something intolerable in the prison regime was with something that 'everyone knew' – that is, recognized – but did not *see* – that is, sense (*TRM* 275). The encounter instigated an entirely new politics in the form of the Group for Information on Prisons (GIP).

In his notebooks, Nietzsche writes: 'Even the *thought of a possibility* can shake and transform us; it is not merely sensations or particular expectations that can do that! Note how effective the *possibility* of eternal damnation was!' (Nietzsche in Heidegger 1979– 87: Vol. 2: 129). For Deleuze, it is the thought of an *incompossibility* that can shake and transform us, by opening us to a multiplicity that is both thought and acted. This domain of incompossible multiplicity is one where negation, law and lack are inapplicable. What matters in it is not the ability to construct an identity or a subject, nor to recognize a truth, but to move beyond both the dogmatic image of thought and this thought's image of action. This means to 'develop action, thought, and desires by proliferation, juxtaposition, and disjunction' and, as molar individuals are products of social and psychological repression, to use groups and collectives as 'a constant generator of "de-individualization"' (Foucault in AO xiii, xiv). Here thought and action seek to become creative and experimental.

The many levels of politics

The eternal return is a repetition of difference, but, as discussed in Chapter 2, this repetition also gives rise to semblances or simulations of identity, opposition and negation. Being semblances does not mean these categories have no purchase on reality; nonetheless, the perspective from which they appear tends to give them more reality than they are due. As categories they are appropriate to the most molar and differenciated domains where microscopic or molecular fluxes appear stable in accordance with the laws of large aggregates. But molar formations also react back upon the forces from which they emerge, attempting to appropriate these molecular forces, though this process 'implies hit-and-miss changes in rhythm and mode rather than any omnipotence; and something always escapes' (ATP 217). In the end, molar categories can only capture and organize what exists on their level – it is people who can be identified and arrested, never desiring-machines, and even successful arrests of molar individuals depend on molecular flows that are always in tension and flux at another level underneath. But these categories also condition the reactive formations of molecular desire that allow them to have purchase. While molecular forces continue to surpass molar formations and flee on all sides, this does not mean that their dynamics are not often occluded by the dominance of molar perspectives, and so an important political task lies in overcoming these perspectives and tapping into molecular desires. But molar formations and categories must also be engaged on their own level, and even though this is the most superficial level of political and social life, it remains significant in its own right.

The molar level is characterized by 'segmentarity', and it comprises diverse coded domains such as family, school and workplace, alongside differenciated categories of identity, such as child, adult, worker, businessman, senior citizen, criminal delinquent and homosexual. There is also a corresponding molar 'line' of movement that goes from one segment to another. One assumes different roles within and across these segments, but under rules that allow only one role to be taken at a time and only under specific relations. Thus an individual passes from childhood to adulthood, and from school to work; the same person can be a father, husband and son simultaneously, but only to different people; one works from nine to five, and becomes a pensioner after 65. In this way, segments are organized by exclusive disjunctions, creating binary choices even where more than two possible options are available: 'if you are neither *a* nor *b*, then you are *c*;...if you are neither black nor white, you are a half-breed; if you are neither man nor woman, you are a transvestite: each time the machine with binary elements will produce binary choices between elements which are not present at the first cutting-up' (*D* 128). While each domain is distinct, an ominous sense pervades them all, in so far as they function on a disciplinary model that polices standards of normal identity. This is made obvious by the way individuals are transitioned from one domain to the next: '[E]ach time, from one segment to the next, they speak to us, saying: "Now you're not a baby any more"; and at school, "You're not at home now"; and in the army, "You're not at school now"' (124).

Codes persist even under a capitalist social machine, as this machine must reterritorialize the flows it decodes and axiomatizes. Coded domains thus point in two directions, one above and one below. On the one hand, they are overcoded by the State, which imposes a 'rigid segmentarity' (*ATP* 212) on them. This does not reduce the domains to homogeneity or unity but instead regulates the transfers and translations from one heterogeneous code to another. The State provides the institutional framework, for example, wherein individuals who are convicted of crimes in the judicial domain are sent to prison, which turns convicts into delinquents, who later re-offend and end up back in court – such is the carceral system Foucault describes in *Discipline and Punish*. The State is thus a 'resonance chamber' (224) rather than a central power holder, and in this regard, while it is an important location of political struggle, it is also an insufficient site for politics: the problem of crime cannot be adequately addressed simply at the State level, since its function as a relay is ultimately rather limited. On the other hand, codes point to molecular or microscopic regimes of power relations that constitute the truths on which they operate. The line of movement here is one of opposition between power and resistance. Power relations constitute the identities of norm and deviant, but it is important to grasp the fuzzy nature of these classifications. If what is normal is meant to apply to the majority of individuals, then ironically no one fits the norm: 'One might say the majority is nobody' (*N* 173). But the forms of deviancy set in opposition to the norm are no more applicable, and largely end up being 'dustbin categories' applied to individuals who cannot be classified any other way.[7] The significance of these classifications thus has little to do with any concrete knowledge they provide of those submitted to them but rather with their use in coordinating the application of disciplinary techniques. Norm and deviant categories thus underpin the deployment of strategies to observe, test, classify, correct and encourage or compel confessions. Nevertheless, this same power creates resistances internal to it, producing the very marginals it struggles to discipline. They are 'the forms of madness which are secret but which nevertheless relate to the public authorities' (*D* 125). Each domain thus intensifies deviancy, which in some respects justifies the further extension of disciplinary power, but which also undermines the entire structure. And each also refers beyond itself to heterogeneous domains, so that molecular power relations of coding elicit State's overcoding.

Opposition also indicates a reactive formation, a stratification of desire that arranges it in exclusive and hierarchical layers. But just as reactive forces depend on active forces in a Nietzschean sense, so these coded formations depend on the production and multiplicity of molecular desiring-machines. In *A Thousand Plateaus*, Deleuze and Guattari introduce various names for this terrain, and its line of movement, which is a 'line of flight'. They call it a 'rhizomatic' plurality, whose relations of inclusive disjunction do not conform to any 'arboreal' model that submits differences to principles of identity (*ATP* 3–25). They also call it a 'smooth space' or 'plane of consistency', which is not an indifferent medium where all differences are the same, but rather a space in which differences or quantitative intensities are not marked or striated by a transcendent identity that puts them into a hierarchical order. It is a space, in other words, that is smooth by virtue of having no transcendent dimension, and so it is also differentiated.[8] Finally, they call it a 'war machine', a name that expresses the agonism of this constitutive domain of difference. In so far as desiring-machines are active in the Nietzschean, noble sense, their productive force 'is not a re-action of *re-sentiment* but the active expression of an active mode of existence; attack and not revenge, the natural aggression of a way of being, the divine wickedness without which perfection could not be imagined' (*NP* 3). Deleuze and Guattari distinguish the war machine from the 'institution of war' used by the State to appropriate the machine into an oppositional schema: '*The State has no war machine of its own*; it can only appropriate one in the form of a military institution, one that will continually cause it problems (*ATP* 355). In this respect, the war machine is the excess that escapes codes and overcodings on all sides.

Molar segments, power relations, desiring-machines and their various lines 'are immanent, caught up in one another' (*D* 125). They form a single assemblage, with molecular levels of desire and power constituting the molar formations that code and axiomatize flows. Nevertheless, molecular desire has an ontological primacy in so far as it constitutes the forms that seem to arrest, divide and control it, and in so far as society is defined not by its segments but its lines of flight: 'It is wrongly said (in Marxism in particular) that a society is defined by its contradictions. That is true only on the larger scale of things. From the viewpoint of micropolitics, a society is defined by its lines of flight, which are molecular' (*ATP* 216). Lines of flight deterritorialize segments and codes. But deterritorialization, which dissolves or surpasses formations of identity, can be partial or absolute. Where partial, these same lines of flight establish new forms of identity into which they are appropriated. As Deleuze and Guattari argue in *Anti-Oedipus*, capitalism's decoding is only a partial deterritorialization. But the same is true of the forms of resistance set in opposition to power relations, for at this level 'the deterritorializations are merely relative, always compensated by reterritorializations which impose on them so many loops, detours, of equilibrium and stabilization' (*D* 136). This limitation of the molecular level of power and resistance

MICROPOLITICS

is attributed to Foucault, but this attribution is problematic for the reasons discussed in the last chapter. Foucault (1977: 230–3) is explicit in criticizing forms of resistance that, through their opposition to the present system, simply replace one system with another. The point remains, however, that absolute deterritorializations or lines of flight must go beyond opposition.

Absolute deterritorializations may not in themselves lead back to reterritorializations, but this does not disconnect them from these formations. Indeed, 'molecular escapes and movements would be nothing if they did not return to the molar organizations to reshuffle their segments, their binary distributions of sexes, classes, and parties' (*ATP* 216–17). If individuals and groups can wage war in conformity with the essence of the war machine, it is '*only on the condition that they simultaneously create something else*, if only new nonorganic social relations' (423). The schizophrenic process of deterritorialization can reach fulfilment only 'insofar as it is capable of creating...a new land' (*AO* 318). All of this points to a transmutation along Nietzschean lines, where negation and opposition are actively destroyed and difference is affirmed. Deleuze and Guattari speak of a revolutionary becoming of desire that is a 'nomadic' becoming or a 'becoming-minor'. The nomadic is opposed to both the sedentary and the migratory, the migrant perhaps being ignorant of his final destination, but nevertheless seeking one, while the nomad moves from point to point, but 'every point is a relay and exists only as a relay' (*ATP* 380). And the minor is opposed to both the majority and the minority, the former being non-existent and the latter being nothing more than a sub-category and therefore an identity formation; becoming-minor breaks with the opposition between majority and minority (105–6). Nomadic and minor becomings are 'false movements', in so far as they can remain stationary and intensive, and also movements at 'infinite speed', which immediately connect heterogeneities. In other words, these becomings are *events*. They are the events of thought as it encounters that which forces it to think, and they create lines of flight that are experimental and thus political: 'Politics is active experimentation since we do not know in advance which way a line is going to turn' (*D* 137).

There is a politics directed towards the State and its molar formations, which seeks to reform or even radically transform them. It is the most recognizable form of politics, and the one most amenable to analysis in terms of groups, interests and power negotiations. But it is hardly a straightforward process, as it testifies 'to a long labour which is not merely aimed against the State and the powers that be, but directly at ourselves' (*D* 138). And though the molar may be superficial, it is hardly dispensable: indeed, 'even if we had the power to blow it up, could we succeed in doing so without destroying ourselves, since it is so much a part of the conditions of life, including our organism and our very reason?' (138). There is a danger that this politics can be overtaken by fear of losing the security of 'the great molar organization that sustains us', leading us to 'flee from flight, rigidify our segments, give ourselves over to binary logic...we reterritorialize on anything available' (*ATP* 227). Through fear, we retreat into this first level of politics, and arrest our (molar) selves there.

There is also a politics directed at constitutive power relations, which seeks to latch onto the resistances immanent to them. The codes could not function without the identities formed in this domain, and the exclusions they entail. Yet there is something of the delinquent, the pervert and the marginal in each of us, and it is in their name that this politics asserts itself. But in so far as it seeks to overturn these standards, this politics risks becoming nothing more than one of opposition, and in this binary logic it risks the danger of a 'microfascism' that reinforces blunt oppositions through a spiteful friend/enemy division. This is a danger of 'clarity', in which 'micro-Oedipuses crop up, microfascisms lay down the law', and where individuals with a certitude of what is good and what is evil assume possession of 'a clarity on their situation, role, and mission even more disturbing than the certitudes' created by the fear of the first politics (*ATP* 228). Microfascisms are reactive formations of desire, and they stretch across all the divisions and categories of contemporary politics, from the liberal to the totalitarian. They are part of a slavish mentality that fails to affirm difference and that clings to identity instead.

This is why a third kind of politics, which is no less collective for being molecular or microscopic, is necessary. It is a politics of creative becoming that in Nietzschean fashion seeks to move 'beyond good and evil'. This creativity is indispensable in so far as the other levels of politics encounter obstacles and blockages that can only be overcome by establishing relays across heterogeneities. And it is necessary because politics must involve changing ourselves as much as changing our world. Here it is a matter of individuals and collectives moving beyond the categories of identity and opposition that seem to exhaust their sense, opening themselves instead to multiplicity and engendering, via repetitions of difference, a multiplicity equal to that which they encounter. Deleuze and Guattari refer to it as a project of turning oneself into a body without organs or BwO, an experimental project using desiring-machines. It too contains dangers, since desire can either affirm difference or reinstate opposition. In this case, the connections across difference that these experiments make may not avoid the black hole of fascism but instead reinforce it by 'augmenting its valence, *turning to destruction, abolition pure and simple, the passion of abolition*' (ATP 229). A line of flight in this way becomes a suicidal line of abolition or death. When desire turns in this direction, it becomes 'realized nihilism' (230) at both the micro and the State level.

As stated before, Deleuze and Guattari offer no firm normative rules to distinguish creative or positive changes from those that are dangerous and destructive. And fascism has certainly often been more creative – and successful – than many forms of affirmative and pluralist politics in organizing all levels of desire. Schizoanalysis asks questions about the desiring-machines we have and how they can be adjusted, but 'schizoanalysis *as such* has strictly no political program to propose' (AO 380). Nevertheless, as an ethos or way of life, and specifically one that aspires towards a 'non-fascist life' (Foucault in AO xiii), it can at least offer a set of ethical considerations. There is an ethical question of the kind of being we can be that precedes that of the kind of politics we must enact.

The place of the subject?

The subject, treated as an individual or a collective, has long been a central focus of political theory. Sometimes it is presupposed as a starting point, as in the case of the hypothetical Rawlsian subject that stands apart from its values, talents and identity in order to choose principles of justice. At other times it is considered a social and cultural construction based on shared histories and understandings, as emphasized by communitarian critiques of liberal thought. Political theories of lack are explicit about the need for some form of temporarily centred subject with a sense of its identity and a capacity to act, even if this subject always ultimately fails to secure itself.[9] In contrast, Deleuze and Guattari state their goal to be 'to reach, not the point where one no longer says I, but the point where it is no longer of any importance whether one says I' (*ATP* 3). This is the point, they maintain, where they 'render imperceptible, not ourselves, but what makes us act, feel, and think' (3). Acting, feeling and thinking certainly exist, and through them subjectivity is introduced into the world. Yet despite being standard trademarks of the subject itself, they do not find their origin in such a being, but instead in something pre-individual or pre-subjective, something not re-cognizable. In this way, Deleuze and Guattari propose a kind of subjectivity without a subject, or one in which the subject is merely an appearance that accompanies subjectivity without in any way being its foundation.

We are used to thinking that some notion of a subject or an 'I' is indispensable to the coherence of our agency and the structure of our selves. Deleuze, however, consistently challenges this belief. An important influence here is Sartre's *The Transcendence of the Ego* (1957). In this early work, Sartre challenges the notion that the unity of consciousness requires an 'I' or ego standing behind it as its governing centre. Following the basic phenomenological principle that consciousness is always consciousness of some object, he maintains instead that unity comes from the syntheses that relate consciousness to objects and to past consciousnesses. In each case the 'I' is extraneous to these constitutive relations, leading Sartre to declare that it is a transcendent object: '[T]he ego is neither formally nor materially *in* consciousness: it is outside, *in the world*. It is a being of the world, like the ego of another' (31). As a consequence, he concludes, the transcendental conditions of consciousness – the conditions that ensure its agency – are impersonal, relating to a field of forces rather than to a transcendental subject: '[T]he transcendental field becomes impersonal; or, if you like, "pre-personal," *without an I*' (36).

All this is evident in simple cases such as reading, where consciousness can be absorbed in its act and aware only of itself and the book being read, the 'I' appearing to it only when consciousness breaks from this activity and asks itself what it is doing. The ego thus arises only in an act of reflection, where consciousness looks at its activity as if from outside: the position it takes when it declares 'I am reading' – or, for that matter 'I am thinking' – is the same perspective it takes when observing another who reads or thinks (Sartre 1957: 44–7), which is why the ego must be given to consciousness as a being that is out in the world. The 'I', then, is the result of a split where separate consciousnesses – such as the one that is thinking and the one that is apprehending the reflection of this activity – never achieve full correspondence. Sartre holds the ego to be dubitable, but not a hypothetical object: 'I do not say to myself, "Perhaps I have an ego," as I may say to myself, "Perhaps I hate Peter"' (76). Undeniably, then, the ego exists on some level. However, Sartre on two occasions explains this existence as the existence of a *simulation*. With reference to the ego's agency, he holds that 'we are dealing here with a semblance only' (79), as consciousness alone is capable of genuine spontaneous activity. And with regard to its central function, he gives the ego a role of disguise, asserting that 'everything happens…as if consciousness constituted the ego as a false representation of itself" (101), because consciousness can function only by masking from itself its own power (100).

Clearly the ego frequently and persistently accompanies our actions. Sartre maintains that this is a matter of the way reflection is needed to sustain various forms of concrete concerted agency: '[W]e must not forget that action requires time to be accomplished. It has articulations; it has moments. To these moments correspond concrete, active consciousnesses, and the reflection which is directed on the consciousnesses apprehends the total action in an intuition which exhibits it as the transcendent unity of the active consciousnesses' (Sartre 1957: 69). Many activities could not endure without the 'I', not because they require some chooser who stands apart from consciousness itself, but because they involve a relation-to-self that fosters the projection of a reference point that *seems* to function as a centre of activity. A person who spends months or even years learning to dance, for example, is changing throughout the process, as posture, footwork, rhythm and technique become intellectually and physically ingrained. In the end, it is not even the same person who has been taught. Nevertheless, the reflective self-to-self relation that is indispensable to the learning activity requires that consciousness apprehend this activity as 'what I am doing', even though this 'I' does not accomplish anything: the 'I' didn't learn to dance, because no 'I' persisted through the process, except as an image appearing to consciousness when it reflected on what it was doing.

Deleuze and Guattari declare that Sartre's discovery of the impersonal transcendental field 'restores the rights of immanence' (*WIP* 47). Nevertheless, Deleuze contends, this achievement is limited in so far as this transcendental field 'is still determined as a field of consciousness and as such it must then be unified by itself through a play of intentionalities or pure retentions' (*LS* 344n. 5). It is enough to note how Hegel's field of forces is similarly impersonal, but its syntheses bring consciousness into correspondence and identity with the world it encounters. In Sartre's case, Deleuze maintains, the theory of the Other developed later in *Being and Nothingness* still falls back onto the duality of subject and object, of the other being another subject, because of this focus on consciousness (307, 344n. 5, 366n. 12). The focus on consciousness, therefore, does not eliminate the subject, but serves to reinforce it. Sartre's thesis that the ego accompanies activities that endure here parallels Bergson's move to preserve the subject by conceiving time as duration, whereby the past's retention in the present becomes the form of an ego that changes without passing away.

In contrast, Deleuze demands a transcendental field that 'does not resemble the corresponding empirical fields' (*LS* 102). This would be a virtual field of forces that is heterogeneous to the actualized differenciations it underpins. Sartre consistently rejects the idea of a pre-personal unconscious, holding that its exponents err similarly to advocates of the transcendental subject by positing an unconscious *me* that unifies states of mind with its own hidden forms of reflection (Sartre 1957: 55–6). For Sartre, pre-personal consciousness spontaneously creates itself *ex nihilo* at every moment (98–9). But Deleuze, in contrast, insists that 'what is neither individual nor personal are...emissions of singularities insofar as they occur on an unconscious surface and possess a mobile, immanent principle of auto-unification through a *nomadic distribution*, radically distinct from fixed and sedentary distributions as conditions of the syntheses of consciousness' (*LS* 102). This unconscious surface, of course, is the field of desiring-production outlined in *Anti-Oedipus*, a self-production or a production of production in which the coherence of the unconscious is a matter of drives and partial objects being related through three inclusive syntheses. The unconscious is structured by a virtual differentiation that unfolds itself in actual differenciations, the latter able to be organized by the categories of identity but only to the extent that their connection to molecular desiring-production is abstracted away. Constants certainly emerge despite the way these machines and their desiring flows are always changing, but only as the somewhat regular results of the varying syntheses and the repetitions of difference that make the machines function.

Like the syntheses of consciousness for Sartre, one constant that arises from these unconscious syntheses is a kind of subject. It comes into being in the conjunctions that reconcile the connective synthesis that makes desiring-machines function and the disjunctive synthesis that repels its components. As explained in the previous chapter, this subject, for Deleuze and Guattari, takes the form of a retroactive 'so *that's* what it was' constituted in the passage through the intensities littering the unconscious. But this is not a subject in the Cartesian, Rawlsian, communitarian or Lacanian sense. It is rather a *dramatization*. And in this way, the conjunctive synthesis of desiring-machines does not constitute a subject so much as actualize an intensity, thereby giving rise to a perspective: '[T]he "I" does not designate a universal but a set of particular positions occupied within a One speaks–One sees, One confronts, One lives' (*F* 115). It is not subjects but perspectives that condition the emergence of subjectivity – that is, acting, feeling and thinking – into the world, and through these perspectives an actual differenciated world is organized, expressing some form of will to power. Each individual and each collective has the perspectives and valuations they ought to have given the structure and dynamic of their desiring-machines, and each will act in accordance with them. But accompanying each perspective will be a 'subject' projected and designated as though it was its foundation.

Of course, even as a projection the subject can have both a reality and a necessary function. Sartre offers a convincing account when outlining the ego's position in concerted or sustained action. Without dismissing that insight, Deleuze suggests another role when he associates the unification of the self around an ego-ideal as a stage in the action that realizes the eternal return, a process discussed at the end of Chapter 3. Nietzsche himself explicitly holds the 'I' or ego to be a simulation or semblance. He refers to it as 'a fiction' (Nietzsche 1968: §370), 'a perspective illusion' (§518), 'only a conceptual synthesis' (§371) and the result of 'our bad habit of taking a mnemonic, an abbreviative formula, to be an entity, finally a cause' (§548). It would seem clear, then, that in formulating the eternal return as a matter of turning every 'it was' into 'thus I willed it' and finally into 'thus I will its eternal return', this 'I' is not carrying out the willing. Nevertheless, this does not make the 'I' a dispensable fiction, as 'it could be useful and important for one's activity to interpret oneself *falsely*' (§492). In the eternal return, the 'I' is a necessary illusion taken up by a self composed of multiple heterogeneous desiring-machines in order to overcome its attachment to the ego and thereby realize in action the multiplicity that it is. To adapt a Kantian ethical formulation here: there is no 'I', but for the sake of the eternal return one must act as if there is, in order finally to leave it behind. To affirm the eternal return is thus to use the image of the subject in order to dissolve it. Sartre's account of consciousness's agency when stripped of the ego is similar: 'This absolute consciousness, when it is purified of the *I*, no longer has anything of the *subject*. It is no longer a collection of representations. It is quite simply a first condition and an absolute source of existence' (Sartre 1957: 106).

Does this not still presuppose that the self must be really unified, at least temporarily, in order to *choose* to act in this way? Such a question, for Deleuze – and certainly also for Nietzsche – forgets that thinking and acting arise only from an *encounter*. Moreover, it overlooks the way that overcoming, like any other action, is realized because it is *desired*, not because of any choice. Subjectivity is introduced into the world, not on account of a subject, but alongside the semblance of a subject that is used to actualize a multiplicity equal to the encounter that forced the self to think. Agency resides in the multiplicity of desiring-machines, whose syntheses project a subject alongside their productive activity.

As noted in Chapter 1, many political theories of lack hold the constitutive exclusions of a friend/enemy antagonism to be necessary for the formation of a collective political subject. Against this, William Connolly, a theorist of abundance, maintains that this view of constitutive antagonism prevents the formulation of an ethics able to support the pluralism all theories of radical democracy seek to promote. The political virtues of agonistic respect and critical responsiveness that Connolly proposes form part of what he calls an 'ethical sensibility', which he attributes to Nietzsche and Foucault. This same term can be applied to Deleuze, whose micropolitical realm, as already mentioned several times, is an ethical domain. What is found here is not a subject but 'a primary sensibility that we *are*' (*DR* 73), ethicality being a 'sensibility before the imperceptible which is indistinguishable from its intensive' (227). To be ethical is to be open to encounters with difference; a subject can only represent these encounters, and hence misses what they are. And again, what emerges from the encounter is a perspective: when Foucault saw what was intolerable in the prison system, he did not recognize a truth or represent a situation to himself as a subject. Rather, he assumed a perspective, from which certain necessities of thought and action followed.

The ethics of making yourself a body without organs

When Foucault explains his turn to study the care of the self, he notes three modes that a genealogy of power relations can take: genealogy can examine the formation of discourses, disciplines and the authoritative positions from which subjects are able to speak, an exploration that corresponds to Foucault's archaeological period; it can explore the mechanisms of disciplinary and normalizing power that manage those who are subjected in these discourses; and, finally, it can investigate the structures in which individuals come to recognize themselves as subjects who relate to these discourses and disciplinary regimes (Foucault 1992: 4–5). This last area of analysis is certainly not a realm free of power, but it is one where power relations delineate a self-to-self relation distinct from other domains of power/knowledge. Here emerges a space of ethical self-formation, which, Foucault maintains, is a necessary complement to any moral code.

A moral code, being a set of rules of conduct, presupposes a subject who relates to the code through obedience (a moral subject) or disobedience (an immoral one). This relation to the code, in turn, presupposes a self that fashions itself as a subject, as an 'I' or ego that takes responsibility for itself and its choices. There must therefore be 'forms and modalities of the relation to self by which the individual constitutes and recognizes himself *qua* subject' (Foucault 1992: 6). These forms and modalities are 'games of truth' – and so products of power relations – that delineate four axes of the self-to-self relation: the 'ethical substance' to be shaped, which could be desire, actions or some combination; the 'mode of subjection', or the form moral obligations take, such as obligation being a matter of divine law, or perhaps the rule of reason; the 'ethical work', or the practices available to shape the self; and the 'telos' or goal of self-formation, which can be for the sake of salvation, self-mastery and so on (24–8). The truths around all of these dimensions vary and the shifts from Greek to Roman to Christian forms are always contingent, as would be expected from a genealogical analysis. As Deleuze says, they set out conditions that are 'not "apodictic" but problematic' (*F* 114), and, in this respect, they engender solutions that must be specific, local and open to mutation. What Foucault excavates by returning to the Greeks, Deleuze maintains, is 'a dimension of subjectivity derived from power and knowledge without being dependent on them' (101). This dimension comes by way of an Outside that is folded into power relations – not a transcendent Outside, but an immanent one that is a fold of force or power, in the Nietzschean sense of will to power (113).

Precisely because a moral subject is the product of these practices of self-formation, the self-to-self relation cannot be that of a subject. Its agency must therefore be of an entirely different order. Foucault turns to the Greek idea of agonism, whereby combative social relations point to 'an agonistic relationship with oneself' (Foucault 1992: 67), and thus to the need to fashion oneself in a project of self-mastery. In this agonistic conception, however, the internal adversary to be fought, no matter how far removed it might seem to the self that struggles with it, 'did not represent a different, ontologically alien power' (68), and so it differs from later Christian conceptions that judge the flesh in terms of corruption and sin. This complex self, embedded in a complex world, shapes itself through its encounters, with a subject arising only as a projection that provides a point of relation to the moral structure. This self is a relational nexus that brings together socially constituted rules, practices, techniques and institutions that intersect with desires, drives, memories and perceptions, none of these being reducible to any of the others, nor strictly separable from them. The quality and the expression of this self's agency follow necessarily from the way these elements are arranged and the ways they shift.

Foucault's step back to the ethical domain, however, would be redundant if the only outcome self-formation ever achieved was to turn this disjointed self into a moral subject relating to an already existing code. Any moral code, however, is replete with points of friction and problematization. One of the Greeks' great ethical problems concerned the status of boys, for even though love of one's own sex and love of the other were not seen as opposites, the sex act itself was conceived in terms of an opposition between masculine activity and feminine passivity, neither of which was suitable to the boy's position.[10] Similar difficulties plague the binaries of every moral system, and where they confront the selves who must relate to them, they compel ethical practice to become more subtle and self-stylization to become more experimental. Ethics becomes the negotiation of moral ambiguities, where the binary oppositions that structure the molar domain reveal their inadequacy and available alternatives cannot be separated into good and bad or right and wrong. It thereby becomes a process of creative overcoming of these limited moral codes. The Greeks, for example, used the problem of boys and the codes, identities and practices at their disposal to expand themselves beyond what they were, inventing new ways to relate to the other and to themselves.[11] Here the ethical project becomes a micropolitical one in the way it works to reshuffle both the molecular and the molar.

When Deleuze and Guattari advise on how to turn oneself into a BwO, they maintain that it is 'a practice, a set of practices' (*ATP* 150) that work to disaggregate the stratifications that schematize us. The body is stratified by the organization of its organs and its BwO into a functioning organism; the unconscious experiences the same when a structure of meaningful signification grounded in a transcendent Master Signifier is imposed on it; and consciousness is stratified by processes of subjectification that embed a fictitious ego and an identity into it (159–60). In such cases, the immanent intensities related through the BwO are 'uprooted' by the introduction of lack and transcendence, and this always signals that 'a priest is behind it' (154). Through these processes, we are given a sense of ourselves that may at times seem exhaustive, but that is ultimately inadequate.

The BwO is not absent from these stratified formations. It 'already exists in the strata as well as on the destratified plane of consistency, but in a totally different manner' (*ATP* 162). There is a BwO wherever there is differentiation or differenciation, but the BwO of differenciation often presents 'terrifying caricatures of the plane of consistency' (163). In each case, it is a matter of desire – '[t]he BwO is desire; it is that which one desires and by which one desires' (165) – but where differenciated desire occludes the virtual differentiations that constitute it, desire comes to desire its repression. The question thus becomes whether the field of immanence, which is an 'absolute Outside that knows no Selves' (156), can be folded into these stratifications so as to open up their limited oppositional relations. This implies an inversion of the forms of the subject, signifier and organism, which appear to be origins but are only semblances or projections.

We therefore begin with the materials given to us, including our seemingly most intimate desires, the socially constituted rules that surround us, our bodies, flesh and even the apparently substantial but ultimately superficial identities and binary oppositions that arise with this assemblage. The BwO is the differenciator that relates these materials through their difference, making it 'necessarily a Place, necessarily a Plane, necessarily a Collectivity (assembling elements, things, plants, animals, tools, people, powers, and fragments of all of these...)' (*ATP* 161). Each of these relations is open to mutation and experimentation.

> This is how it should be done: Lodge yourself on a stratum, experiment with the opportunities it offers, find an advantageous place on it, find potential movements of deterritorialization, possible lines of flight, experience them, produce flow conjunctions here and there, try out continuums of intensities segment by segment, have a small plot of new land at all times. It is through a meticulous

MICROPOLITICS

relation with the strata that one succeeds in freeing lines of flight, causing conjugated flows to pass and escape and bringing forth continuous intensities for a BwO. Connect, conjugate, continue: a whole 'diagram,' as opposed to still signifying and subjective programs. (161)

This process is not a matter of subjective choice. Indeed, it is dependent entirely on the existing structure of one's desiring-machines, and thus their active or reactive quality, their affirmative or negative expression and the distribution of cracks that can open them to change. We react to stratified formations and the possibility of destratification in the way appropriate to who and what we are at any given time. Some individuals and collectives, therefore, may only have within them a capacity to transition from one segment to another: 'For perhaps there are people who do not have this line [of flight], who have only the two others, or who have only one, who live on only one' (*D* 125). In another sense, however, the line of flight 'has always been there' (125), and in the encounters that can spur thinking, it can always be released. But a line of flight can also end up returning to the very strata that code and overcode it. Regardless, what makes the 'choice' is not a subject but the BwO, in so far as the form it takes determines what can and cannot be attached to it, and thus what the self is able to do or become (165–6).

In this regard, Deleuze and Guattari only offer the advice of caution: 'Not wisdom, caution. In doses. As a rule immanent to experimentation: injections of caution' (*ATP* 150). This is because in creating one's BwO, 'you can botch it' (149) in many ways, and in the end, 'staying stratified – organized, signified, subjected – is not the worst that can happen' (161). An experiment that ends up clinging reactively and resentfully to stratifications can end in a cancerous or fascist BwO, while one that destratifies too quickly and violently can lead to an empty 'black hole'. Even though 'dismantling the organism has never meant killing yourself, but rather opening the body to connections that presuppose an entire assemblage' (160), many experiments ended badly because '*they had emptied themselves of their organs* instead of looking for the point at which they could patiently and momentarily dismantle the organization of the organs' (160–1). The challenge is thus 'distinguishing within desire between that which pertains to stratic proliferation, or else too-violent destratification, and that which pertains to the construction of the plane of consistency (keep an eye out for all that is fascist, even inside us, and also for the suicidal and the demented)' (165).

If more specific guidelines for self-creation cannot be provided, it is precisely because the uncertainties surrounding the project of making oneself a BwO make it something political – not in the narrow institutional sense of politics, but in the broader sense of a contest and engagement with difference. Self-formation is ethical, but also political, not simply because it involves a direct connection to social and political formations, but more profoundly because any experimentation with molecular fluxes and creative deterritorializations can either reify or problematize these social and political forms. Absent foundational standards, the construction of a BwO is a matter of pragmatism and strategy in relation to the obstacles we encounter and the relays we establish, and so is dependent on context and contingencies. Through our thought and practice at this level, Deleuze and Guattari maintain, we negotiate the impasses imposed on us by the very formations of identity that often provide us with reassurance but that are ultimately inadequate to our lives.

* * *

Nietzsche writes of the noble self: 'a well-constituted human being, a "happy one", *must* perform certain actions and instinctively shrinks from other actions, he transports the order of which he is the physiological representative into his relations with other human beings and with things' (Nietzsche 1990: 'The Four Great Errors' §2). The practices of the self formulated by Foucault, Deleuze and Guattari all rest on this ethical wager: that by working to constitute ourselves in certain ways, necessities of a political nature follow. Neither self-formation nor the politics it can entail can rest on the categories of identity and the subject; where these are treated as essentials to politics, the encounters necessary to engender self-formation are lost. Such theses are not part of the classical sense of political theory as the thoerization of either an ideal state or normative political concepts such as justice, order and equality. But they are consistent with the recent ontological turn in political thought and its exploration of human and extra-human being. What is affirmed in this way is pluralism, as an ethic that feeds into politics, and as a strategy of political engagement. A crucial political upshot of Deleuze's ontology is that it shows how pluralization can become a way of both individual and collective life. But it must be disengaged not only from the structures of representation, identity and the subject, but from approaches that see the constitution of these structures as a political and ethical necessity.

6

Conclusion: Pluralism and 'a life'

Everyone experiences identity crises, often several times in life, and when they occur molar social structures provide numerous answers to the question 'Who am I?'. These answers may involve any or all of the positive and negative categories of identity, including religious (you are Christian, Jewish, Muslim, Hindu), sexual (you are straight, gay, bisexual), national (you are American, British, Chinese) and those related to social norms (you are a law-abiding citizen, a delinquent, a pervert). Of course, the way that none of these categories or any combination of them is sufficient to delineate one's identity is the reason it is in crisis in the first place. Yet this does not alleviate the pressure to shift towards some sort of new identification, as though it were the only route out of this quandary.

The centrality of identity in political theory's ontological turn has meant that many theorists treat it as a problematic but still indispensable category. While the displacement of identity – and with it the political subject – is considered crucial for the development of a pluralist and democratic politics,[1] it is still treated as a *sine qua non* for politics, ethics, meaning and even thinking as such. In so far as identity holds this status, so too do the categories associated with it, including opposition, negation and, in the case of theories of identity associated with dialectics or theories of lack, some form of constitutive exclusion. Thus even post-identity political theories, which are critical of the anti-pluralism and rigorous policing of identity borders found in many forms of identity politics, seek to moderate this tendency and make connections across diverse identities, but nevertheless maintain the necessity for some form of exclusion.[2] For these theorists, if identity crises are ubiquitous, it is because these exclusions can never be final, making the construction of these exclusions and their inevitable failure matters of continual negotiation and renegotiation.

Deleuze accepts the important role of identity in life, but his thinking and his ontology are decidedly not so identity-centred. Identity for him is a projection or a semblance, though one that certainly plays a role in organizing important aspects of the political and social world. Constituencies could not press their interests in an institutional setting without the markers of identity that allow them to present a united front; real forms of social inequality and disavowal could not be analyzed and challenged unless logics of exclusion manifested themselves in a social universe arranged according to these markers; and certain kinds of politics that may at times be really necessary cannot consolidate themselves without resort to antagonistic positioning. But precisely because it is a projection, and not a construction, Deleuze rejects the idea of constitutive exclusion. Much like Foucault's criticism that 'juridico-discursive' models of power give power the same negative form at all levels (Foucault 1990: 84–5), he maintains that at the molecular level desire operates by different rules, and this introduces another form of politics, ethics, meaning and thought. The rejection of constitutive exclusion does not mean that Deleuze's ontology affirms a wholly inclusive unity, as some critics have maintained. But it does mean that the difference and disjunction found at the molecular level are misinterpreted when treated as forms of constitutive negation, lack or exclusion. For Deleuze, there is a productivity at this level that is not that of an identity generated through exclusion, but rather that of desiring-machines that differentiate and differenciate themselves. Where identity falls into crisis, it is not that its exclusionary matrix has broken down, but rather that, as the result of an encounter, it

CONCLUSION: PLURALISM AND 'A LIFE'   151

has become at least temporarily impossible to conceal an always already existing disconnect between the usual molar interpretation of ourselves as beings with some sort of pregiven or constituted identity and the concrete reality of our molecular multiplicity. Deleuze's last publication, 'Immanence: a Life' (*TRM* 384–9), draws out an important link between this multiplicity and an ethical pluralism. There is an impersonal, pre-subjective life, he maintains, which is simply a transcendental field that is a field of immanence. In a manner similar to the early Sartre's analysis of consciousness without an ego, Deleuze holds that this field is given to us 'as pure a-subjective stream of consciousness, as pre-reflexive impersonal consciousness, or as the qualitative duration of consciousness without a self' (384). But this is only a conceptual presentation of the field, the way it is given to consciousness, and consciousness itself is in fact a 'transcendent' that lies outside this field, coming into being 'only if a subject is produced simultaneously with its object' (384–5). Contra Sartre, consciousness for Deleuze is inseparable from the subject, in so far as its syntheses are syntheses of unity. And so while the transcendental field is coextensive with consciousness and its experiences, it cannot be defined by them; rather, it is what gives sense to them while being something quite different (385).[3] 'A Life' is consciousness's immanent Outside.

While a subject's life is defined by its traits and by the accidents and occurrences that happen to it, 'a life' is determined by singularities and events, which are the intensive states that constitute the field of immanence. These events are not ordered chronologically, as is the case with the subject's life, but in accordance with a structure in which they are out of sync with themselves and never properly present to consciousness: 'This indefinite life does not itself have moments, however close they may be, but only between-times, between-moments. It does not arrive, it does not come after, but presents the immensity of an empty time where one sees the event to come and already past, in the absolute of an immediate consciousness' (*TRM* 387). Impersonal life is no less determinate for being defined by these untimely events, nor for being designated with the indefinite article, 'a'. But it is determined as a singularity rather than particular being, a 'difference in itself' rather than an identity that is specified and individuated within a generic category. And if '*a life* is everywhere, in every moment which a living subject traverses and which is measured for the objects that have been experienced' (387), it is because, beyond the categories of genus, species and specific and individual difference through which the subject is organically represented and classified, there is a difference that speaks to the concrete and fundamental uniqueness of each life.

Uniqueness does not imply separateness and atomization. Indeed, as difference, it invokes connection. There is a connection made between us by virtue of the indefinite life that in some sense we share. Deleuze explains by way of a common theme in Dickens:

> A scoundrel, a bad apple, held in contempt by everyone, is found on the point of death, and suddenly those charged with his care display an urgency, respect, and even love for the dying man's least sign of life. Everyone makes it his business to save him. As a result, the wicked man himself, in the depths of his coma, feels something soft and sweet penetrate his soul. But as he progresses back toward life, his benefactors turn cold, and he himself rediscovers his old vulgarity and meanness....The life of the individual has given way to an impersonal and yet singular life, which foregrounds a pure event that has been liberated from the accidents of internal and external life, from the subjectivity and the objectivity of what comes to pass: a '*homo tantum*' with whom everyone sympathizes and who attains a kind of beatitude; or an ecceity which is no longer an individuation, but a singularization, a life of pure immanence, neutral, beyond good and evil, since only the subject that incarnated it in the midst of things made it good or bad. (386–7)

It would be easy to confuse this ethical connection to others with a humanist universalism. But it does not invoke a shared identity, some way that all of us are 'the same', nor does it promise a relation free of agonism and strife. Rather, it points to a 'shared' difference surpassing the oppositional or contrary differences that distinguish only in relation to a higher identity. It thereby establishes not a universalism but a *univocity* that links different pre-personal lives through their difference. This ethical connection may appear fleeting in so far as, like the dying scoundrel and those around him, we seem eventually to return to the identities that stratify us in everyday life. But this does not make it insignificant. And it only seems fleeting from a perspective in which the categories of identity take on undue importance. But is a perspective that clings to identity in this way not one of *ressentiment*?

There are important political questions today, such as how to motivate ourselves and others into political action, how to build effective political movements and how to decide specific courses of action. There may even be situations in which we must decide whether it is time to stage a revolution of some sort or another, or at the very least smash up something fundamental. And there are persistent questions about what ought to be kept and what ought to be thrown away in any new political future. It would be presumptuous and in poor taste to think that a work of political theory could provide answers to these questions like some sort of recipe book or instruction manual for political life. They must obviously be determined collectively – that is to say, politically – and they will differ across the multiple, interpenetrating layers of political and social life, all the while being quite specific in terms of time and place. But there is another more basic question that must also be asked, an ethical question that lies at the intersection of ethics and politics: what is it to be a 'political animal', and particularly one that does not suffer (too much at least) from *ressentiment*? Without providing firm and final answers to the other questions, the answer to this one does suggest something about what these others can and must be. And in this regard the contribution Deleuze's philosophy makes is to answer the question with a powerful and unwavering insistence that a 'political animal' must be something different than a political subject. At an ontological level, it is a matter of immanence: in so far as the subject depends on negation and lack, it is incompatible with the completion of immanence, and therefore must be sacrificed. And at an ethical and political level, it is a matter of pluralism: in so far as the subject and its identity must be constituted through some ultimate friend/ enemy binary, its pluralism remains quite limited, and arguably not very useful in a world where collective solutions remain temporary, never exhaust the problems to which they respond and always generate new and quite different problems to negotiate. Deleuze's explorations of sense and difference, time and repetition, force and will to power, molecular desiring-production and the micropolitical together offer ways to think beyond the subject and the crude but still influential categories of identity that surround it. The political animal they present is a micropolitical animal that uses the images of identity and the subject to become something new.

Notes

Chapter 1

1 See Aristotle (1933–5: 1003a), Heidegger (1962:1), Parmenides, quoted in Barnes (1987: 133–5), and Plato (1961: *Sophist* 244a).
2 The classic example is that of the addict who is deemed unfree because he does not *really* want to be taking drugs; restraining the drug user to wean him off his addiction can therefore be said to liberate him in the sense of giving him the kind of self-control required under the positive concept of freedom.
3 This certainly does not mean that Berlin's thought is immune from the charge of being metaphysical. Indeed, his so-called empirical claims are often as rigid, universalist and baseless as the metaphysical ones he dismisses, as when he holds that the principle that negative liberty must be limited is obvious 'simply because respect for the principles of justice...is as basic in men as the desire for liberty' (Berlin 1969: 170). Moreover, when justifying his liberal view that individual freedom should be maximized, Berlin reels off a list of classical metaphysical grounds, apparently thinking that his own position does not invoke a metaphysic because it is indifferent to which metaphysical crutch is used: 'Different names or natures may be given to the rules that determine these frontiers [of individual liberty]: they may be called natural rights, or the word of God, or Natural Law, or the demands of utility or of the "permanent interests of man"; I may believe them to be valid *a priori*, or assert them to be my own ultimate ends, or the ends of my society or culture. What these rules or commandments will have in common is that they are accepted so widely, and grounded so deeply in the actual nature of men as they have developed through history, as to be, by now, an essential part of what we mean by being a normal human being' (164–5).
4 So, for example, society would be justified in allowing certain medical occupations to be highly paid if, as a result of attracting the most talented individuals to these careers, it benefits all in society, and if everyone has an equal and fair opportunity to pursue a medical career.

5 Similar critiques have been levelled against the conception of the agent in Berlin's negative theory of freedom. See, for example, Taylor (1985).
6 In this respect it is noteworthy that once Rawls strips his fictitious rational agents of their self-knowledge through the veil of ignorance, he must then carefully supply them with knowledge so that they can make a choice in favour of his principles, and if the knowledge imparted does not yield the principles sought, it is the former, not the latter, that is to be changed: 'We want to define the original position so that we get the desired solution' (Rawls 1971: 141). Thus he holds that agents in the original position must have knowledge of 'the general facts about human society', such as 'political affairs and the principles of economic theory' and 'the laws of human psychology' (137), all of which Rawls necessarily leaves vague, as any specification of these laws and principles would surely be controversial. Moreover, he contends that agents will follow a 'just savings principle' based on concern for at least the next two generations, which is necessary to construct principles of justice that will not exhaust all resources in a single generation. Finally, despite arguing that agents will not have any knowledge of their own 'aversion to risk' (137), Rawls contends that the choice of principles will be consistent with the 'maximin rule'. He insists that 'the essential thing is not to allow the principles chosen to depend on special attitudes toward risk' (172). Yet he never explains why the maximin principle is *not* a special attitude towards risk.
7 The early Rawls holds that the conditions placed in the original position should match ideas of fairness that can be worked out by real people in a state of 'reflective equilibrium', where they put aside their particular self-interests and values in order to consider what would be fair to all parties. The principles of justice derived in the original position are similarly meant to accord with judgements reached in a state of reflective equilibrium.
8 White takes this last term from Charles Taylor (1989).
9 See Larmore (2005: 67). This comes out particularly when White differentiates the politics of strong and weak ontologies in terms of the difference between the 'extreme example' of George W. Bush's self-righteous 'mantra of evil' and an affirmation of contestability that White sees expressed in the admission of the television evangelist, the Reverend Billy Graham, that despite the clearly evil nature of the events of 9/11, evil itself 'remained always shrouded in mystery, and he [Graham] ultimately could not speak articulately about it' (White 2005: 15).
10 This is suggested by the way White, in his own treatment of Connolly, never identifies a place where Connolly acknowledges the contestability of his fundamental claim that 'it is hard, indeed impossible, to become detached as such' (Connolly, quoted in

White 2000: 106), and, when turning to Connolly's later work on 'neuropolitics', the way he unproblematically asserts that while the disengaged subject relies 'on outdated notions of a single, unified center of reason and will,. . .in reality there are multiple "brains"' (White 2000: 110).

11 Indeed, White's portrayal is belied by a range of philosophical traditions linked to Aristotle in particular that distinguish the domain of speculative reason, which works out universal truths that are metaphysical or ontological in nature, from that of practical reason, which, concerned with moral and political matters, involves contingent and often primarily pragmatic truths.

12 White mentions Deleuze rarely and only in relation to Connolly's use of his thought (see, for example, White 2000: 140; 2003: 213). However, although he associates Deleuze with his strongest articulator of weak ontology, it would not be surprising if White considered Deleuze's thought on its own to be a variant of strong ontology, since Deleuze does little or nothing explicitly to problematize his ontological claims.

13 White holds George Kateb to be a liberal theorist who carries out a weak ontological turn and Charles Taylor to be a representative of the communitarian camp who does the same.

14 Some would question whether Deleuze can rightly be linked to democratic theory as he never offers a theory of democracy as such and at times is highly critical of current democratic politics, but the same is true of many other Continental philosophers who inspire current radical democratic theory debates. Moreover, the focus of these debates goes beyond the standard field of democratic theory, and in many respects concerns not so much institutional politics but a democratic or pluralist ethos. In this regard Deleuze's philosophy is highly appropriate to the discussions. On Deleuze's relation to democratic theory and politics, see Patton (2005).

15 These are the terms used by Tønder and Thomassen (2005) to organize these debates.

16 The foundational text in this regard, from which many political theories of lack take their basic cues, remains that of Laclau and Mouffe (1985).

17 Carl Schmitt's (2007) thesis that the establishment of the friend/enemy antagonism is the foundation of the political and underpins all other social relations has been developed in political theory particularly by Mouffe (1993).

18 For example: 'I do not see "lack" and "excess" as two opposite categories, so that asserting the priority of one would necessarily exclude the other, but as being two necessary moments of a unique ontological condition. It is because there is lack, conceived as deficient being, that excess becomes possible' (Laclau 2005: 256).

19 Agonism denotes strife, aggression and combat, but not necessarily the denigration of the other as enemy or threat to be destroyed, which is why theorists such as Connolly can assert that agonism can involve respect. The difference between agonism and antagonism is perhaps best illustrated by Nietzsche, a thinker of agonism from whom Connolly draws extensively, and the distinction he draws between how the noble and slave conceive of their enemies: 'How much reverence has a noble man for his enemies! – and such reverence is a bridge to love. – For he desires his enemy for himself, as his mark of distinction; he can endure no other enemy than one in whom there is nothing to despise and *very much* to honor! In contrast to this, picture "the enemy" as the man of *ressentiment* conceives him – and here precisely is his deed, his creation: he has conceived "the evil enemy," "*the Evil One*," and this in fact is his basic concept' (Nietzsche 1967: 1.10).

20 See, for example, Connolly's (1995b) criticism that Chantal Mouffe's reliance on Schmittian antagonism and her treatment of the incompleteness of social identity as a lack prevents her from developing, albeit in a never complete and uncontestable way, 'a positive conception of ethics' (130) that would underpin the pluralism she also wishes to support.

21 See Hardt and Negri (2000: 393–413).

22 For example: 'Reforms in justice depend upon a more general ethos of critical responsiveness to new social movements, and the practice of justice invokes relations of agonistic respect between contending identities already on its register' (Connolly 1995a: 187). The subsequent pages detail the importance of the ethos of responsiveness towards inchoate constituencies as they emerge and develop to the point at which 'a new social identity is consolidated' (193). I am hesitant to press this point too forcefully as Connolly seems to have moved somewhat from the terminology of identity in later works. Whatever the notion of identity to which he is or was committed, however, it is certainly not one in which an identity is defined by a strict and singular negative division that separates it from others; rather, Connolly conceives identity always as something complex and multiple.

23 There have been occasional and rather problematic attempts to read Deleuze in the opposite way as a philosopher of transcendence. See, for example, Hallward (2006).

24 Along these lines, Kant defines his critical philosophy as an immanent critique of reason by reason itself – that is, an exploration, by reason, of its own fundamental limits.

25 Laclau (2001) levels such criticisms against Hardt and Negri's 'Nietzschean/Deleuzian' and Spinoza-inspired political theory of immanence.

26 In this respect, it is not surprising to find critics of Deleuzian immanence holding that Deleuze himself does not actually have a politics or that his philosophy ultimately leads to the sacrifice of politics. See, for example, Žižek (2004: 32) and Badiou (2000: 90–1).
27 The idea of the 'beautiful soul' comes from Hegel (1977: §§632–71), who uses it to describe the figure who, refusing to sully himself in the world, pretends to be able to withdraw from the world and judge it from afar.
28 Also: 'But noology is confronted by counterthoughts, which are violent in their acts and discontinuous in their appearances, and whose existence is mobile in history. These are the acts of a "private thinker," as opposed to the public professor. . . . "Private thinker," however, is not a satisfactory expression, because it exaggerates interiority, when it is a question of *outside thought*. To place thought in an immediate relation with the outside, with the forces of the outside, in short to make thought a war machine, is a strange undertaking whose precise procedures can be studied in Nietzsche (the aphorism, for example, is very different from the maxim, for a maxim, in the republic of letters, is like an organic State act or sovereign judgment, whereas an aphorism always awaits its meaning from a new external force, a final force that must conquer or subjugate it, utilize it)' (*ATP* 376–7).

Chapter 2

1 'Everything I've written is vitalistic, at least I hope it is' (*N* 143).
2 See, for example, Bennett (2001, 2009); Coole and Frost (2010).
3 Deleuze, for example, identifies an 'enterprise of "demystification"' that stretches from Lucretius to Nietzsche (*LS* 278–9). A notable exception to Deleuze's general opposition to mysticism is found in the last pages of *Bergsonism*, where Deleuze offers an analysis of the figure of the mystic in Bergson's *Two Sources of Morality and Religion* (*B* 106–12). However, Deleuze never returns in a serious way to this Bergson text.
4 'Sense is this wonderful word which is used in two opposite meanings. On the one hand it means the organ of immediate apprehension, but on the other hand we mean by it the sense, the significance, the thought, the universal underlying the thing. And so sense is connected on the one hand with the immediate external aspect of existence, and on the other hand with its inner essence' (Hegel, quoted in Hyppolite 1997: 24).
5 Hyppolite makes a similar link when he rejects anthropological readings of Hegel's thought that would treat collective human spirit as

the Absolute Subject: 'In the *Phenomenology*, Hegel does not say man, but self-consciousness. The modern interpreters who have immediately translated this term by man have somewhat falsified Hegel's thought. Hegel is still too Spinozistic for us to be able to speak of a pure humanism; a pure humanism culminates only in skeptical irony and platitude' (Hyppolite 1997: 20).

6 'Definition is said not only to express the nature of what is defined, but to *involve* and *explicate* it. . . . To explicate is to evolve, to involve is to implicate' (*EPS* 16).
7 See Spinoza 1992: *The Ethics*, Part I, Proposition 16.
8 On the Aristotelian origins and subsequent history of the thesis of univocity that informs Deleuze's concept, see Widder (2001, 2009a).
9 'By substance I mean that which is in itself and is conceived through itself; that is, that the conception of which does not require the conception of another thing from which it has to be formed' (Spinoza 1992: *The Ethics*, Part I, Definition 3). In contrast, 'By mode I mean the affections of substance; that is, that which is in something else and is conceived through something else' (Part I, Definition 5).
10 See Aristotle (1933–5: 1018a) and *DR* (30–2).
11 On the distinction between contraries and contradictories, see Aristotle (1933–5: 1055a–b).
12 Deleuze's portrayal of Hegelian dialectics involving contradiction within a thing's essence (*NP* 8–9; *DR* 45–6) seems to contradict his own acknowledgement that Hegel's is an ontology of sense rather than essence. However, these passages become clearer when linking them to Hyppolite's (1997: 119) thesis that contradiction is an 'essential difference' because it determines the identity of a thing through its opposition to all others.
13 Infinitely small difference is defined by its approach to zero, but, crucially, *the difference cannot reach zero* or a definitive value for the curve at the point in question will not be obtained, since division by zero yields infinity. As is well known, this quandary led Leibniz, Newton and other founders of calculus to invoke the concept of the 'infinitesimal', a positive number so small that it cannot be distinguished from zero, but that also cannot be multiplied by any number, even by infinity, in order to yield the number 1. The use of this mathematical and metaphysical curiosity, as Leibniz himself acknowledged, kept calculus in the realm of the approximate, and resulted, Russell (1937: §303) maintains, in its philosophical underpinnings being left 'in a somewhat disgraceful condition'. The task of a great deal of mathematical theory, and particularly set theory, as it progressed from the nineteenth century onwards, was to eliminate the assumption of infinitesimals in the name of establishing both the continuity of the calculus and the exactitude of its results. The

axiomatization of mathematics and the displacement of geometry in favour of number theory were the predominant results of this effort. While Alain Badiou celebrates these developments when he equates ontology and mathematics, Deleuze can be seen to challenge them by examining alternative traditions and figures in the history of mathematics. On this point, see Smith (2003b).

14 In this sprit, Deleuze counterpoises Leibniz's world of an infinity of compossible perspectives to that of fiction writer Jorge Luis Borges's short story, 'The Garden of Forking Paths' (1993: 67–78). The story recounts a novel of the same title that reads as a confused muddle in which 'the hero dies in the third chapter, while in the fourth he is alive' (73) because its author, Ts'iu Pên, chooses to include in it all possible and incompossible storylines. 'This is Borges's reply to Leibniz: the straight line as force of time, as labyrinth of time, is also the line which forks and keeps on forking, passing through *incompossible presents*, returning to *not-necessarily true pasts*' (*C2* 131).

15 'In pressing forward to its true existence, consciousness will arrive at a point at which it gets rid of its semblance of being burdened with something alien, with what is only for it, and some sort of "other", at a point where appearance becomes identical with essence, so that its exposition will coincide at just this point with the authentic Science of Spirit. And finally, when consciousness itself grasps this its own essence, it will signify the nature of absolute knowledge itself' (Hegel 1977: §89).

16 See Duns Scotus (1987: 4–8).

17 In the original French text of *Difference and Repetition*, Deleuze makes use of the distinction 'between *différencier*, to make or become different, and *différentier*, which is restricted to the mathematical operation' (*DR*, Translator's Preface, xi). The English translation follows this terminology with the terms 'differentiate' and 'differenciate'.

18 'To repeat is to behave in a certain manner, but in relation to something unique or singular which has no equal or equivalent. And perhaps this repetition at the level of external conduct echoes, for its own part, a more secret vibration which animates it, a more profound, internal repetition within the singular' (*DR* 1).

19 In the psychoanalytic variant of this thesis, traumatic experiences that can be repressed but never eliminated return in the form of repetitive neurotic behaviours, where the patient might dream the same dream every night or constantly wash his hands. In short: we repeat because we repress. In freeing repetition from being a repetition of the same, Deleuze reverses this order, so that what is repressed is precisely the repetition of difference that would subvert the notion of identity persisting over time. Repetition of difference is

now the form of concrete lived experience, although it is repressed in order to experience life in terms of identity, similarity and continuity: 'I do not repeat because I repress. I repress because I repeat, I forget because I repeat. I repress, because I can live certain things or certain experiences only in the mode of repetition. I am determined to repress whatever would prevent me from living them thus: in particular, the representation which mediates the lived by relating it to the form of a similar or identical object' (*DR* 18).

20 'The term "Temporality" is intended to indicate that temporality, in existential analytic, represents the horizon from which we understand being' (Heidegger 1982: 228).

21 'Time is no longer defined by succession because succession concerns only things and movements which are in time. If time itself were succession, it would need to succeed in another time, and on to infinity' (*KCP* vii). Kant himself states: 'For change does not affect time itself, but only appearances in time. . . . If we ascribe succession to time itself, we must think yet another time, in which the sequence would be possible' (Kant 1965: A183/B226).

22 The three syntheses of time are arguably the centre of Deleuze's entire ontology and philosophy, but they can only be addressed here in brief detail. Book length studies have been produced by Faulkner (2006) and Williams (2011). See also Widder (2008: 86–99).

23 The most extensive and grand formulation of this thesis is Bergson's *Creative Evolution* (1998), but it is also found in his early work, *Time and Free Will* (1910), where Bergson defines freedom not in terms of a free will that would break with the past but as a unity of action that expresses the fundamental character of the self as an enduring being that compresses its entire past into its present existence and moves into the future.

24 This emerges in the way Deleuze links Bergson's conception of duration to Plato's notion of reminiscence and holds the latter to invoke a transcendent and unrepresentable ground for representation (*B* 59 and *DR* 88).

25 For example: 'Pure duration is the form which the succession of our conscious states assumes when our ego lets itself *live*, when it refrains from separating its present state from its former states' (Bergson 1910: 100). See also Bergson (1998: 3–4).

26 The paradox of the first two syntheses of time is that the subject that constitutes time also exists within it. Deleuze uses Kant's critique of Descartes's 'I think, therefore I am' (*cogito ergo sum*) to introduce this idea. Kant maintains that all experiences, including the subject's experience of itself, must be organized within an order of time intuited prior to all experience (that is, *a priori*) and must be conceived as the effect of a prior cause. This means, however, that when the subject perceives the spontaneous activity of thinking

from which it then declares 'I think', it strangely encounters something that it both can and cannot assign to itself: 'the spontaneity of which I am conscious in the "I think" cannot be understood as the attribute of a substantial and spontaneous being, but only as the affection of a passive self which experiences its own thought – its own intelligence, that by virtue of which it can say *I* – being exercised in it and upon it but not by it' (*DR* 86).

27 'Following Nietzsche we discover, as more profound than time and eternity, the untimely: philosophy is neither a philosophy of history, nor a philosophy of the eternal, but untimely, always and only untimely – that is to say, "acting counter to our time and thereby acting on our time and, let us hope, for the benefit of a time to come"' (*DR* xxi).

28 'The processes of the system *Ucs.* are *timeless*; i.e. they are not ordered temporally, are not altered by the passage of time; they have no reference to time at all. Reference to time is bound up. . .with the work of the system Cs.' (Freud 1957b: 187).

29 MacKenzie (2008) examines this and related issues with respect to political events, focusing primarily on the differences between Badiou's and Deleuze's conceptualizations of the event.

30 See, for example, Gillespie (2008: ch. 1), although this reading of Deleuze limits his understanding of change and novelty to that which is presented in the second synthesis of time.

31 Badiou is, once again, the leading figure from whom many of these critics take their lead, at one point asking 'whether this Event with a capital "E" might not be Deleuze's Good' (2000: 27) and declaring that 'if the only way to think a political revolution, an amorous encounter, an invention of the sciences, or a creation of art as distinct infinities. . .is by sacrificing immanence (which I do not actually believe is the case, but that is not what matters here) and the univocity of Being, then I would sacrifice them' (91–2).

32 'What history grasps in an event is the way it's actualized in particular circumstances; the event's becoming is beyond the scope of history. History isn't experimental, it's just the set of more or less negative preconditions that make it possible to experiment with something beyond history. Without history the experimentation would remain indeterminate, lacking any initial conditions, but experimentation isn't historical. In a major philosophical work, *Clio*, Péguy explained that there are two ways of considering events, one being to follow the course of the event, gathering how it comes about historically, how it's prepared and then decomposes in history, while the other way is to go back into the event, to take one's place in it as in a becoming, to grow both young and old in it at once, going through all its components or singularities. Becoming isn't part of history; history amounts only [*sic*] the set of preconditions,

however recent, that one leaves behind in order to "become," that is, to create something new. This is precisely what Nietzsche calls the Untimely. . . . It's fashionable these days to condemn the horrors of revolution. It's nothing new; English Romanticism is permeated by reflections on Cromwell very similar to present-day reflections on Stalin. They say revolutions turn out badly. But they're constantly confusing two different things, the way revolutions turn out historically and people's revolutionary becoming. These relate to two different sets of people. Men's only hope lies in a revolutionary becoming: the only way of casting off their shame or responding to what is intolerable' (*N* 170–1).

33 'May 1968 in France was molecular, making what led up to it all the more imperceptible from the viewpoint of macropolitics. . . . [T]hose who evaluated things in macropolitical terms understood nothing of the event because something unaccountable was escaping. The politicians, the parties, the unions, many leftists, were utterly vexed: they kept repeating over and over again that "conditions" were not ripe. It was as though they had been temporarily deprived of the entire dualism machine that made them valid spokespeople' (*ATP* 216; see also *TRM* 233–6). On the complexity of Deleuze and Guattari's assessment of the May 1968 events, see Buchanan (2008: 7–19).

34 Foucault considers the Iranian Revolution in these terms: 'In rising up, the Iranians said to themselves – and this perhaps is the soul of the uprising: "Of course, we have to change this regime and get rid of this man, we have to change this corrupt administration, we have to change the whole country, the political organization, the economic system, the foreign policy. But above all, we have to change ourselves. Our way of being, our relationship with others, with things, with eternity, with God, etc., must be completely changed and there will only be a true revolution if this radical change in our experience takes place"' (Foucault 1988b: 217–18).

35 'The rhizome is reducible neither to the One nor the multiple. It is not the One that becomes Two or even directly three, four, five, etc. It is not a multiple derived from the One, or to which One is added $(n + 1)$' (*ATP* 21).

36 See, for example, Plato (1961: *Parmenides* 141a–b and 154a–155c; also *Phaedo* 102b; *Republic* 479a–b).

37 One particular theme taken up from Bergson and Deleuze in recent theory is that of multiple paces or speeds of duration. William Connolly (2005, 2011), in particular, has used the idea to theorize a world of diverse open systems, ranging from the human to the natural, moving at different temporal speeds and interacting in ways that can give rise to sudden and sometimes unpredictable changes.
One can consider, for example, the pace at which a densely populated city might spring into being over a geological fault whose

durational change is comparably slow until a sudden catastrophic shift takes place, or the rapid rate of pollution-generating capitalist industrial development in relation to an environmental system that may remain stable for decades until a tipping point is reached. In terms of chronological time, the same clock can measure all these systems, from the tectonic plates moving a few inches a year to the metropolis built in a handful of generations. But the lived temporalities or durations of each system remain qualitatively irreducible and out of sync with one another. Bergson himself seems ambiguous and ambivalent about the thesis. In *Matter and Memory* (1991: 204–6) and *An Introduction to Metaphysics: The Creative Mind* (1983: 187–8) he theorizes multiple levels of duration above and below that of human consciousness, but in *Duration and Simultaneity* (1999: 32) he dismisses the idea. Deleuze himself takes the idea up positively in his early writings on Bergson (*B* 76–89; *DI* 32–51), but it does not play a significant role in his elaboration of the three syntheses of time and so has not been addressed in this chapter.

38 Thus Žižek takes the virtual to be 'the pure flow of experience, attributable to no subject, neither subjective nor objective' and the actual to be a world of 'fixed entities, just secondary "coagulations" of this flow' (2004: 22), and Badiou takes this supposed relatively inert or 'passive' (2000: 33) nature of the actual to indicate that actual beings are nothing more than unreal simulations of a fully real virtual.

39 Bergson (1998: 247) thus portrays the relationship between spirit and matter through the image of a jet of steam thrown into the air, with droplets forming and falling back to earth, though they are still pressed upwards by the continuous force of the uncondensed part of the steam jet.

Chapter 3

1 Constantin Boundas's (1996: 81) view that it is 'curious that the centrality that Bergson has in Deleuze's work...has not yet found among Deleuze's readers the attention it deserves' certainly appears dated in light of numerous more recent publications that read Deleuze and Bergson largely through each other. In many cases moves away from Bergson by Deleuze are treated as moves either to deepen Bergson's thought or to 'Bergsonize' the thought of other key figures in Deleuze's work, such as Nietzsche (see Ansell-Pearson 2002: chapter 7; Borradori 2001; and Moulard 2002). Bergson is thus taken implicitly, and sometimes even explicitly, to be the centre of Deleuze's own thought: Moulard-Leonard, for example, refers to these instances where Deleuze moves away from Bergson as 'departure[s] from his master' (2008: 103, also 146), and Badiou's (2000: 39) statement that 'Deleuze is a marvellous reader of Bergson, who, in my opinion, is his real master, far more than Spinoza, or perhaps even Nietzsche' is quoted, seemingly favourably, by Ansell-Pearson (1999: 20). Given Deleuze's engagements with so many figures in the history of Western thought, it is not surprising that his thought has been categorized in various ways, particularly outside the circles focused on Deleuze scholarship. Vincent Descombes, for example, declares Deleuze to be 'above all a post-Kantian' (Descombes 1980: 152), although one critical of the post-Kantian tradition that culminates with Hegel, while others hold that Deleuze returns to a pre-Kantian position that asserts the full intelligibility of God, the self and the world (see, for example, Hallward 2006: 11–12). Of course, many others have justifiably seen the attempt to locate Deleuze's key inspiration or orientation (anti-Hegelian, pro-Nietzschean) to be rather pointless (see, for example, Buchanan 2000: 10–15).

2   On this point, see Widder (2011).
3   'But I suppose the main way I coped with it at the time was to see the history of philosophy as a sort of buggery or (it comes to the same thing) immaculate conception. I saw myself as taking an author from behind and giving him a child that would be his own offspring, yet monstrous. It was really important for it to be his own child, because the author had to actually say all I had him saying. But the child was bound to be monstrous too, because it resulted from all sorts of shifting, slipping, dislocations, and hidden emissions that I really enjoyed. I think my book on Bergson's a good example. . . .It was Nietzsche, who I read only later, who extricated me from all this. Because you just can't deal with him in the same sort of way. He gets up to all sorts of things behind *your* back. He gives you a perverse taste – certainly something neither Marx nor Freud ever gave anyone – for saying simple things in your own way, in affects, intensities, experiences, experiments. It's a strange business, speaking for yourself, in your own name, because it doesn't at all come with seeing yourself as an ego or a person or a subject. . . .So anyway, I got to work on two books along these meandering lines, *Difference and Repetition* and *The Logic of Sense*' (*N* 6–7).
4   See, for example, Appel (1999: 8–12).
5   This is Habermas's (1987) general line of critique against Nietzsche and all he considers to be Nietzsche's heirs, and he identifies Deleuze as the mediator who brings Nietzsche's theory of power into French structuralist and post-structuralist thought (127).
6   See, for example, Houlgate (1986: 5–8, 24–5) and Malabou (1996).
7   In addition to the early Deleuze's praise of (Hyppolite's) Hegel,

NOTES

Deleuze and Guattari also positively link Hegel's understanding of the Concept with their own (*WIP* 11–12). Houlgate displays his ignorance of Deleuze's account when he attributes to him the claim 'that Nietzsche knew Hegel's texts well' (1986: 24), whereas Deleuze actually states: 'It has been said that Nietzsche did not know his Hegel. In the sense that one does not know one's opponent well. On the other hand we believe that the Hegelian movement, the different Hegelian factions were familiar to him. Like Marx he found his habitual targets there' (*NP* 8). Jurist (2000: 27) similarly misses the point.

8 It is notable that Hyppolite (1997) directs various Hegelian criticisms at Bergson, Leibniz, Hume and Spinoza, all of whom are marshalled by Deleuze against Hegel.

9 'The search for new means of philosophical expression was begun by Nietzsche and must be pursued today in relation to the renewal of certain other arts, such as the theatre or the cinema' (*DR* xxi).

10 'How far the perspective character of existence extends or indeed whether existence has any other character than this; whether existence without interpretation, without "sense," does not become "nonsense"; whether, on the other hand, all existence is not essentially actively engaged in *interpretation* – that cannot be decided even by the most industrious and most scrupulously conscientious analysis and self-examination of the intellect. . . . But I should think that today we are at least far from the ridiculous immodesty that would be involved in decreeing from our corner that perspectives are permitted only from this corner' (Nietzsche 1974: §374).

11 'The Nietzschean typology brings into play a whole psychology of "depths" or "caves". . . .We must nevertheless be careful not to give Nietzschean concepts an exclusively psychological significance. It is not just that the type is also a biological, sociological, historical and political reality, not only that metaphysics and the theory of knowledge themselves belong to typology. But that Nietzsche, through this typology, develops a philosophy which must, in his view, replace the old metaphysics and transcendental critique and give a new foundation to the sciences of man: genealogical philosophy, that is to say the philosophy of the will to power. The will to power must not be interpreted psychologically, as if the will to power wanted power because of a motive; just as genealogy must not be interpreted as a merely philosophical genesis' (*NP* 145).

12 As Nietzsche says, 'it should be kept in mind that "strong" and "weak" are relative concepts' (Nietzsche 1974: §118).

13 See, for example, Nietzsche (1968: §§512, 521, 532, 568 and 1986: §§11, 18–19).

14 In a precursor to what he later calls genealogy, in *Human, All too Human*, Nietzsche writes of the need for 'a *chemistry* of the moral, religious and aesthetic conceptions and sensations, likewise of all the agitations we experience within ourselves in cultural and social intercourse, and indeed even when we are alone' (Nietzsche 1986: §1).

15 Nietzsche also draws an experiential connection between quantitative differences and qualities: 'Our "knowing" limits itself to establishing quantities; but we cannot help feeling these differences in quantity as qualities. Quality is a perspective truth for *us*; not an "in itself"...we sense bigness and smallness in relation to the conditions of our existence...with regard to making possible our existence we sense even relations between magnitudes as qualities' (Nietzsche 1968: §563).

16 'There is a deep affinity, a complicity, but never a confusion, between action and affirmation, between reaction and negation. Moreover, the determination of these affinities brings the whole art of philosophy into play. On the one hand, it is clear that there is affirmation in every action and negation in every reaction. But, on the other hand, action and reaction are more like means, means or instruments of the will to power which affirms and denies, just as reactive forces are instruments of nihilism. And again, action and reaction need affirmation and negation as something which goes beyond them but is necessary for them to achieve their own ends. Finally, and more profoundly, affirmation and negation extend beyond action and reaction because they are the immediate qualities of becoming itself. Affirmation is not action but the power of becoming active, *becoming active* personified. Negation is not simple reaction but a *becoming reactive*' (*NP* 54).

17 As Kojève (1969: 3–5) argues in his famous lectures on Hegel, this 'animal Desire' is not enough to confirm one's humanity.

18 'This type of man *needs* to believe in a neutral independent "subject," prompted by an instinct for self-preservation and self-affirmation in which every lie is sanctified. The subject (or, to use a more popular expression, the *soul*) has perhaps been believed in hitherto more firmly than anything else on earth because it makes possible to the majority of mortals, the weak and oppressed of every kind, the sublime self-deception that interprets weakness as freedom, and their being thus-and-thus as a *merit*' (Nietzsche 1967: 1.13).

19 As Nietzsche writes regarding the priests in whom *ressentiment* finds its birth: 'As is well known, the priests are the *most evil enemies* – but why? Because they are the most impotent. It is because of their impotence that in them hatred grows to monstrous and uncanny proportions, to the most spiritual and poisonous kind

of hatred. The truly great haters in world history have always been priests; likewise the most ingenious haters: other kinds of spirit hardly come into consideration when compared with the spirit of priestly vengefulness' (Nietzsche 1967: 1.7).

20 'That lambs dislike great birds of prey does not seem strange: only it gives no ground for reproaching these birds of prey for bearing off little lambs. And if the lambs say among themselves: "these birds of prey are evil; and whoever is least like a bird of prey, but rather its opposite, a lamb – would he not be good?" there is no reason to find fault with this institution of an ideal, except perhaps that the birds of prey might view it a little ironically and say: "*we* don't dislike them at all, these good little lambs; we even love them: nothing is more tasty than a tender lamb"' (Nietzsche 1967: 1.13).

21 'Rather, it was "the good" themselves , that is to say, the noble, powerful, high-stationed and high-minded, who felt and established themselves and their actions as good, that is, of the first rank, in contradistinction to all the low, low-minded, common and plebeian. It was out of this *pathos of distance* that they first seized the right to create values and to coin names for values: what had they to do with utility!' (Nietzsche 1967: 1.2). See also Nietzsche (1989: §257).

22 'When the noble mode of valuation blunders and sins against reality, it does so in respect to the sphere with which it is *not* sufficiently familiar, against a real knowledge of which it has indeed inflexibly guarded itself: in some circumstances it misunderstands the sphere it despises, that of the common man, of the lower orders; on the other hand, one should remember that, even supposing that the affect of contempt, of looking down from a superior height, *falsifies* the image of that which it despises, it will at any rate still be a much less serious falsification than that perpetrated by its opponent – *in effigie* of course – by the submerged hatred, the vengefulness of the impotent' (Nietzsche 1967: 1.10).

23 See Nietzsche (1967: 1.13).

24 See Nietzsche (1967: 2.21–2).

25 'What is to be feared, what has a more calamitous effect than any other calamity, is that man should inspire not profound fear but profound *nausea*; also not great fear but great *pity*. Suppose these two were one day to unite, they would inevitably beget one of the uncanniest monsters: the "last will" of man, his will to nothingness, nihilism' (Nietzsche 1967: 3.14).

26 'When would they [men of *ressentiment*] achieve the ultimate, subtlest, sublimest triumph of revenge? Undoubtedly if they succeeded in *poisoning the consciences* of the fortunate with their own misery, with all misery, so that one day the fortunate began to be ashamed of their good fortune and perhaps said one to another: "it is disgraceful to be fortunate: *there is too much misery!*"' (Nietzsche 1967: 3.14).

27 The reference is to the story of Diogenes the Cynic, who wandered the streets of Athens carrying a lantern during the daytime and told others he was searching for an honest man.

28 'You see what it was that really triumphed over the Christian god: Christian morality itself, the concept of truthfulness that was understood ever more rigorously, the father confessor's refinement of the Christian conscience, translated and sublimated into a scientific conscience, into intellectual cleanliness at any price. Looking at nature as if it was proof of the goodness and governance of a god; interpreting history in honor of some divine reason, as a continual testimony of a moral world order and ultimate moral purposes; interpreting one's own experiences as pious people have long enough interpreted theirs, as if everything were providential, a hint, designed and ordained for the sake of the salvation of the soul – that is *all over* now, that has man's conscience *against* it, that is considered indecent and dishonest by every more refined conscience' (Nietzsche 1974: §357).

29 Deleuze (*DR* 92) maintains that Zarathustra's death is only implied because Nietzsche did not live to write the final part of the story. However, it is explicitly connected to overcoming in the existing text, where Zarathustra, having counselled others that the eternal return is the path to their redemption, declares: "Now I wait for my own redemption – that I may go to them for the last time. For I want to go to men once more; under their eyes I want to go under; dying, I want to give them my richest gift' (Nietzsche 1966: 'On Old and New Tablets', 198).

30 The most obvious example is in the aphorism entitled 'The greatest weight': 'What, if some day or night a demon were to steal after you into your loneliest loneliness and say to you: "This life as you live it and have lived it, you will have to live once more and innumerable times more; and there will be nothing new in it, but every pain and every joy and every thought and sigh and everything unutterably small or great in your life will have to return to you, all in the same succession and sequence – even this spider and this moonlight between the trees, and even this moment and I myself. The eternal hourglass of existence is turned upside down again and again, and you with it, speck of dust!' (Nietzsche 1974: §341).

31 Deleuze cites Kierkegaard, Pascal and Péguy as thinkers who similarly counselled an overcoming of oneself but who 'were not ready to pay the necessary price' (*DR* 95) because their version of overcoming 'is supposed to restore everything to us' (*C1* 116).

32 'To "give style" to one's character – a great and rare art! It is practiced by those who survey all the strengths and weaknesses of their nature and then fit them into an artistic plan until every one of them appears as art and reason and even weaknesses delight the eye. Here a large mass of second nature has been added; there a piece of original nature has been removed – both times through long practice and daily work at it. Here the ugly that could not be removed is concealed; there it has been reinterpreted and made sublime. Much that is vague and resisted shaping has been saved and exploited for distant views; it is meant to beckon toward the far and immeasurable. In the end, when the work is finished, it becomes evident how the constraint of a single taste governed and formed everything large and small. Whether this taste was good or bad is less important than one might suppose, if only it was a single taste!' (Nietzsche 1974: §290).

Chapter 4

1 Critics often treat the 'Docile Bodies' chapter in *Discipline and Punish* (1979) as proof that Foucault's thesis erroneously holds modern power to force individuals into passivity. Foucault, however, actually says that docility is an ideal of a military model of society that developed in the early modern period and inspired the formation of disciplinary institutions. He never holds the ideal to have been realized: 'Historians of ideas usually attribute the dream of a perfect society to the philosophers and jurists of the eighteenth century; but there was also a military dream of society; its fundamental reference was not to the state of nature, but to the meticulously subordinated cogs of a machine, not to the primal social contract, but to permanent coercions, not to fundamental rights, but to indefinitely progressive forms of training, not to the general will but to automatic docility' (169).
2 Deleuze (*N* 174–5, 177–82) suggests that Foucault's thesis of a disciplinary society functioning through technologies of confinement has been overtaken and replaced by a new 'control society' working with open spaces and instant communication, and managing diverse flows of people, technology and information. This criticism of Foucault has been taken up by others, including Hardt and Negri (2000: 24, 330). But the distinction it draws between discipline and control is rendered problematic by the passage from *Discipline and Punish* just quoted, and it hardly seems that disciplinary techniques have in any sense diminished in open spaces – one need only notice the prevalence of CCTV cameras throughout these spaces, for example. Deleuze nevertheless contends that '[c]ontrol is not discipline. You do not confine people with a highway. But by making highways, you multiply the means of control I am not saying this is the only aim of highways, but people can travel infinitely and "freely"

without being confined while being perfectly controlled. That is our future' (*TRM* 322). There is undoubtedly truth to these claims, as long as one also notes the overt presence of speed cameras and the fact that people had better already be disciplined (which, again, need not require confinement) before they are let loose on these high-speed motorways.

3 'Power relations are both intentional and nonsubjective. If in fact they are intelligible, this is not because they are the effect of another instance that "explains" them, but rather because they are imbued, through and through, with calculation: there is no power that is exercised without a series of aims and objectives. But this does not mean that it results from the choice or decision of an individual subject' (Foucault 1990: 94–5).

4 With respect to the prison, for example: 'The delinquent is an institutional product. It is no use being surprised, therefore, that in a considerable proportion of cases the biography of convicts passes through all these mechanisms and establishments, whose purpose, it is widely believed, is to lead away from prison' (Foucault 1979: 301). The consistency of this failure leads Foucault to conclude that the prison's real purpose is not to reform delinquents but instead to manage their deviance: 'For the observation that prisons fail to eliminate crime, one should perhaps substitute the hypothesis that the prison has succeeded extremely well in producing delinquency, a specific type, a politically or economically less dangerous – and, on occasion, usable – form of illegality' (277).

5 According to the model, 'Power over sex is exercised in the same way at all levels. From top to bottom, in its over-all decisions and its capillary interventions alike, whatever the devices or institutions on which it relies, it acts in a uniform and comprehensive manner; it operates according to the simple and endlessly reproduced mechanisms of law, taboo, and censorship: from state to family, from prince to father, from the tribunal to the small change of everyday punishments, from the agencies of social domination to the structures that constitute the subject himself, one finds a general form of power, varying in scale alone. This form is the law of transgression and punishment, with its interplay of licit and illicit' (Foucault 1990: 84–5).

6 On this and the previous point, see Widder (2004).

7 This is not as straightforward as many seem to believe, given that in Plato's *Symposium*, the famous dialogue on love, Socrates reports that his teacher Diotima scoffed at his suggestion that love is a desire for a quality or thing that one lacks, holding instead that a middle position exists between fullness and lack (Plato 1961: *Symposium*, 200a, 202a–206a).

8 Chronologically, for Lacan, the beginnings of subjectivity appear at the 'mirror stage', when the infant, apprehending its reflection,

recognizes itself as a singular and unified being. While this unity is already compromised by the fact that it is really only an image conveyed from outside, it nonetheless creates the conditions under which 'the *I* is precipitated in a primordial form, prior to being objectified in the dialectic of identification with the other, and before language restores to it, in the universal, its function as subject' (Lacan 2006: 76). This image of unity prepares the way for the traumatic experience of castration anxiety, which in turn retroactively gives meaning to the mirror stage as a memory of a now missing wholeness.

9 The last of these is Žižek's (1989) favourite formulation, and one he uses to attack 'post-structuralists' who, he says, absorb everything into a deconstructive play of signifiers, failing to recognize that the lack both resists deconstruction and remains outside signification, without for all that becoming a positive form.

10 Indeed, after noting that Freud refers to the drives as psychoanalysis's 'myths', Lacan declares: 'For my part, I will ignore this term myth – indeed, in the same text, in the first paragraph, Freud uses the word *Konvention*, convention, which is much closer to what we are talking about and to which I would apply the Benthamite term, *fiction*, which I have mapped for my followers' (Lacan 1981: 163). On the other hand, while drives are conventions, the libido is a myth through which we approach the Real: 'The libido is the essential organ in understanding the nature of the drive. This organ is unreal. Unreal is not imaginary. The unreal is defined by articulating itself on the real in a way that eludes us, and it is precisely this that requires that its representation should be mythical, as I have made it. But the fact that it is unreal does not prevent an organ from embodying itself' (205).

11 Positing an instinct for self-preservation, for example, 'masks its ignorance by assuming the existence of morals in nature'; in contrast to this, 'the drive – the Freudian drive – has nothing to do with instinct (none of Freud's expressions allows for confusion here)' (Lacan 2006: 722).

12 'In the theory of psycho-analysis we have no hesitation in assuming that the course taken by mental events is automatically regulated by the pleasure principle. We believe, that is to say, that the course of those events is invariably set in motion by an unpleasurable tension, and that it takes a direction such that its final outcome coincides with a lowering of that tension – that is, with an avoidance of unpleasure or a production of pleasure' (Freud 1957a: 7). While investment alone, independent of aims and objects, is sufficient to attain pleasure, this can be frustrated when 'individual instincts or parts of instincts turn out to be incompatible in their aims or demands with the remaining ones' (11), and in this conflict certain drives are repressed, although this repression ultimately serves the

pleasure principle. Freud, of course, is nevertheless led towards a theorization of a drive or instinct operating 'beyond' the pleasure principle: Thanatos, or the 'death instinct'.

13 'The best formula seems to me to be the following – that *la pulsion en fait le tour* [the drive goes around it]. . . . *Tour* is to be understood here with the ambiguity it possesses in French, both *turn*, the limit around which one turns, and *trick*' (Lacan 1981: 168).

14 In this way the drives' objects are a subset of desire's objects: '[T]he object of desire is the cause of the desire, and this object that is the cause of desire is the object of the drive – that is to say, the object around which the drive turns. . . . It is not that desire clings to the object of the drive – desire moves around it, in so far as it is agitated in the drive. But all desire is not necessarily agitated in the drive. There are empty desires or mad desires that are based on nothing more than the fact that the thing in question has been forbidden you' (Lacan 1981: 243).

15 'Say that it's Oedipus, or you'll get a slap in the face. The psychoanalyst no longer says to the patient: "Tell me a little bit about your desiring-machines, won't you?" Instead he screams: "Answer daddy-and-mommy when I speak to you!"' (*AO* 45).

16 'Oedipus depends on this sort of nationalistic, religious, racist sentiment, and not the reverse: it is not the father who is projected onto the boss, but the boss who is applied to the father, either in order to tell us "you will not surpass your father," or "you will surpass him to find our forefathers"' (*AO* 104).

17 See *AO* (53, 73, 83, 171, 175, 217, 268, 308–11, 363). Žižek takes the standard Lacanian line that *Anti-Oedipus* is 'arguably Deleuze's worst book' (2004: 21) while singularly ignoring evidence that Lacan approved of – or at least did not dismiss – the work. On this point, see Smith (2004: 635–6).

18 'But the problem is not to know whether desire is alien to power, whether it is prior to the law as is often thought to be the case, when it is not rather the law that is perceived as constituting it. This question is beside the point. Whether desire is this or that, in any case one continues to conceive of it in relation to a power that is always juridical and discursive, a power that has its central point in the enunciation of the law. . . . We must construct an analytics of power that no longer takes law as a model and a code' (Foucault 1990: 89–90).

19 Hence the English translators of *Anti-Oedipus* explain their translation of *objets partiels* as 'partial objects' rather than part-objects, as is standard in translations of Klein's work (*AO* 309n). Klein also features prominently in the last 50 pages of *The Logic of Sense*, where Deleuze uses her account of psychic development to trace the unfolding of an ontology of sense to the point where the self

is overcome. Despite this more positive treatment of Klein in this earlier solo text, however, Deleuze levels the same criticism that she treats reality as being composed of whole objects to which the psyche adapts itself. On the earlier Deleuze's relation to Klein, see Widder (2009b).

20 *The Logic of Sense* presents three syntheses with the same names, albeit in the order of connective, conjunctive and disjunctive (see Deleuze 1990: 47, 174–6, 231–2). In both cases these syntheses can be related back to the three syntheses of time in *Difference and Repetition*, with the differences in order of presentation being linked to the place given to the subject and to sense in each analysis (in all three cases, the subject is associated with the conjunctive synthesis, and sense with the disjunctive synthesis). Having said this, the syntheses in *Anti-Oedipus* cannot be equated with those of the earlier texts, as Williams (2011: 172n. 20) quite correctly notes.

21 This shorthand is only introduced in *A Thousand Plateaus*, but there seems no reason it cannot be used when referring to *Anti-Oedipus*. Deleuze originally introduces the idea of the body without organs, which he takes from Antonin Artaud, in a somewhat different form in *The Logic of Sense*.

22 Moreover, just as Deleuze links his ontology of expressive sense to Spinoza's conception of infinite substance and its attributes, he and Guattari write: 'The body without organs is the immanent substance, in the most Spinozist sense of the word; and the partial objects are like its ultimate attributes, which belong to it precisely insofar as they are really distinct and cannot on this account exclude or oppose one another' (*AO* 327).

23 'It is not a question of denying the vital importance of parents or the love attachment of children to their mothers and fathers. It is a question of knowing what the place and the function of parents are within desiring-production, rather than doing the opposite and forcing the entire interplay of desiring-machines to fit within . . . the restricted code of Oedipus' (*AO* 47).

24 Deleuze and Guattari hold that psychoanalysis illicitly turns the unconscious into a theatre of representation – 'a classical theater was substituted for the unconscious as a factory' (*AO* 24) – in which parental and other figures take the form of 'global persons' with established meanings, referring desire to these persons.

25 Daniel Paul Schreber was a German judge whose memoirs were analyzed by Freud as a case of paranoid schizophrenia. For Deleuze and Guattari, 'Freud . . . stresses the crucial turning point that occurs in Schreber's illness when Schreber becomes reconciled to becoming-woman and embarks upon a process of self-cure that brings him back to the equation Nature = Production (the production of a new humanity)' (*AO* 17).

26 Of course, as the ideal gas law is ideal, it can only approximate the behaviour of real gases.
27 'Although it is true that the molecular works in detail and operates in small groups, this does not mean that it is any less coextensive with the entire social field than molar organization' (*ATP* 215). Also: 'the molar and the molecular are distinguished not by size, scale, or dimension but by the nature of the system of reference envisioned' (217).
28 See Protevi (2006a), which links Deleuze and Guattari's ontological concepts to the idea of emergence in scientific complexity theory, and also Protevi (2006b), which brings the principles of this 'political physiology' to bear on a study of Hurricane Katrina, wrapping into it discussion of the complex social, historical, environmental and other elements at play in the events that were wrought.
29 'You will have guessed *what* has really happened here, *beneath* all this: that will to self-tormenting, that repressed cruelty of the animal-man made inward and scared back into himself, the creature imprisoned in the "state" so as to be tamed, who invented the bad conscience in order to hurt himself after the *more natural* vent for this desire to hurt had been blocked – this man of the bad conscience has seized upon the presupposition of religion so as to drive his self-torture to its most gruesome pitch of severity and rigor' (Nietzsche 1967: 2.22).
30 'Transgression, guilt, castration: are these determinations of the unconscious, or is this *the way a priest sees things?* Doubtless there are many other forces besides psychoanalysis for oedipalizing the unconscious, rendering it guilty, castrating it. But psychoanalysis reinforces the movement, it invents a last priest' (*AO* 112).
31 'Oedipus would be nothing if the symbolic position of an object from on high, in the despotic machine, did not first make possible the folding and flattening operations that will constitute Oedipus in the modern social field: the triangulation's *cause*' (*AO* 267–8).
32 Nietzsche makes clear that *ressentiment* directed against others who are blamed for suffering creates the moral opposition between good and evil, but guilt comes from blame being turned back on the self: '"I suffer: someone must be to blame for it" – thus thinks every sickly sheep. But his shepherd, the ascetic priest, tells him: "Quite so, my sheep! someone must be to blame for it: but you yourself are this someone, you alone are to blame for it – *you alone are to blame for yourself!*" – This is brazen and false enough: but one thing at least is achieved by it, the direction of *ressentiment* is *altered*' (Nietzsche 1967: 3.15).
33 Deleuze thus writes to Michel Cressole: 'There's a piece you know that explains this innate spitefulness of people who come from the militant left: "If you like big ideas, then try talking about kindness and fraternity at a leftist meeting. They specialize in all forms

of carefully calculated animosity, in greeting anybody, present or absent, friend or foe, and anything they say, with aggressiveness and put-downs. They don't want to understand people, but to check them over"' (*N* 4). Along similar lines, I am reminded of a former student reporting that at the Socialist Worker's Party meetings he used to attend, no one was allowed to ask questions.

Chapter 5

1 I owe my knowledge of these events to a former student's conference paper. See Harrison (2006).
2 'Furthermore: might not this "struggle" that one tries to wage against the "enemy" only be a way of making a petty dispute without much importance seem more serious than it really is? I mean, don't certain intellectuals hope to lend themselves greater political weight with their "ideological struggle" than they really have? . . . And then I'll tell you: I find this "model of war" not only a bit ridiculous but also rather dangerous. Because by virtue of saying or thinking "I am fighting against this enemy," if one day you found yourself in a position of strength, and in a situation of real war, in front of this blasted "enemy," wouldn't you actually treat him as one? Taking that route leads directly to oppression, no matter who takes it: that's the real danger' (Foucault 1991: 180–1).
3 Nietzsche provides a concise response to these lazy populist assumptions: 'There are still harmless self-observers who believe that there are "immediate certainties"; for example, "I think". . . .When I analyze the process that is expressed in the sentence "I think," I find a whole series of daring assertions that would be difficult, perhaps impossible, to prove; for example, that it is *I* who think, that there must necessarily be something that thinks, that thinking is an activity and operation on the part of a being who is thought of as a cause, that there is an "ego," and, finally, that it is already determined what is to be designated by thinking – that I *know* what thinking is. For if I had not already decided within myself what it is, by what standard could I determine whether that which is just happening is not perhaps "willing" or "feeling"? In short, the assertion "I think" assumes that I *compare* my state at the present moment with other states of myself which I know, in order to determine what it is; on account of this retrospective connection with further "knowledge," it has, at any rate, no immediate certainty for me" (Nietzsche 1989: §16).
4 Deleuze takes these examples from Plato's *Theaetetus* (1961: 193a–196d), but contends that the same model that ties thought to

recognition is evident in Descartes and even Kant, whose critique of reason in no way undermines the model's implicit presumptions (*DR* 134–7). Although the dialogue ends in aporia, without any resolution to the question of what knowledge is, Deleuze contends that it 'presents simultaneously both a positive model of recognition or common sense, and a negative model of error' (148) that in a quite different context governs the search for Forms in Plato's *Republic* (148–9).

5 'But who can believe that the destiny of thought is at stake in these acts, and that when we recognise, we are thinking?' (*DR* 135).
6 Deleuze's reference is to Plato (1961: *Republic* 523b–524d).
7 An example is provided by Foucault's (1975) case study of Pierre Rivière, who murdered his mother, sister and one of his brothers in 1835 and, in advance of his trial, wrote a long memoir to explain and take responsibility for his actions, although it was used instead to demonstrate his insanity and institutionalize him. The memoir nevertheless raised the question of whether Pierre was indeed rational or insane, the only psychological category available at the time for the latter being 'monomania', and this would be discarded within decades. A monomaniac was conceived as a person maniacally committed to a single idea or emotion but who pursued it relentlessly yet seemingly rationally, so that he would appear sane to others. But it also came to be thought that acting out the mania would cure the monomaniac of his mental illness, and, in Pierre's case, this would explain how he could write his seemingly rational account. In this way, however, since its pathology dictated that no sign of madness would be detectable either before or after the act, the diagnosis of monomania came to hang only on the act itself, and as a result it ended up being used simply to account for the most heinous murders where no other reason could be given.
8 'A field, a heterogeneous smooth space, is wedded to a very particular type of multiplicity: nonmetric, acentered, rhizomatic multiplicities that occupy space without "counting" it and can "be explored only by legwork." They do not meet the visual condition of being observable from a point in space external to them; an example of this is the system of sounds, or even of colors, as opposed to Euclidean space' (*ATP* 371).
9 In some theories the subject designates a conscious agency able to make choices and assume responsibility that emerges from a temporary stabilization of this subject's identity achieved through the constitutive exclusions that separate it from what it is not (see, for example, Butler 1993: 3). In other approaches, the subject is the unconscious agent of lack that constitutes itself through acts that both determine and subvert it – so, for example, Žižek (2008: 83–4) speaks of the victim of a swindle who is not deceived by his swindler but who instead, desiring a quick fortune through a cheat,

NOTES

allows himself to be suckered; the apparent loss of subjectivity is actually its confirmation, as the subject's own desire did this to him and he has no one else to blame. The necessity for some sort of at least temporary stabilization of both the subject and the discourse it takes up to identify itself is most often asserted alongside the claim that without partial stability there would be no meaning but only chaos, and that the subject would be reduced to a mere 'subject position' unable to escape the determining forces of power (this reduction is often attributed to Foucault). Expressing the first assertion, Ernesto Laclau maintains that 'a discourse in which meaning cannot possibly be fixed is nothing else but the discourse of the psychotic' (Laclau 1990: 90); reflecting the second, he holds that 'if the subject was a mere subject position within the structure [of relations that constitutes its identity], the latter would be fully closed', and that this closure can only be superseded by 'the *subject*, who can only exist as a will transcending the structure', even if this subject is established only through this structure's relational network (Laclau 1996: 92). Comparable claims can be found in Marchart (2007: 80–2), Newman (2001: 138–40), Stavrakakis (1999: 13–15) and Žižek (1989: 72, 173–5). Žižek also, following Lacan, proclaims himself to be one of the 'partisans of Cartesian subjectivity' (2008: xxiv) on the grounds that unless a 'unique scene of the Self' is affirmed, the self will be reduced to 'a pandemonium of competing forces' (xxiii). In all these cases, what is invoked is what Deleuze calls the 'summary law of all or nothing' that creates a false alternative between organized being and chaos (*LS* 106, 306).

10 See Foucault (1992: 185–225). As Foucault says in response to a comment that the ancients were more tolerant of homosexuality: 'It might look that way. Since there is an important and large literature about loving boys in Greek culture, some historians say, "Well, that's the proof that they loved boys." But I say that proves that loving boys was a problem. Because if there were no problem, they would speak of this kind of love in the same terms as love between men and women' (Foucault 1984: 344).

11 I am grateful to a former student, Matthew Hammond, who presented this idea in an unpublished graduate conference paper. See Hammond (2003).

Conclusion

1 For example: 'There are significant differences among us on the question of the "subject", and this comes through as we each attempt to take account of what constitutes or conditions the failure of any claim to identity to achieve final or full determination. What

remains true, however, is that we each value this "failure" as a condition of democratic contestation itself' (Butler, Laclau and Žižek 2000: 2).

2 Thus Judith Butler (1993), for example, after calling into question an identity politics that demands the coherence of its identities even at the cost of excluding and abasing other identity positions deemed abject, maintains: 'None of the above is meant to suggest that identity is to be denied, overcome, erased. None of us can fully answer to the demand to "get over yourself!" The demand to overcome radically the constitutive constraints by which cultural viability is achieved would be its own form of violence. But when that very viability is itself the consequence of a repudiation, a subordination, or an exploitative relation, the negotiation becomes increasingly complex. What this analysis does suggest is that an economy of difference is in order in which the matrices, the crossroads at which various identifications are formed and displaced, force a reworking of that logic of non-contradiction by which one identification is always and only purchased at the expense of another. . . . Thus every insistence on identity must at some point lead to a taking stock of the constitutive exclusions that reconsolidate hegemonic power differentials, exclusions that each articulation was forced to make in order to proceed' (117–18). By the same token, however, Butler contends that a denial of the need for constitutive exclusion would engender an insipid politics that subordinates difference in the name of a secretly violent unity: 'The ideal of transforming all excluded identifications into inclusive features – of appropriating all difference into unity – would mark the return to a Hegelian synthesis which has no exterior and that, in appropriating all difference as exemplary features of itself, becomes a figure for imperialism, a figure that installs itself by way of a romantic, insidious, and all-consuming humanism' (116).

3 This formulation is certainly enough to put to bed Žižek's (2004) erroneous contention that Deleuze's ontology never entirely freed itself from – and, due to Guattari's negative influence, fatally came to embrace – an 'empiriocriticist' and idealist conception of the virtual as 'the pure flow of experience, attributable to no subject, neither subjective nor objective – subject and object are, as all fixed entities, just secondary "coagulations" of this flow' (22).

Bibliography

Ansell-Pearson, K. (1999), *Germinal Life: The Difference and Repetition of Deleuze*. London: Routledge.
—. (2002), *Philosophy and the Adventure of the Virtual: Bergson and the Time of Life*. London: Routledge.
Appel, F. (1999), *Nietzsche Contra Democracy*. Ithaca: Cornell University Press.
Aristotle. (1933–5), *Metaphysics*. Trans. H. Tredennick. 2 vols. Cambridge, MA: Loeb Classics.
Badiou, A. (2000), *Deleuze: The Clamor of Being*. Trans. L. Burchill. Minneapolis: University of Minnesota Press.
Barnes, J. (1987), *Early Greek Philosophy*. London: Penguin.
Bennett, J. (2001), *The Enchantment of Modern Life: Attachments, Crossings, and Ethics*. Princeton: Princeton University Press.
—. (2009), *Vibrant Matter: A Political Ecology of Things*. Durham: Duke University Press.
Bergson, H. (1910), *Time and Free Will: Essays on the Immediate Data of Consciousness*. Trans. F. L. Pogson. London: George Allen and Unwin.
—. (1983), *An Introduction to Metaphysics: The Creative Mind*. Trans. M. L. Andison. Totowa, NJ: Rowman & Allanheld.
—. (1991), *Matter and Memory*. Trans. N. M. Paul and W. S. Palmer. New York: Zone Books.
—. (1998), *Creative Evolution*. Trans. A. Mitchell. Mineola, NY: Dover Publications.
—. (1999), *Duration and Simultaneity: Bergson and the Einsteinian Universe*. Ed. R. Durie. Trans. L. Jacobson, with M. Lewis and R. Durie. Manchester, UK: Clinamen Press.
Berlin, I. (1969), *Four Essays on Liberty*. Oxford: Oxford University Press.
Boradori, G. (2001), 'The Temporalizatioin of Difference: Reflections on Deleuze's Interpretation of Bergson'. *Continental Philosophy Review*. 34.1, 1–20.
Borges, J. L. (1993), *Ficciones*. Intro. John Sturrock. New York: Everyman's Library.
Boundas, C. (1996), 'Deleuze-Bergson: An Ontology of the Virtual'. In P. Patton (ed.), *Deleuze: A Critical Reader*. Oxford: Blackwell, pp. 81–106.

Buchanan, I. (2000), *Deleuzism: A Metacommentary*. Edinburgh: Edinburgh University Press.
—. (2008), *Deleuze and Guattari's Anti-Oedipus: A Reader's Guide*. London: Continuum.
Butler, J. (1993), *Bodies that Matter: On the Discursive Limits of "Sex"*. London: Routledge.
Butler, J., Laclau, E. and Žižek, S. (2000), *Contingency, Hegemony, Universality: Contemporary Dialogues on the Left*. London: Verso.
Connolly, W. (1993), *The Augustinian Imperative: A Reflection on the Politics of Morality*. Newbury Park, CA: Sage Publications.
—. (1995a), *The Ethos of Pluralization*. Minneapolis: University of Minnesota Press.
—. (1995b), 'Twilight of the Idols'. *Philosophy and Social Criticism*. 21.3, 127–37.
—. (2005), *Pluralism*. Durham: Duke University Press.
—. (2011), *A World of Becoming*. Durham: Duke University Press.
Coole, D. and Frost, S. (eds) (2010), *New Materialisms: Ontology, Agency, and Politics*. Durham: Duke University Press.
Deleuze, G. (1983), *Nietzsche and Philosophy*. Trans. H. Tomlinson. London: Athlone Press.
—. (1984), *Kant's Critical Philosophy*. Trans. H. Tomlinson and B. Habberjam. London: Athlone Press.
—. (1986), *Cinema 1: The Movement-Image*. Trans. H. Tomlinson and B. Habberjam. London: Athlone Press.
—. (1988), *Foucault*. Trans. S. Hand. London: Athlone Press.
—. (1989), *Cinema 2: The Time-Image*. Trans. H. Tomlinson and R. Galeta. London: Athlone Press.
—. (1990), *The Logic of Sense*. Ed. C. V. Boundas. Trans. M. Lester, with C. Stivale. New York: Columbia University Press.
—. (1991), *Bergsonism*. Trans. H. Tomlinson and B. Habberjam. New York: Zone Books.
—. (1992), *Expressionism in Philosophy: Spinoza*. Trans. M. Joughin. New York: Zone Books.
—. (1993), *The Fold: Leibniz and the Baroque*. Trans. T. Conley. Minneapolis: University of Minnesota Press.
—. (1994), *Difference and Repetition*. Trans. P. Patton. London: Athlone Press.
—. (1995), *Negotiations, 1972–1990*. Trans. M. Joughin. New York: Columbia University Press.
—. (1998), *Essays Critical and Clinical*. Trans. D. W. Smith, with M. A. Greco. London: Verso.
—. (2004), *Desert Islands and Other Texts, 1953–1974*. Ed. D. Lapoujade. Trans. M. Taormina. New York: Semiotext(e).
—. (2006), *Two Regimes of Madness: Texts and Interviews, 1975–1995*. Ed. D. Lapoujade. Trans. A. Hodges and M. Taormina. New York: Semiotext(e).

BIBLIOGRAPHY

Deleuze, G. and Guattari, F. (1983), *Anti-Oedipus: Capitalism and Schizophrenia*. Trans. R. Hurley, M. Seem, and H. R. Lane. Minneapolis: University of Minnesota Press.
—. (1987), *A Thousand Plateaus: Capitalism and Schizophrenia*. Trans. B. Massumi. Minneapolis: University of Minnesota Press.
—. (1994), *What is Philosophy?* Trans. H. Tomlinson and G. Burchell. New York: Columbia University Press.
Deleuze, G. and Parnet, C. (1987), *Dialogues*. Trans. H. Tomlinson and B. Habberjam. New York: Columbia University Press.
Descombes, V. (1980), *Modern French Philosophy*. Trans. L. Scott-Fox and J. M. Harding. Cambridge: Cambridge University Press.
Duns Scotus, J. (1987), *Philosophical Writings* (second edn). Trans. A. Wolter, OFM. Indianapolis: Hackett.
Faulkner, K. (2006), *Deleuze and the Three Syntheses of Time*. New York: Peter Lang.
Foucault, M. (1975), *I Pierre Rivière, Having Slaughtered My Mother, My Sister, and My Brother: A Case of Parricide in the 19th Century*. Trans. F. Jellinek. Lincoln: University of Nebraska Press.
—. (1977), 'Revolutionary Action: "Until Now"'. In D. F. Bouchard (ed.), *Language, Counter-Memory, Practice*. Ithaca: Cornell University Press.
—. (1979), *Discipline and Punish: The Birth of the Prison*. Trans. A. Sheridan. New York: Vintage Books.
—. (1980), *Power/Knowledge: Selected Interviews and Other Writings, 1972–1977*. Ed. C. Gordon. Trans. C. Gordon, L. Marshall, J. Mepham, and K. Soper. Brighton: Harvester.
—. (1984), 'On the Genealogy of Ethics: An Overview of Work in Progress'. In P. Rabinow (ed.), *The Foucault Reader*. New York: Pantheon Books, pp. 340–72.
—. (1988a), 'Critical Theory/Intellectual History'. In L. D. Kritzman (ed.), *Politics, Philosophy, Culture*. New York: Routledge, pp. 17–46.
—. (1988b), 'Iran: The Spirit of a World Without Spirit'. In L. D. Kritzman (ed.), *Politics, Philosophy, Culture*. New York: Routledge, pp. 211–24.
—. (1990), *The History of Sexuality, Volume One: An Introduction*. Trans. R. Hurley. New York: Vintage Books.
—. (1991), *Remarks on Marx: Conversations with Duccio Trombadori*. Trans. R. J. Goldstein and J. Cascaito. New York: Semiotext(e).
—. (1992), *The History of Sexuality, Volume Two: The Use of Pleasure*. Trans. R. Hurley. Harmondsworth: Penguin Books.
Freud, S. (1957a), 'Beyond the Pleasure Principle'. In *The Standard Edition of the Complete Psychological Works of Sigmund Freud*. Ed. and Trans. J. Strachey. 24 vols. 18:3–64. London: Hogarth Press and the Institute for Psycho-Analysis.
—. (1957b), 'The Unconscious'. In *The Standard Edition of the Complete Psychological Works of Sigmund Freud*. Ed. and Trans. J. Strachey. 24 vols. 14:161–215. London: Hogarth Press and the Institute for Psycho-Analysis.

Gillespie, S. (2008), *The Mathematics of Novelty: Badiou's Minimalist Metaphysics*. Melbourne: re.press.
Habermas, J. (1987), *The Philosophical Discourse of Modernity*. Trans. F. Lawrence. Cambridge: Polity Press.
Hallward, P. (2006), *Out of this World: Deleuze and the Philosophy of Creation*. London: Verso.
Hammond, M. (2003), 'How Does One Think with What Is Already Thinking?' Paper delivered at the School of Historical, Political and Sociological Studies (SHiPPS) Graduate Conference, 28 May. Exeter University, Exeter, UK.
Hardt, M. and Negri, A. (2000), *Empire*. Cambridge, MA: Harvard University Press.
Harrison, C. (2006), 'Problems of Negotiation in the London ESF: Horizontals versus Verticals'. In C. Barker and M. Tyldesley (eds.), *Conference Papers of the Eleventh International Conference on 'Alternative Futures and Popular Protest' held at Manchester University 19–21 April 2006 Vol. II*. Manchester: Faculty of Humanities and Social Science.
Hegel, G. W. F. (1975), *Hegel's Logic: Being Part One of the Encyclopaedia of the Philosophical Sciences*. Trans. W. Wallace. Foreword by J. N. Findlay. Oxford: Oxford University Press.
—. (1977), *Phenomenology of Spirit*. Trans. A. V. Miller. Foreword by J. N. Findlay. Oxford: Oxford University Press.
Heidegger, M. (1962), *Being and Time*. Trans. J. Macquarrie and E. Robinson. Oxford: Blackwell.
—. (1979–87), *Nietzsche*. Ed. David Farrell Krell. 4 vols. San Francisco: Harper-Collins.
—. (1982), *The Basic Problems of Phenomenology* (revised edn). Trans. A. Hofstadter. Bloomington: Indiana University Press.
Houlgate, S. (1986), *Hegel, Nietzsche and the Criticism of Metaphysics*. Cambridge: Cambridge University Press.
Hyppolite, J. (1997), *Logic and Existence*. Trans. L. Lawlor and A. Sen. Albany: State University of New York Press.
Jurist, E. (2000), *Beyond Hegel and Nietzsche: Philosophy, Culture, and Agency*. Cambridge, MA: MIT Press.
Kant, I. (1965), *Critique of Pure Reason* (unabridged edn). Trans. N. Kemp Smith. New York: St. Martin's Press.
Kojève, A. (1969), *Introduction to the Reading of Hegel*. Assembled by Raymond Queneau. Trans. James H. Nichols, Jr. Ed. Allan Bloom. New York: Basic Books.
Lacan, J. (1981), *The Four Fundamental Concepts of Psycho-Analysis*. Trans. A. Sheridan. Ed. Jacques-Alain Miller. New York: W. W. Norton.
—. (2006), *Écrits: The First Complete Edition in English*. Trans. B. Fink, in collaboration with H. Fink and R. Grigg. New York: W. W. Norton.

BIBLIOGRAPHY

Laclau, E. (1990), *New Reflections on the Revolution of our Time*. London: Verso.
—. (1996), *Emancipation(s)*. London: Verso.
—. (2001), 'Can Immanence Explain Social Struggles?' *Diacritics*. 31.4, 3–10.
—. (2005), 'The future of radical democracy'. In L. Tønder and L. Thomassen (eds.), *Radical Democracy: Politics Between Abundance and Lack*. Manchester: Manchester University Press, pp. 256–62.
Laclau, E. and Mouffe, C. (1985), *Hegemony and Socialist Strategy: Towards a Radical Democratic Politics*. London: Verso.
Larmore, C. (2005), 'Respect for Persons'. *The Hedgehog Review: Critical Reflections on Contemporary Culture*. 7.2, 66–76.
Leibniz, G. W. (1973), 'Monadology'. In G. H. R. Parkinson (ed.), *Leibniz: Philosophical Writings*. Trans. M. Morris and G. H. R. Parkinson. London and Melbourne: Everyman's Library, pp. 179–94.
MacKenzie, I. (2008), 'What is a Political Event?' *Theory & Event*. 11.3.
Malabou, C. (1996), 'Who's Afraid of Hegelian Wolves?' In P. Patton (ed.), *Deleuze: A Critical Reader*. Oxford: Blackwell, pp. 114–38.
Marchart, O. (2007), *Post-Foundational Political Thought: Political Difference in Nancy, Lefort, Badiou and Laclau*. Edinburgh: Edinburgh University Press.
Mouffe, C. (1993), *The Return of the Political*. London: Verso.
Moulard, V. (2002), 'The Time-Image and Deleuze's Transcendental Empiricism'. *Continental Philosophy Review*. 35.3, 325–45.
Moulard-Leonard, V. (2008), *Bergson-Deleuze Encounters: Transcendental Experience and the Thought of the Virtual*. Albany: State University of New York Press.
Newman, S. (2001), *From Bakunin to Lacan: Anti-Authoritarianism and the Dislocation of Power*. Lanham, MD: Lexington Books.
Nietzsche, F. (1966), *Thus Spoke Zarathustra: A Book for All and None*. Trans. W. Kaufmann. New York: Viking Press.
—. (1967), *On the Genealogy of Morals*. Trans. W. Kaufmann. New York: Vintage Books.
—. (1968), *The Will to Power*. Trans. W. Kaufmann and R. J. Hollingdale. New York: Vintage Books.
—. (1974), *The Gay Science, with a Prelude in Rhymes and an Appendix of Songs*. Trans. W. Kaufmann. New York: Vintage Books.
—. (1982), *Daybreak: Thoughts on the Prejudices of Morality*. Trans. R. J. Hollingdale. Cambridge: Cambridge University Press.
—. (1986), *Human, All Too Human: A Book for Free Spirits*. Trans. R. J. Hollingdale. Cambridge: Cambridge University Press.
—. (1989), *Beyond Good and Evil: Prelude to a Philosophy of the Future*. Trans. W. Kaufmann. New York: Vintage Books.
—. (1990), *Twilight of the Idols/The Anti-Christ*. Trans. R. J. Hollingdale. Harmondsworth: Penguin Books.

Patton, P. (2005), 'Deleuze and Democracy'. *Contemporary Political Theory*. 4.4, 400–13.
Plato. (1961), *The Collected Dialogues of Plato, Including the Letters*. Ed. E. Hamilton and H. Cairns. Princeton: Princeton University Press.
Protevi, J. (2006a), 'Deleuze, Guattari and Emergence'. *Paragraph*. 29.2, 19–39.
—. (2006b), 'Katrina'. *Symposium: Canadian Journal of Continental Philosophy*. 10.1, 363–81.
Rawls, J. (1971), *A Theory of Justice*. Cambridge, MA: Harvard University Press.
—. (1985), 'Justice as Fairness: Political not Metaphysical'. *Philosophy and Public Affairs*. 14.3, 223–51.
Russell, B. (1937), *The Principles of Mathematics* (second edn). London: George Allen & Unwin.
Sandel, M. J. (1998), *Liberalism and the Limits of Justice* (second edn). Cambridge: Cambridge University Press.
Sartre, J.-P. (1957), *The Transcendence of the Ego: An Existentialist Theory of Consciousness*. Trans. F. Williams and R. Kirkpatrick. New York: Noonday Press.
Schmitt, C. (2007), *The Concept of the Political* (expanded edn). Trans. G. Schwab. Chicago: University of Chicago Press.
Smith, D. W. (2003a), 'Deleuze and Derrida, Immanence and Transcendence: Two Directions in Recent French Thought'. In P. Patton and J. Protevi (eds.), *Between Deleuze and Derrida*. London: Continuum, pp. 46–66.
—. (2003b), 'Mathematics and the Theory of Multiplicities: Badiou and Deleuze Revisited'. *Southern Journal of Philosophy*. 41.3, 411–49.
—. (2004), 'The Inverse Side of the Structure: Žižek on Deleuze on Lacan'. *Criticism*. 46.4, 635–50.
Spinoza, B. (1992), *The Ethics, Treatise on the Emendation of the Intellect, and Selected Letters*. Trans. S. Shirley. Ed. S. Feldman. Indianapolis: Hackett Publishing Company.
Stavrakakis, Y. (1999), *Lacan and the Political*. London: Routledge.
Taylor, C. (1985), 'What's Wrong with Negative Liberty'. In C. Taylor (ed.), *Philosophical Papers, Vol. II*. Cambridge: Cambridge University Press, pp. 211–29.
—. (1989), *Sources of the Self: The Making of Modern Identity*. Cambridge: Cambridge University Press.
Tønder, L. and Thomassen, L. (2005), 'Rethinking radical democracy between abundance and lack'. In L. Tønder and L. Thomassen (eds.), *Radical Democracy: Politics Between Abundance and Lack*. Manchester: Manchester University Press, pp. 1–13.
White, S. (2000), *Sustaining Affirmation: The Strengths of Weak Ontology in Political Theory*. Princeton: Princeton University Press.

—. (2003), 'After Critique: Affirming Subjectivity in Contemporary Political Theory'. *European Journal of Political Theory*. 2.2, 209–26.
—. (2005), 'Weak Ontology: Genealogy and Critical Issues'. *The Hedgehog Review: Critical Reflections on Contemporary Culture*. 7.2, 11–25.
Widder, N. (2001), 'The Rights of Simulacra: Deleuze and the Univocity of Being'. *Continental Philosophy Review*. 34.4, 437–53.
—. (2004), 'Foucault and Power Revisited'. *European Journal of Political Theory*. 3.4, 411–32.
—. (2008), *Reflections on Time and Politics*. University Park, PA: Penn State University Press.
—. (2009a), 'Duns Scotus'. In G. Jones and J. Roffe (eds.), *Deleuze's Philosophical Lineage*. Edinburgh: Edinburgh University Press, pp. 27–43.
—. (2009b), 'From Negation to Disjunction in a World of Simulacra: Deleuze and Melanie Klein'. *Deleuze Studies*. 3.2, 207–23.
—. (2011), 'Deleuze on Bergsonian Duration and Nietzsche's Eternal Return'. In B. Herzogenrath (ed.), *Time and History in Deleuze and Serres*. London: Continuum.
Williams, J. (2011), *Gilles Deleuze's Philosophy of Time: A Critical Introduction and Guide*. Edinburgh: Edinburgh University Press.
Žižek, S. (1989), *The Sublime Object of Ideology*. London: Verso.
—. (2004), *Organs without Bodies: On Deleuze and Consequences*. London: Routledge.
—. (2008), *The Ticklish Subject: The Absent Centre of Political Ontology* (revised edn). London: Verso.

Index

actual *see* virtual
actualization 39–41, 46, 49–50, 58, 110, 138–9
  of the Event 50
  of events 49
  of a perspective 139
  see also virtual
agonism 15, 66, 74, 141–2, 158n. 19
  Connolly on 15, 141, 158n. 19
  Nietzschean forces and 66, 74
antagonism 14–15, 124–5, 141
  agonism versus 15, 141, 158n. 19
  radical democratic theory and 14
Aristotle 1, 7, 27–30
  Deleuze on 28–30

Badiou, Alain 27, 159n. 26, 163n. 31
Bergson, Henri 21, 37–8, 43, 45–7, 58, 61–3, 138
  Deleuze's turn from 46–7, 58, 61–2
  on duration 37–8, 43, 45–6
  on the ego 47, 138
  on élan vital 21
  on the virtual 37–8
Berlin, Isaiah 2–3, 6, 154n. 3, 156n. 5
body without organs (also BwO) 107–8, 111, 114, 135, 143–6
Borges, Jorge Luis 161n. 14
Butler, Judith 178n. 9, 180n. 2

capitalism 89, 94, 104, 113–16, 118–21, 130–2
  its axiomatic 115, 119
  Oedipus and 104, 113
  as partial deterritorialization 119–22
  relation to earlier social machines 115–16, 118
Connolly, William E. 8–9, 15–16, 141, 158nn. 19–20, 22
contradiction *see* dialectics, opposition
creativity *see* novelty

Descartes René 102, 124
desire 13–14, 72–3, 94–102, 105–21, 131, 140, 143–4
  capitalism and 118–21
  Deleuze on 92–4
  Deleuze and Guattari on 13, 92, 103–22, 144
  desiring its own repression 112–14
  desiring-production 106, 110–14, 139, 154
  deterritorialization and 115, 119–20
  drives and 100–2
  Hegel on 72–3, 94–5
  Lacan on 13, 95–102
  (micro)fascism and 122, 134
  need and 95–6, 102–3, 106

overcoming and 140
Plato on 94, 105, 172n. 7
  revolutionary character of 115, 121–2
  transcendence and 94, 103, 115
desiring-machines 105–14, 129, 140, 145 *see also* desire, social machines
deterritorialization 50, 92–3, 117, 119–22, 132–3
  partial versus absolute 119–22, 132–3
reterritorialization and 120, 133
dialectics 11–12, 19, 30, 35–7, 62–3, 65, 67–8, 71–4, 78, 84–5, 94–5, 97, 102, 150
  Deleuze on 19, 62–3, 67, 74, 84–5
  dialectic of consciousness 35–7, 65, 71
  dialectic of lordship and bondage 71, 73–4, 78, 95
  dialectic of self-consciousness 36–7, 71–4
  identity and 11–12, 19, 30–1, 36–7, 65, 71–2, 150
  opposition and 11–12, 19, 30
  Otherness and 12
difference (*see also* Otherness)
  actual and virtual 37–8
  as contradiction or opposition 11–12, 71
  as contrariety 28–9
  as difference in itself or differenciator 27–5, 38, 41, 48, 53, 57, 64, 70, 77, 108, 127
  as difference in quantity 67–9, 109
  Hegel and 11–12, 30–1, 63
  as individuating difference 29
  infinitely large 30–1
  infinitely small 31–2, 39, 48
  intensive 32, 67, 108–9
  repetition and 41–3, 129
  as specific difference 28
  thought and 127
  versus dialectics 85
differenciation and differentiation 24–5, 39–41, 70, 110–12, 139, 144
differenciator 24, 35, 38–9, 41, 47–8, 57–8, 70, 77, 107–8, 111, 144
  body without organs (BwO) as 107, 111, 144
  Oedipal trauma as 48
  sense and 24
  virtual 38–9
  will to power as 70, 77
disjunction, disjunctive synthesis *see* synthesis
dramatization 40–1, 66, 79, 109, 139
drives 66, 69, 100–2, 106, 109, 112–14, 143
  desiring-machines and 106
  Lacan on 100–2
  the subject and 100–3, 109, 113
  their repression 112–14
  will to power as 69, 113
Duns Scotus, John 25–6, 37
  on univocity 25–6
  on the virtual 37

ego (also 'I') 47, 49, 65, 86–8, 95, 109–10, 136–41, 144, 151
  see also subject, the
  Bergson on 47, 138
  Deleuze and Guattari on 136, 144
  dissolution in eternal return 86–8

INDEX

fractured by time 47
Klein on 106–7
Lacan on 104
Nietzsche on 140
out of sync with itself 49
Sartre on 136–40, 151
   as semblance 139–40
eternal return 27, 47, 49–50, 86–8,
   127, 129, 140
   Deleuze on 27, 49–50,
      86–8
   Nietzsche on 86–7, 140
   novelty and 50, 86–8, 127
   as third synthesis of time
      47, 49–50
   univocity and 27
ethics 10, 16, 63, 88, 94, 141–7,
   151–3
   as ethos 52, 141–7
   overcoming and 63, 88
   relation to politics and
      micropolitics 10, 52–3, 88,
      94, 143, 146–7
event(s) 33–4, 38–44, 47–51, 59,
   66, 81–3, 86–8, 98, 128,
   133, 151–2
   actualization of 49
   eternal return and 86–8
   the Event and 50–1
   an idea as a rare 128
   incompossibility of 33–4,
      38, 39
   of nihilism 81–3
   Oedipal 47–8, 98
   virtual 38

fascism 2, 52, 122, 134–5, 145
   microfascism (or molecular
      fascism) 122, 134
fold 18–20, 24, 31, 34, 38, 43, 47,
   52, 92, 93, 108

immanence and 18–19
   misinterpreted by philosophies
      of transcendence 19–20
   Otherness as 18–19, 31, 108
   resistance as 93
   sense and 18–20, 31, 38
   virtual 38
force(s) 36–7, 63–71, 74–9, 82–4,
   109, 113, 154
   active and reactive 66, 68–9,
      71, 74–9, 82–4, 109, 113
   Hegel on 36–7
   Nietzsche on 63–71, 74, 109, 113
   perspective and 40–1
   sense and 37, 64–5, 70
   virtual 37, 65, 138
Foucault, Michel 7, 21, 52–3,
   89–94, 105, 111, 125, 128,
   133, 141–3, 146, 150
   on the care for the self 141–3
   Deleuze on 92–4, 133, 141, 142
   on the Group for Information
      on Prisons (GIP) 52–3, 128
   on modern power relations
      89–94, 105, 111
Freud, Sigmund 47–8, 100–2, 112
   Deleuze on 47–8

genealogy 61, 64, 66, 70–1, 74,
   79, 82, 141

Hegel, Georg Wilhelm Friedrich 7,
   11–12, 22–4, 27, 30–2, 35–8,
   62–3, 65–6, 71–4, 94–5, 138
   on desire 72, 94–5
   dialectic of consciousness
      35–7, 65, 71
   dialectic of lordship and
      bondage 71, 73–4, 78, 95
   dialectic of self-consciousness
      71–4

on dialectics 11–12, 30–1
on force 36–7, 65–6
orgiastic representation and 30–1
radical democracy and 11–12
on sense 22–4, 36–7
Heidegger, Martin 1, 7, 21, 43–4, 63
on time 43–4
humanism 24–5, 64
Hyppolite, Jean 22–3, 159–60n. 5, 167n. 8

identity,
constituted by opposition 13–14, 16, 31, 74–5
Deleuze on 16–17, 150–1
dialectics and 11–12, 19, 30–1, 36–7, 65, 71–2, 150
eternal return and 49, 86
identity crises 149–51
incompossibility and 34–5
micropolitics and 59, 88, 125, 134–5, 144–7
as a molar formation 129–30
ontology of essence and 22
organic representation and 28–30
orgiastic representation and 30–5
possible/real and 39
power relations and 91–2, 131
radical democratic theory and 13–14, 16–17, 98–9
in relation to thought 125–6
repetition and 42, 68
semblance and 56–9, 129, 150
as a slavish value 77–8
the subject and 11–14, 97
transcendence and 20, 26

immanence 17–20, 25, 38–9, 142, 144, 151–4
causality and 25
critique and 17–18
Deleuze on 17–20
ethics and 151–4
folds and 18–20, 38
the Outside and 18–19, 142, 144
sense and 25, 38–9
Spinoza and 25–6
transcendence and 17–20, 25
incompossibility 33–5, 39, 47–9, 128
intensity, intensive difference 32, 67, 108–9, 132

Kant, Immanuel 43–4, 104–5, 140, 158n. 24, 162n. 21
Klein, Melanie 106–7, 118, 174–75n. 19

Lacan, Jacques 7, 13, 21, 95–105, 108, 117
Deleuze and Guattari on 104–5, 117–18
on lack 13, 98–9
on the Other 13, 95–9, 117
radical democratic theories and 13, 98–9
on the subject 13, 95–9, 100–3
lack 13–14, 17–18, 94–9, 101–2, 110, 128, 136, 150, 153
Deleuze and Guattari on 103–4, 106, 110
ontology and 13, 98–9, 150
Otherness as 13–14, 17
radical democratic theory and 13–14, 17, 98–9, 136, 150
transcendence and 17–18

Laclau, Ernesto 157n. 18, 158n. 25, 178–9n. 9
Leibniz, Gottfried 30–5, 39, 47, 57, 63, 67
  on infinitely small difference 31–2
line of flight 50, 131, 135, 145

MacKenzie, Iain 163n. 29
Marx, Karl 114, 121
master–slave relation 40, 71, 73–9, 95
  Deleuze on 40
  Nietzsche on 40, 71, 74–9
  Hegel on 71, 73–4, 95
micro(scopic) 38, 90–1, 111, 131
micropolitics 16, 20, 52, 59, 88, 94, 125, 134–5, 141, 143, 145–7, 154
  identity and 59, 88, 125, 135, 143
  molar and molecular 38, 94, 104, 106, 110–12, 114, 129–35, 150, 154

Nietzsche, Friedrich 7, 17, 21, 25, 27, 40, 46–7, 49, 51, 58, 61–88, 109–10, 113, 116, 125, 128, 132–4, 141, 146
  on bad conscience 61, 113
  Deleuze's use against Hegel 62–3, 71
  on eternal return 86–7, 140
  on master–slave relation 40, 71, 74–9
  on nihilism 78, 80–4, 113
  ontology of force 63–70
  on quantity and quality 66–9, 109
  on will to power 63, 69–71, 74–8, 109
  on the will to truth 79, 125
nihilism 78, 80–4, 113, 135
  Deleuze on 80, 83–4
  fascism as 135
  Nietzsche on 80–4, 113
novelty 42–3, 50–3, 86–8, 127–9, 133
  eternal return and 50, 86–8, 127
  problem of 42, 51–2
  repetition and 42–3, 50, 88
  in thought and action 127–9

objet a 13, 96, 98, 99, 101
Oedipus (also Oedipal) complex, the 47–8, 98, 103–5, 110, 113, 116–18, 120–1, 134
  capitalism and 104, 113, 120–1
  Deleuze on 47–9
  Deleuze and Guattari on 103–4, 105, 110, 113, 116
  as event 48
  Klein on 107
  Lacan on 98, 117–18
ontology,
  abundance and lack 13–16
  conflation with metaphysics 2–4, 6
  Deleuze on 10, 16–17, 51–2, 150
  of essence 22–4, 64
  memory and 45
  nihilism and 82–3
  ontological turn in political theory 1–2, 7–11, 20, 146–7
  radical democratic theory an 11–17
  of sense 22–7, 53
  of transcendence 17

univocity and 25–7
vitalism and 20
'weak' versus 'strong' 8–10, 51
opposition 11–14, 16, 18–19, 31, 36, 38, 52–3, 58–9, 65–6, 71, 74–8, 92, 125, 129, 131, 134, 149 *see also* difference
   abstract nature of 16, 19, 58–9
   dialectics and 11–12, 19, 30, 36, 38, 53, 66
   identity constituted by 13–14, 16, 31, 74–5
   politics and 125, 134
   power relations and 92, 131
   sense and 16, 18–19, 23–4, 31
   as slavish value 74, 76–8
   versus difference and disjunction 38, 65, 71
Other, the (also Otherness) 12–17, 19, 24, 55–6, 95–9, 107, 117, 138
   as abundance 14–15
   the BwO as 107
   Deleuze on 16
   as differenciator 38
   escapes representation 12, 14
   exceeding dialectical opposition 12, 19
   as fold 18–19, 24, 107
   immanence and 18–20
   Lacan on 13, 95–9
   as lack 13–14, 19
   Sartre on 138
   sense and 16, 24, 108
   simulacra and 55–6
   the subject and 12, 17–18, 95–8
   transcendence and 14, 17–18, 117
Outside, the 18–19, 142, 144, 151
   thought and 18–19

overcoding 117, 130–2, 145
overcoming 27, 61, 63, 77–8, 83–8, 94, 140, 143
   as active destruction 84–5
   desire and 140
   differs from dialectical sublation 84–6

partial objects 106–8, 111, 114, 139
perspectivism 33, 40–1, 64, 71, 74, 76, 139–41
   the emergence of subjectivity and 41, 64, 139–41
   force and 40, 74, 76
   Leibniz and 33
   semblance or simulation and 40–1
   truth and 40–1
phallus 13, 97, 104
Plato 1, 7, 17, 26, 54–5, 57, 94, 105, 126–7, 172n. 7
   Deleuze on 17, 54–5, 126–7
   on desire 94, 105, 172n. 7
   on simulacra 54–5, 57
   on transcendence 17, 26
Protevi, John 176n. 28

quality 1, 29, 37, 63, 66–9
   as category of Being 1, 29, 37
   Deleuze and Nietzsche on 66–9
   as difference in quantity 68–9
   Hegel on 67–8
quantity 1, 29, 37, 63, 66–9, 108–9, 132 *see also* difference in quantity
   as category of being 1, 29, 37
   Deleuze and Nietzsche on 66–9, 109
   Hegel on 67–8
   mechanism and 67–8

INDEX

radical democratic theory 11–17, 58, 62, 98–9
  abundance and 13–15, 58
  Deleuze and 11, 16–17, 62
  identity and 13–14
  Lacan and 13, 98–9
  lack and 13–14, 98–9
  Otherness and 12–15
  the subject and 13–14, 98–9
Rawls, John 3–7, 11, 125, 156nn. 6–7
  Michael Sandel's critique of 4–5, 11
repetition 41–53, 55–6, 68, 86, 88, 98, 129, 154
  Lacan on 98
  novelty and 42–3, 50, 88
  as repetition of difference 42–3, 129
  of selves in the unconscious 48–9
  simulacra as 55–6
  as structure of time 44
  traditional concept of 42, 68
representation 12, 14, 16, 28–32, 34, 39, 41–2, 57, 66, 68, 71, 103, 110, 127–8, 147, 152
  organic 28–30, 39, 152
  orgiastic 30–2
  repetition and 42
  thought and 127–8
ressentiment 75–7, 82–3, 86–7, 114, 118, 122, 153
reterritorialization *see* deterritorialization
revolution (*also* revolutionary politics) 51–2, 115, 121–2
  Deleuze on 51–2
  Desire and 115, 121–2
rhizome 53, 57, 131

Sartre, Jean-Paul 136–140, 151
  Deleuze and Guattari on 138
schizoanalysis 94, 106, 135
sense 16, 19–20, 22–7, 31, 36–7, 49–51, 56, 58, 64–6, 70, 82–4, 108, 126–7, 154
  differs from essence and appearance 22–3
  events and 49–51
  expression and 24–7
  force and 37, 64–5, 70
  Hegel on 22–4, 36–7
  of nihilism 82–4
  ontology of 22–7, 58
  opposition and 16, 18–19, 23–4, 31
  Otherness and 16, 24, 108
  recording synthesis and 108
  simulacra and 56
  synthesis and 23–4, 31
  thinking and 126–7
  the virtual and 37
  will to power and 70
simulacra 54–8, 81
  Deleuze on 54, 55–7
  Plato on 54–5, 57
  simulation of identity and 56–7
  the will to truth and 81
social machines 110, 111–12, 114–21 *see also* desire, desiring-machines
  codes versus axiomatic 115
  socius as recording surface of 114–15
Spinoza, Baruch 17, 25–6, 58, 61, 63, 104–5, 175n. 22
  expressive sense and 25–6
  immanence and 17
  Lacan on 104–5

State, the 91, 115, 117–18, 120, 130–1, 134
   capitalist 115, 120, 130–1
   despotic 117–18
   Foucault on 91
Stoicism 17
subject, the (*also* subjectivity) 1, 3–6, 8, 11–14, 16–18, 35–7, 40–1, 47, 75–6, 85–7, 95–9, 100–3, 106, 108–10, 113, 125–6, 135–43, 145–7, 151–4
   consciousness and 35–7
   Deleuze and Guattari on 106, 108–10, 113, 139, 145
   dialectics and 11–14, 35–7, 85–6, 95–7
   drives and 100–3, 109, 113
   eternal return dissolves 96–7
   Foucault on 141–3
   fractured by time 47
   identity and 11–14, 97
   Lacan on 13, 95–9, 100–3, 139
   lack and 13–14, 17, 95–9, 121, 136
   Nietzsche on 75–6, 86, 140
   the Other and 95–8
   perspectivism and the emergence of 40–1, 44, 64, 139
   Rawls on 3–6, 135, 139
   subjectivity without a subject 88, 136, 139–41
   thinking and 125–6
   transcendence and 17–18, 98–9
substance 1, 22, 25–6, 28–30, 32, 37, 142
   Aristotle on 28–30
   ethical 142
   Leibniz on 32–3
   Spinoza on 25–6, 32
synthesis 11–12, 24, 26, 30–1, 36, 38, 40–1, 43–50, 53, 56–7, 61, 65, 71, 87, 107–12, 114–15, 128, 136, 138–140, 151
   conjunctive 108–10, 139
   connective 107, 139
   of consciousness 136, 139
   disjunctive 24, 26, 38, 40, 47, 53, 65, 107–8, 111, 114, 139
   Hegelian 11–12, 30–1, 36, 41
   inclusive versus exclusive 110, 114
   machinic desire and 107–11, 114–15
   molecular versus molar 110–12
   sense and 23–4, 31
   three syntheses of time 44–50, 61, 87
   of the unconscious 110, 138–9

thinking (*also* thought) 18–19, 79, 125–9
   an encounter and 126
   the Outside and 18
   the will to truth and 79
time 1, 19, 37–8, 41–53, 58, 61, 82, 127, 151, 154
   Bergson on 37–8
   chronological or linear 37–8, 43–4
   as duration 37–8
   the Event and 50–1
   novelty and 50–3, 127
   the problem of its passage 45–6
   repetition as the structure of 43–4
   three syntheses of 44–50, 61
   the untimely and 47–50, 52, 82, 151

INDEX

transcendence 10, 14, 17–20, 22, 25–7, 46, 57, 75, 78, 81–2, 94, 98–9, 103, 108, 115, 132, 136–7 see also immanence
  Deleuze on 17, 19–20, 57
  desire and 94, 103
  of the ego 136–7
  identity and 20, 26
  immanence and 17–20, 25
  lack and 98–9
  Otherness and 14, 17–18, 117
  Plato and 12, 57
  slave morality and 75, 77, 78
  the subject and 17–18, 98–9, 103
  univocity and 25–6
  the will to truth and 81–2
trauma 47–9, 98
  Deleuze on 47–9, 98
  as event 48
  Freud on 48
  Lacan on 98
  Oedipal 47–9, 98
truth 35–7, 40–1, 79–81, 125–6, 142 see also will to truth
  dialectic of consciousness and 35–7
  the dogmatic image of thought and 125–6
  games of 142
  perspectivism and 40–1
  the will to truth and 79–81

univocity 22, 25–7, 30, 37, 48, 51, 61, 127, 152
  Aristotle's categories and 30
  of being 22, 25–7, 37, 61
  confusion with the One 22, 26–7
  as disjunctive synthesis 26
  Duns Scotus and 25–6, 37
  eternal return and 27, 127
  and the Event 50–1
  Oedipus as univocal enigma 48
  sense and 25–7, 50
  Spinoza and 25–6
  transcendence and 25–6
untimely see time

vice-diction 32, 34–5, 39, 67, 110
virtual 34, 37–41, 45–6, 48–50, 53, 58, 65, 70, 110–11, 138–9, 144 see also actualization
  actual and 38–41, 49, 58
  Bergson on 37–8
  Deleuze on 37–41
  and differenciation/differentiation 39–40, 111, 144
  Duns Scotus on 37
  Event 50
  force and 37, 65, 70, 138
  past as 38, 45–6
  the unconscious and 48, 110, 139
  virtual and actual differs from possible and real 38–40
vitalism 21–2, 58, 66

war machine 132–3
White, Stephen 8–10, 51
will to power 63, 69–71, 74–7, 82–4, 109, 154
  as differenciator 70
will to truth 79–83, 126

Žižek, Slavoj 159n. 26, 165n. 38, 173n. 9, 179n. 9, 180n. 3

www.ingramcontent.com/pod-product-compliance
Lightning Source LLC
Chambersburg PA
CBHW052043300426
44117CB00012B/1952